BETWEEN

THE

LINES

BETWEEN
THE
LINES

Understanding Yourself and Others Through
HANDWRITING ANALYSIS

REED HAYES

Destiny Books
Rochester, Vermont

Destiny Books
One Park Street
Rochester, Vermont 05767

Library of Congress Cataloging-in-Publication Data
Hayes, Reed C.
    Between the lines: understanding yourself and others through handwriting
    analysis / Reed Hayes.
        p.   cm.
    Includes bibliographical references and index.
    ISBN 0-89281-371-7
    1. Graphology. I. Title.
BF891.H393 1992
155.2'82—dc20   92-19458
                                                                               CIP

Printed and bound in the United States

10   9   8   7   6   5   4   3   2   1

Text design by Charlotte Tyler

Destiny Books is a division of Inner Traditions International, Ltd.

Distributed to the book trade in the United States by American International Distribution Corporation (AIDC)

Distributed to the book trade in Canada by Book Center, Inc., Montreal, Quebec

For Kim Iannetta,
my partner, handwriting playmate, critic, and friend

And for Avery Freed,
in appreciation for his support, patience, and friendship

AUTHOR'S NOTE

The handwriting samples in this book are for instructional purposes only. Comments about the writers are not intended to be complete reports or to defame the subjects in any way.

TABLE OF
CONTENTS

PREFACE: HOW TO USE THIS BOOK   xi

INTRODUCTION   1

1. GRAPHOLOGY: A REFLECTION OF YOUR INNER SELF   5
   Practical Applications of Handwriting Analysis   10
   What Handwriting Does Not Reveal   12

2. HISTORY OF HANDWRITING ANALYSIS   14

3. BASICS OF HANDWRITING ANALYSIS   19
   Regularity or Irregularity   19
   Size of Writing   22
   Spacing   24
      Line Spacing
      Word Spacing
      Letter Spacing
   The Baseline   33
   Line Direction   36
   Handwriting Form   39
      Arcades

Angles
Garlands
Threads

4. ZONAL DISTRIBUTION AND DIRECTIONAL TRENDS 42
 Middle Zone 44
 Upper Zone 46
 Lower Zone 49
 Directional Trends 53

5. YOUR SLANT ON LIFE 56
 Emotional Responsiveness 56
 Emotional Permanence 62

6. HOW YOU THINK 67
 The Methodical Thinker 71
 The Investigative–Analytical Thinker 73
 The Perceptive Thinker 75
 The Adaptable Thinker 76
 Is the Writer Logical or Intuitive? 80
 Traits That Reveal Clear Thinking 82
  Simplification
  Attention to Detail
  Concentration

7. YOUR SIGNATURE: THE FACE YOU SHOW THE WORLD 85

8. PREPARATION FOR HANDWRITING ANALYSIS 97
 How to Look at Handwriting 99

9. STROKE BASICS 110

10. BEGINNING AND ENDING STROKES 114

11. YOUR WRITING FITS YOU TO A *T* 123

12. ARE YOU INSECURE? 134
 Self-Consciousness 135
 Jealousy 137

Repression   139
Self-Underestimation   141
Sensitivity to Criticism   142

13. HANDWRITING REVEALS YOUR SOCIAL LIFE   144
    Do You Lean Toward People?   145
    Do You Connect With People?   146
    Do You Seek Out Social Activity?   147
    How Do You Choose Your Friends and Acquaintances?   148
    Are You Generous?   150
    Are You Easily Angered?   151
        Irritability
        Resentment
        Temper
        Sarcasm
        Argumentativeness
    Are You Open-Minded?   157
    How Do You Communicate?   158
        Frankness
        Talkativeness
        Secretiveness
        Self-Deceit
        Deliberate Deceit
    Do You Have a Sense of Humor?   161

14. YOUR LOWER LOOPS ARE SHOWING   163
    Energy, the Underlying Force   164
    Secrets of the Lower Zone   165
    So What's Normal?   166

15. IS THE WRITER HONEST?   174
    Dishonesty Has Many Faces   176
    Twenty-five Signs of Dishonesty   177
    Handwriting Samples Showing Dishonesty   180

16. HANDWRITING REVEALS YOUR SPECIAL APTITUDES   182
    Sense of Rhythm   183

Imagination   184
Cultural Aptitudes   185
    Literary Interest
    Color Sense
    Talent for Music
    Simplicity of Expression
    Line Value
Mechanical Aptitudes   191
    Manual Dexterity
Business Skills   192
    Organizational Skills
    Decisiveness
    Determination
    Diplomacy
    Initiative
Scientific Aptitude   195

DICTIONARY OF PERSONALITY TRAITS   197

SUGGESTED READING LIST   210

HANDWRITING ANALYSIS WORKSHEET   212

INDEX   220

PREFACE:
HOW TO
USE THIS BOOK

You are about to begin a journey into the world of handwriting analysis. If you follow the signposts presented in this book, you will begin to look at yourself, your family, and your friends in a new way—from the inside out.

The purpose of this book is to give you a fundamental understanding of graphology based on both American and European methods. The information presented comes from many years of experience and is therefore dependably accurate. However, you will want to prove to yourself that graphology really works. Your own handwriting is a good place to start, as you probably know yourself quite well already. Once you have read this book, you may be somewhat self-conscious about how you write, so before reading further, sit down and write yourself a letter in your natural handwriting.

As you read through the book, check to see which character traits apply to you and which do not. You will probably also be interested in what the handwriting of your friends and relatives reveals about them.

You may start collecting every scrap of handwriting you can get your hands on. As you study the writing of the people in your life you will probably encounter traits that do not seem to correspond to their personalities. If so, wait until you have read further before deciding that a trait does or does not fit. Consider that additional traits may mask or alter those in question—or perhaps you do not know the person as well as you had thought.

Handwriting never lies, but sometimes we do not interpret it correctly. I suggest you read through the entire book and then come back to those traits of which you are uncertain. The details about handwriting that you gain later in the book will help to clarify the more generic or global traits presented in the first few chapters.

The worksheet provided at the back of this book is to help you interpret a handwriting sample. For your convenience, it follows the text chapter by chapter. Make extra copies of the worksheet so you can use it for more than one handwriting sample.

The Dictionary of Personality Traits at the end of the book will help you to determine specific character traits in handwriting. It shows the primary stroke indications of each trait mentioned in this book and others as well.

You have now taken your first step on the road of handwriting analysis, a road with interesting twists, turns, and side paths. After you have completed this book, you may wish to read others, using the suggested reading list as a guide. Best of luck on your journey!

INTRODUCTION

My own fascination with handwriting analysis started more than two decades ago when a graphologist offered to analyze my writing. Like others who are not aware of the value and accuracy of this art and science, I was prepared merely to have my fortune told or at best to hear general statements about my personality. When the graphologist, who had not known me previously, told me absolutely correct things about myself that she could not have known otherwise, I was both amazed at her accuracy and curious to know how she arrived at her conclusions.

In my search to discover how handwriting reflects personality, I soon realized that no magic is involved and that the interpretation of writing is quite logical and systematic. All actions, writing included, start in the brain. When a person picks up a pen or pencil to write, the brain sends messages to the hand and arm muscles and directs the marking of the paper. The lines, curves, loops, and dots that result are all reflections of the inner self. Although the writing instrument is held by the hand, it is the brain that impels us to write.

Like facial expressions and body language, handwriting expresses personal characteristics. Watching a conversation from a distance, we can tell a great deal about the participants by noting their gestures and the looks on their faces. Likewise, we can observe the individualized gestures of handwriting as reflections of personality.

Handwriting analysis is no longer a parlor game or an occult subject. It is a logical method of personality assessment that is supported by statistical and empirical research. In handwriting analysis we look for specific writing signs that indicate specific personality traits and then carefully evaluate them against one another before drawing final conclusions. No analysis is based on a single handwriting indication, and no personality trait is considered positive or negative on its own, because each characteristic in the writing is influenced by all the others.

Handwriting is so closely tied to impulses from the brain that it is a barometer of moods and of physical, emotional, and mental health. It evolves as you do, maturing with growth, disintegrating with age, and changing as a result of physical, mental, or emotional illness. Although your writing differs somewhat from one day to another according to mood, physical health, and environment, your basic personality indications remain constant and allow your writing to be analyzed accurately.

In addition to other characteristics, handwriting reflects the following:

- Moods and feelings
- Personal tastes
- Physical and emotional health
- Thinking styles
- Social traits
- Goal orientation and achievement potential
- Talents and aptitudes
- Insecurities
- Integrity (honesty)
- Sexual attitudes
- Communication and social skills

Handwriting analysis is an invaluable tool that can be utilized in many areas:

• *Self-understanding.* Graphology can give a very accurate and nonbiased look at who you are—your strengths, weaknesses, and special skills.

• *Interpersonal relationships.* Compatibility for marriage and social or business arrangements can be enhanced by a deeper understanding of the people involved. Knowing your mate's thoughts, feelings, and insecurities can help you make your relationship work better. Understanding your family members, partner, co-workers, and friends from the inside out allows you to relate to them on a personal and honest level.

• *Psychology and counseling.* Handwriting, as external evidence of emotional makeup, thought processes, and personality integration, can be used to validate other psychological tests. Emotional problems, fears, inhibitions, and general social traits are all indicated by writing, often more efficiently than with other methods.

• *Education.* The value of handwriting analysis to instructors and teachers far surpasses that of any other projective test. Handwriting is easily observed and can be monitored regularly. Teachers find that their students' handwriting reveals thinking styles as well as mental or emotional problems that may not be otherwise apparent, and they can tailor their instructional methods accordingly.

• *Business and industry.* Personnel selection, employee promotion and counseling, and motivation of staff can be enhanced by the use of graphology: Small businesses and Fortune 500 companies claim that it is both legitimate and effective. Time and money are saved by matching the right person with the right skills and personality to a position.

• *Law.* Handwriting is an effective method for screening prospective jurors. In Hawaii, lawyers consult with members of our corporation, Trial Run Ink, to aid them in jury selection and in understanding clients, jury members, key witnesses, opposing counsel, and judges.

• *Criminology.* Graphology can be used to determine dishonesty as well as potential dangerousness. Document examiners use graphological training to evaluate forged signatures and spurious or altered contracts, and to compare one handwriting with another.

Handwriting uses universal symbols and movements, rendering the analysis of writing cross-cultural.* For example, we say that things are "looking up" or that we are "feeling down." Regardless of the cultural origin of the writer, looking up (literally or figuratively) implies hope and optimism, whereas feeling down implies a negative approach. Both conditions are clearly indicated in handwriting when the line of writing is buoyed up by elation or pressed down with depression. We push forward in our activities or we draw back, represented in handwriting strokes that drive to the right (the future) or pull to the left (the past). In *Between the Lines* you will learn to recognize these and other less obvious movements.

Although this book will not prepare you to be a professional graphologist, it will give you a solid introduction to the world of handwriting. The first few chapters discuss the basics of handwriting analysis: overall personality organization; moods and attitudes toward life; emotional makeup; thinking styles; emphasis on the spiritual, the mundane, or the physical; and personalized expression of signatures. You will learn how to collect samples for analysis and how to prepare a thumbnail personality sketch from the information gleaned thus far. In succeeding chapters the details of personality will be explored by examination of individual writing strokes (*t* crosses, *i* dots, beginning and ending strokes, loops, and so on). You will look at indications of insecurities, talents, and natural aptitudes and learn how to determine dishonesty. You will also consider the sexual implications of writing.

This book will provide an objective look at *you*. By looking at yourself honestly you can deal more effectively with your weaknesses and build on your strengths. When you know yourself well you can better understand others, and when you understand other people you can accept them as they are.

---

*However, it is important to know the model from which the person learned to write. Handwriting that is not based on the Latin alphabet (for example, Chinese, Japanese, Hebrew, and Vietnamese) can be analyzed accurately only after specialized study, which is not within the scope of this book.

1
GRAPHOLOGY:
A REFLECTION OF
YOUR INNER SELF

Graphology is the evaluation of handwriting to determine character, disposition, and aptitudes. Like facial expressions, bodily movements, and other mannerisms, handwriting expresses personality: As a series of highly personalized gestures, it reflects the thoughts, feelings, and habits present at the moment the writer puts pen to paper.

Each person's handwriting is unique and indicates individualized expression. Pressure patterns, slant, letter size, punctuation, and loop formations allow each person to be recognized as an individual with a visibly unique character. Although most people learn to write by following a schoolroom model, no one is able to copy it exactly. Even with hours of practice and after learning the mechanics, people write according to their own dispositions and their own personalities, adding individual movements and dropping those that feel uncomfortable or alien.

How far from the schoolroom model your writing deviates is significant. If your writing strongly resembles the model, you tend to be conventional and to base your thinking on societal rules and expectations. On the other hand, if you deviate from the writing style you were

5

taught, you probably follow your own thinking and act according to self-prescribed standards. In graphology it is the deviations from the norm that are the most revealing about the writer's individuality.

Sigmund Freud said, "There is no doubt that men also express their character through handwriting," and the 19th-century British prime minister Benjamin Disraeli wrote, "Handwriting bears an analogy to the character of the writer, as all voluntary actions are characteristic." Others who understood handwriting as an expression of personal characteristics were Albert Einstein, George Sand, Robert Browning and Elizabeth Barrett Browning, and Edgar Allan Poe. Thomas Gainsborough went so far as to keep the handwriting of the person he was painting in front of him so that he could "feel" his subject's character and portray the personality more accurately. As the German researcher William Preyer said at the turn of the century, "Handwriting is brainwriting."

Handwriting is a vast resource of information to those who know how to interpret it. Even the casual observer who knows nothing about graphology can, with reasonable accuracy, see personality traits in handwriting.

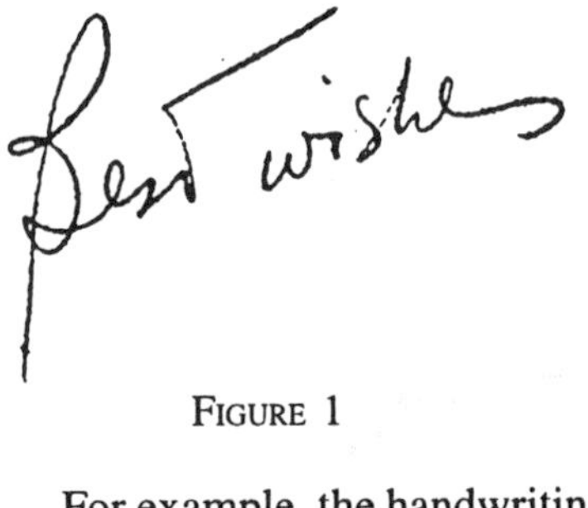

FIGURE 1

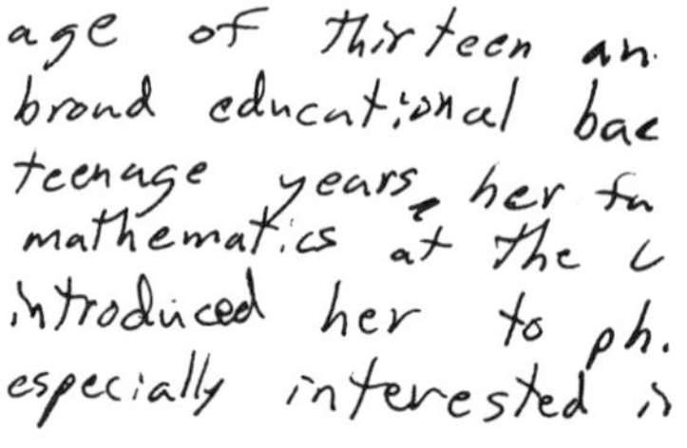

FIGURE 2

For example, the handwriting of Fig. 1 portrays a strong, confident, dynamic person in the firm writing strokes, the enlarged size, and the forward movement. Fig. 2, on the other hand, is the writing of an uncertain, less secure person, as indicated by the uncertain letter formations; the changeable size, spacing, and line direction; and the general lack of stroke stability.

Fig. 3 illustrates extravagance in the expansive movements, whereas Fig. 4 is more thrifty in its conservation of space.

FIGURE 3
Extravagant

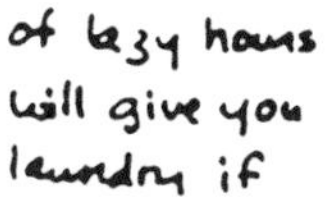

FIGURE 4
Thrifty

The next two samples (Figs. 5, 6) show organization (even line spacing) and disorganization (uneven line spacing).

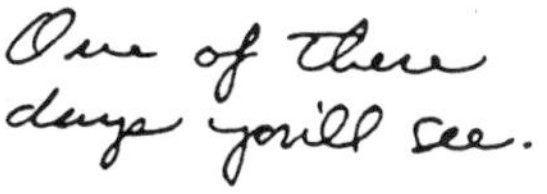

FIGURE 5
Organized

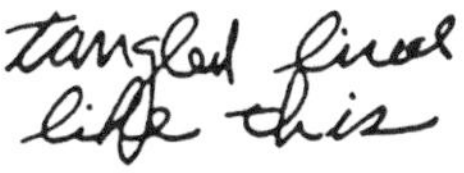

FIGURE 6
Disorganized

The degree of patience is suggested by the speed of the handwriting (Figs. 7, 8).

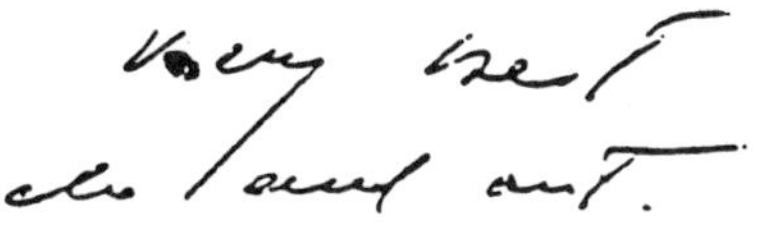

FIGURE 7
Impatient

FIGURE 8
Patient

Slant shows whether the writer is outgoing or reserved (Figs. 9, 10).

FIGURE 9
Reserved

FIGURE 10
Outgoing

How far the writer deviates from the classroom style of writing shows the degree of originality (Figs. 11, 12).

FIGURE 11
Conventional

FIGURE 12
Original

Careful letter formations suggest self-discipline (Figs. 13, 14).

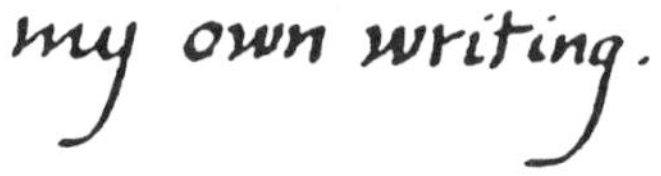

my own writing.

FIGURE 13
Self-disciplined

FIGURE 14
Spontaneous

Well-formed letters show clarity of thought (Figs. 15, 16).

FIGURE 15
Clear thinking

FIGURE 16
Unclear thinking

Handwriting analysis is more complicated than these examples suggest. The intricacies of the nervous system and physical disposition, added to the diversities of life, render graphology a complex subject. The chemical, mechanical, and electrical processes produced by the brain, plus the influences of heredity and environment, form the uniqueness and complexity of every person and every person's writing.

The evaluation of writing involves great care, and there can be no accurate appraisal of handwriting that attempts to "pigeonhole" the writer. Eleanor Vivian, dean emeritus of the International Graphoanalysis Society in Chicago, says that "any attempt to form a scale of measurement would not succeed, for where there is life there is variability and the lack of predictability, and as writing depicts life, it cannot be mechanized or put on a mathematical scale. To try to do so is to destroy the integrity of the analysis."

From the study of thousands of handwriting samples, it is clear that people often have similar personality traits. Such traits as emotional responsiveness, anger, pride, or talkativeness are common, but differences of intensity as well as other characteristics either diminish or support the findings. For example, a talkative person might speak critically (with sarcasm), exaggeratedly (with too much imagination), argumentatively (with contention), emotionally (with responsiveness), excitedly (with enthusiasm), and so on.

The limitless combinations of characteristics in varying intensities make it impossible for a personality report to be made on the basis of a single trait or handwriting feature. Likewise, no trait can be considered positive or negative on its own before the entire evaluation is complete.

A frequent argument against handwriting analysis is that a person's writing varies from day to day. Because handwriting is closely governed by the nervous system, the writer produces a variable, "living" handwriting that reflects subtle physical, emotional, and environmental changes. Handwriting evolves as personality does, but it always retains certain distinctive marks of the writer.

In handwriting analysis, individual life-styles, environments, and unique situations must be considered, as well as physical conditions (for example, an odd writing position, quality of pen, poor writing surface, writer's age and health, temperature, being jostled in a vehicle).

A few words of caution are in order: A little knowledge about handwriting can do a lot of damage. No single book can teach you how to analyze handwriting professionally. To analyze handwriting after reading one book on the subject would be like trying to speak French after reading a French dictionary. The nuances of personality are so varied that to understand this science thoroughly requires years of dedicated study, observation, and application of graphological principles.

However, this book *will* give you an introduction to the examination and interpretation of handwriting for personal use, provide a basic but accurate method of graphology based on both European and American techniques, and set you on the path to the art and the science of graphology.

Handwriting analysis will give you a key to the people around you. Most important, it will deepen your self-understanding which can bring joy to your life.

Handwriting is:

- Brainwriting
- An expression of personality
- A record of mental, emotional, and spiritual tendencies
- A diagram of the unconscious

- An outward reflection of inner functions
- A record of psychomotor impulses
- Crystallized expressive movement
- A unique and individual art form
- A picture of the psyche
- A reflection of needs and desires
- An indication of potential and liabilities
- An objective picture of the subjective
- An indication of psychic health
- A way of communicating Me to You

PRACTICAL APPLICATIONS
OF HANDWRITING ANALYSIS

Because handwriting reveals thinking patterns, social traits, emotional makeup, integrity, goal orientation, fears, defense mechanisms, aptitudes, and a host of other personality traits, it is certain to be useful in any situation involving people. It is an efficient and objective reflection of the personalities of the people you meet daily.

Compatibility for marriage, social, or business arrangements can be enhanced by a deeper understanding of the people involved. You can check out your realtor before buying a home, examine a salesperson before signing a contract, decide which attorney will work best for you, or evaluate a possible marriage partner. Graphology can enable you to cultivate worthwhile friends and avoid false ones. It can improve relationships between husband and wife, children and parents. Friction between people is reduced when understanding replaces emotional bias.

The use of handwriting analysis in business by personnel departments and management is growing rapidly as small businesses and Fortune 500 companies alike recognize it as a legitimate and effective tool for hiring and management. Statistics indicate that 80 percent of today's work force (including management) are unhappy with their jobs.

Time and money may be saved by using handwriting analysis to choose the person whose skills and personality match the position.

Employers can also avoid hiring dishonest, incompetent, or unreliable employees. Applicants do their best to convince employers they would be an asset to the company. Resumes list experience, and interviews may reveal skills, but neither uncovers personality traits, innate aptitudes, and the prospective employee's ability to fit in. An evaluation of the applicant's handwriting reveals characteristics that may not surface during the interview. On the basis of what is shown in the applicant's handwriting, an employer can know in advance whether he or she fits the position.

Conversely, an employer can avoid firing a potentially good employee who may be performing poorly only because of temporary problems. Graphology can help determine candidates who are most deserving of job promotions, orient people to work best suited to their particular skills, and eliminate people who are square pegs desperately trying to fit into round holes.

Graphology also has a place in the legal field. Document examiners use graphological training as background in determining spurious or altered contracts and in comparing one handwriting with another. It is also a basis for dealing with anonymous letters.

Handwriting analysis is becoming an invaluable tool for attorneys. In Hawaii, my partner and I consult with lawyers who use graphology as a jury screening tool and an aid in the understanding of clients, jury members, key witnesses, opposing counsel, and judges. Positive feedback tells us that this method gives them a competitive edge.

Because handwriting reveals personality regardless of the writer's age, it can be highly beneficial in understanding the thinking patterns, emotions, and problems of children. The value of handwriting analysis to instructors and teachers far surpasses that of any other projective test. Academic progress can be regularly monitored, learning skills and social adjustment better understood, and special aptitudes discovered. Teachers who know their students well can tailor their instruction methods accordingly.

Graphology is a highly useful tool in the helping professions. It is used by counselors, priests, and psychiatrists, who find they can pinpoint personality or behavioral problems. All types of emotional abnormalities, from slight disturbances to schizophrenia, paranoia, and sexual deviations, are discernible in handwriting. The advantages of using handwriting as a diagnostic aid are that the subject need not be present to be tested and is not influenced to give the expected answers; the writing is also a permanent record, unlike body language or facial gestures. (Note: No competent graphologist attempts to diagnose illness, either mental or physical. Although illness is sometimes suggested by handwriting, diagnosis should be made only in conjunction with other tests and after consultation with other professionals.)

Graphology can also act as an insurance policy that signals possible danger. To the trained graphologist, handwriting reveals dishonesty as well as potential for violence. And, although there is not a so-called criminal type, handwriting discloses those traits that, when carefully evaluated, point toward possible criminal behavior.

One of the most useful areas for the application of graphology is that of self-knowledge. It has been said that people have three characters: the one they exhibit, the one they actually have, and the one they think they have. Few people can accurately discover the truth about themselves without input from objective sources, especially since we tend to believe only what we want to believe about ourselves. Socrates said, "The unexamined life is not worth living." Graphology can help you to examine your life by providing an accurate and objective look at who you are and how you can make use of your most positive traits.

WHAT HANDWRITING
DOES NOT REVEAL

In spite of its usefulness and accuracy, graphology has its limits.

Handwriting does not reveal gender. Writing indicates qualities that can belong to either sex; there is no certain way of knowing from the script whether the writer is male or female. There are some men who have a delicate handwriting and some women whose writing is bold. To be fair and accurate in the final report, the graphologist should know the writer's sex before starting the analysis (for example, you would want to know the sex of the writer to interpret lower loops pulling toward "mother" or "father").

Handwriting does not reveal age or physical characteristics. Some children think like adults and some adults are childlike. The handwriting of a precocious child will show adult characteristics, whereas a childish adult has immature writing. Old age can affect handwriting, causing it to be shaky, fragile, or brittle. Since these signs can be easily confused with signs of emotional or mental disease, it is important for the analyst to be informed of the subject's age, as well as any physical problems. Physical characteristics, such as body shape or size, cannot be determined through writing.

Handwriting does not reveal the future. Handwriting indicates characteristics present only at the time of writing. The graphologist cannot peer into the future and answer questions about success, money, or love. Graphology is in no way linked to the occult; it is based instead on careful observation and evaluation of specific personality traits indicated by specific handwriting signs. Handwriting analysis can suggest how a person is likely to react in a given situation, but it is not predictive. The graphologist who relies on guesswork or speculation is cheating the client for whom the analysis is prepared.

Handwriting does not reveal the writer's occupation. A handwriting report can indicate innate talents and aptitudes, but it cannot tell with certainty how or whether the writer uses those abilities.

2
HISTORY
OF HANDWRITING
ANALYSIS

Modern handwriting analysis is grounded in antiquity. The ancient Chinese knew that handwriting was a measure of personality, as did the early Romans.

In perhaps the earliest known acknowledgment of the diversity of handwriting, Aristotle (384–322 B.C.E.) wrote: "Spoken words are the symbols of mental experience, and written words are the symbols of spoken words. Just as all men have not the same speech sounds, so all men have not the same writing." The Roman emperor Nero (37–68 B.C.E.) is reported to have said of a man at court, "His writing shows him to be treacherous." During the following century, the Roman historian Suetonius remarked on the tie between character and writing in the handwriting of Emperor Augustus. Other outstanding figures who claimed that handwriting reveals character included Aesop, Julius Caesar and Cicero. Jo-Hau (1060–1110), the Chinese philosopher and artist, declared that "handwriting infallibly shows us whether it comes from a noble minded person or a vulgar one." In 1270 Roger Bacon twice mentioned handwriting as an indicator of personality in his *Compendium Studii Philosophiae.*

Although a general interest in handwriting and personality dates to ancient times, no organized system of writing analysis appeared until the 17th century. In 1622 Camillo Baldi, an Italian scholar and physician of the University of Bologna, published a book entitled *Treatise on a Method to Recognize the Nature and Quality of a Writer from His Letters.* Although this book aroused interest among the educated classes, it could not be widely used because relatively few people at that time could read and write.

Typically, handwriting analysis continued to be of interest to intellectuals. The next published work on the subject (1778) was by Johann Kasper Lavater, a Univeristy of Zurich scholar, poet and theologian, who concluded that "everybody has his own individual and inimitable handwriting." He found that "the handwriting of a person is congruent with his actual situation and state of mind" and that there exists a "remarkable analogy between the voice, gait, and handwriting of most people."

After Lavater's publication, handwriting analysis became popular among writers, artists, statesmen, and other public figures. Sometimes with more art than science, handwriting analysis was practiced (often with amazing intuitive skill) by Dumas *père*, Emile Zola, George Sand, the Brownings, Alphonse Daudet, Nikolai Gogol, Anton Chekhov, Albert Einstein, Thomas Mann, and Edgar Allan Poe, among others.

By the first half of the 19th century, handwriting analysis was more than just a parlor game. It was studied seriously in France by Abbé Louis J. H. Flandrin—the bishop of Amiens—and the archbishop of Cambrai, whose greatest contribution to handwriting analysis was the training of their assistant, Abbé Jean-Hippolyte Michon. In 1875 Michon published the most scholarly work then extant about handwriting analysis, *The Practical System of Graphology*, thus giving the term "graphology" to that study. Michon tirelessly studied thousands of handwriting samples to make a list of hundreds of graphic signs that identified individual personality traits. His method became known as "the school of fixed signs."

A disciple of Michon, Jean Crépieux-Jamin, enlarged upon Michon's studies, revising and reclassifying the material and establishing new laws relating to the analysis of writing. In 1888 Crépieux-Jamin published his well-known book, *L'Ecriture et le Caractère,* which by 1975 was in its 17th edition.

Near the turn of the 20th century, Crépieux-Jamin interested the eminent psychologist Alfred Binet in graphology as a personality testing technique. Several years before bringing out his first intelligence test in 1905, Binet experimented with handwriting analysis, using seven analysts. Each analyst was given 37 handwritings of men who had achieved success and 37 of men at the same social level who were not outstanding for their achievements. Asked to identify the handwritings belonging to each group, they all scored well above the chance level.

Meanwhile, in Germany, other scientific experiments were being conducted at the university level. William Preyer, a professor at the University of Berlin, studied the essential similarity between handwriting, footwriting, mouthwriting, opposite-handwriting, and crook-of-the-elbow writing. Preyer discovered that no matter how the writing instrument was held, an individual's writing still showed the same essential characteristics. As a result of this study Preyer coined the phrase "Handwriting is brainwriting."

For many years the foremost practitioner of graphology in Germany was Ludwig Klages, whose term "expressive movement" covered all common activities that the average person performs almost automatically and with little conscious thought: walking, running, talking, making gestures and facial expressions, and especially handwriting. Klages interpreted each handwriting as positive or negative by evaluating the "formlevel," a sum total of the organization, spontaneity, originality, dynamism, harmony, and rhythm of the writing. A high formlevel results in positive application of the traits indicated, while a low formlevel yields negative results.

At the same time, Professor Max Pulver in Switzerland gave handwriting analysis the flavor of Carl Jung's analytic psychology. Pulver devised the "symbolism of space" approach and divided handwriting into three zones: the upper zone (upper loop area), symbolizing mental and spiritual orientations; the middle zone (letters resting on the baseline), indicating emotional makeup; and the lower zone (lower loop area), suggesting materialistic interests and biological drives. In England, Robert Saudek quantified handwriting by use of ruler, protractor, caliper, pressure board, microscope, and even slow-motion pictures. Hans Jacoby also furthered graphological study in England and wrote a marvelous and informative book, *Analysis of Handwriting* (1939).

Little important graphological work was conducted in the United States until June Downey, professor of psychology at the University of Wyoming, researched resemblances of family members' handwritings and published a small book on the psychology of handwriting in 1919.

Milton Bunker made perhaps the greatest contribution to American handwriting analysis. A master shorthand teacher who had done some cursory reading about graphology, Bunker noticed that his students all wrote their shorthand lessons differently from one another in spite of his careful instruction. Intrigued by this fact, he set out to investigate. His studies led him to realize that it does not matter whether the person is writing actual letters; it is the basic pen strokes constituting the letters and shapes that are important. Bunker studied the minute details of handwriting (as opposed to the gestalt of the script) and gave his method the name "graphoanalysis" to distinguish it from other approaches. In the 1920s he set up a school to teach graphoanalysis, which today is the International Graphoanalysis Society (Chicago), the largest handwriting analysis school in existence. The school is characterized by conservative and strict methods, and its research department focuses strongly on statistical validation of handwriting analysis.

In the 1930s the prominent U.S. psychologist Gordon Allport of Harvard and his co-worker Philip Vernon contributed their authority to the subject. In *Studies in Expressive Movement* they wrote, "[Handwriting] is a crystallized form of gesture, an intricate but accessible prism which reflects many, if not all of the inner consistencies of personality. . . . Handwriting provides material that is less artificial than tests and more convenient for analysis; and since it can be studied at leisure, it is superior to facial expression, gesture, and gait, which are so fleeting and difficult to record."*

Werner Wolff, a psychologist and teacher at Bard College, ex-

---

*Allport, Gordon, and Philip Vernon. *Studies in Expressive Movement.* New York: Macmillan, 1933.

plored the configuration of signatures and concluded that all the signatures of an individual follow an inherent rhythm that is beyond conscious control. Wolff published his research in a book entitled *Diagrams of the Unconscious* (1948).

One of the most distinguished graphologists was Klara Roman, who taught graphology at the New School for Social Research in New York City. Roman devised an instrument to measure pen pressure and did considerable work with the handwriting of people suffering from speech disturbances. Her book *Handwriting: A Key to Personality* (1952) is still a classic in the field.

Many other graphologists made their individual contributions to graphology in this century, and several published important works. They include Ulrich Sonnemann, Daniel Anthony, Felix Klein, Nadya Olyanova, Thea Stein Lewinson, Alfred O. Mendel, and Irene Marcuse, to name but a few.

3
BASICS
OF HANDWRITING
ANALYSIS

Handwriting analysis is both a science and an art. The science involves careful examination of the most minute details of the writing to determine the writer's individualized expressions. It also involves enumeration of these details and arrangement of the findings to discover which characteristics are more prominent (and therefore the most influential in the personality) and which are less prominent.

Graphology develops into an art as the handwriting analyst moves from the mere observation of isolated signs to evaluation of the indications as a whole, thereby creating a meaningful and accurate report. The art of graphology comes with experience and results in understanding oneself and others, which is the real satisfaction of handwriting analysis.

REGULARITY OR IRREGULARITY

The long road leading to the art of graphology starts with understanding the picture of the writing as a whole—its gestalt or formlevel. All details gleaned later are subject to the overall regularity and organization of the writing, which reveals whether the details are positive or negative. For example, large handwriting in a regular and organized setting indicates confidence, self-expression, energy, and activity, whereas the same writing in an irregular and poorly coordinated milieu implies arrogance, brusqueness, and impulsiveness. Small writing that is also regular and organized points toward focused and concentrated energies and an ability to think in great detail; in a poorly organized script it suggests lack of confidence, shyness, and a tendency to focus on a very small inner world.

The first thing that strikes us when we look at a page of handwriting is the overall balance and regularity (or irregularity) of the script. A person who is consistent and determined expresses these characteristics in consistent and determined ways: certainty of thought and action, a self-assured walk, or consistency of speech, for example. When he or she takes up a pen, the handwriting will also be regular and stable. Writing movements can never be entirely regular, of course, but the relative regularity of each handwriting can be determined.

Regularity is indicated when writing is balanced on the page with somewhat equal margins on all four sides, capital and lowercase letters are in good proportion to one another, letters slant consistently, lines follow evenly across the page, letters are equal in height, pressure is even throughout, and the writing is simple, clear, and legible. The arrangement of regular writing as a whole is pleasing to the eye (Fig. 17).

Regularity, when combined with other supportive indications, is a positive sign for the overall personality. It lends balance and stability to a person's inner life and promotes consistency in thought, feeling, and effort. People with this type of handwriting are reliable and dependable; you can expect their feelings and expressions to be similar each time you meet them.

In irregular writing, margins are unbalanced, capital and lowercase letters are out of proportion to one another, slant is inconsistent, lines are uneven, letters are of unequal height, pressure is changeable. The arrangement of irregular writing is discordant (Fig. 18).

Irregular handwriting suggests that the writer's life is inconsistent and uncertain, even haphazard. Thoughts and feelings are changeable and lack clarity; there is a lack of self-discipline and an unreliable approach to life.

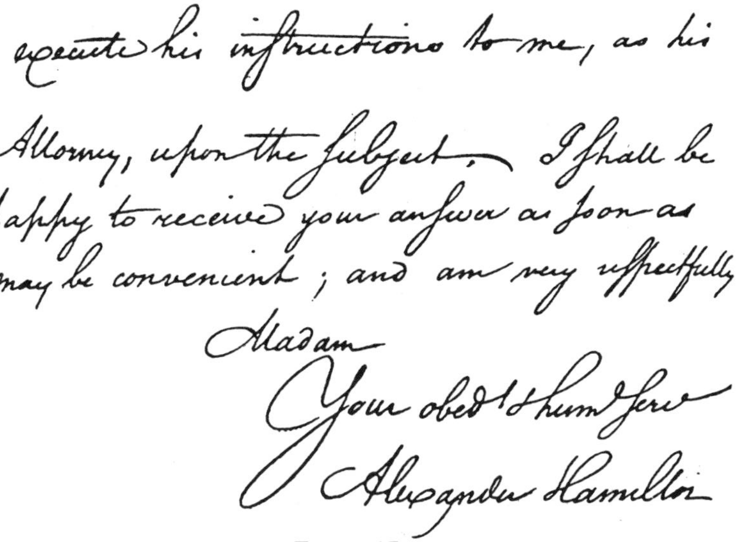

FIGURE 17
Regularity: Alexander Hamilton, U.S. statesman

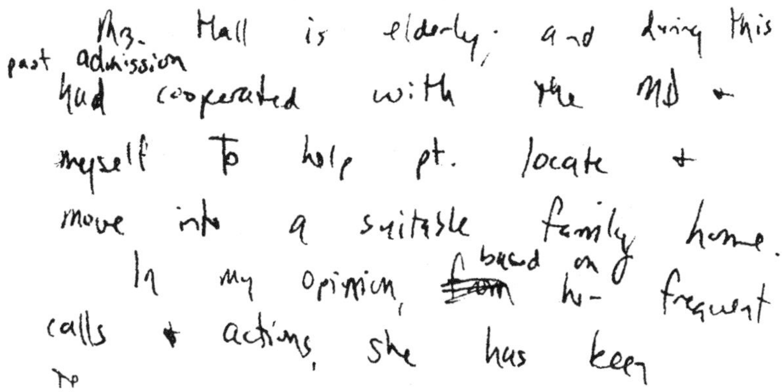

FIGURE 18
Irregularity

If all the signs of regularity mentioned earlier are consistently precise, the writing is considered to be overly regular and the interpretation is less than positive. Overly regulated writing points toward monotony, artificiality, and perfectionism. A certain amount of "give" to the writing is desirable, as it suggests healthy adaptability and spontaneity, which are not a part of the overly consistent writer's makeup (Fig. 19).

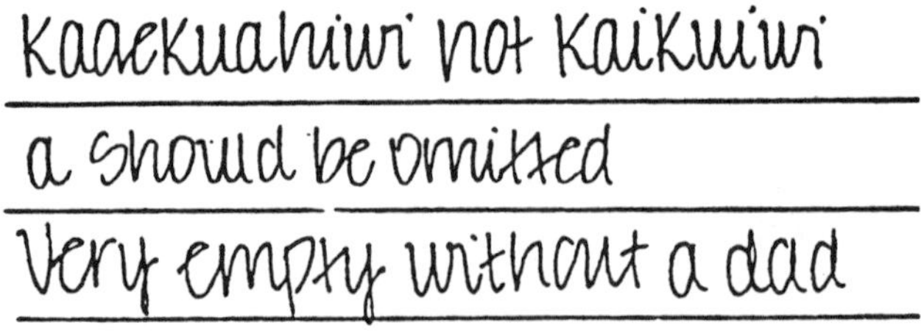

Kaaekuahiwi not Kaikuiwi

a should be omitted

Very empty without a dad

Figure 19
Excessive regularity

SIZE OF WRITING

Handwriting size shows how you impress yourself on the environment and how you feel about your relationships to other people. It also shows the amount of importance you place on yourself (ego emphasis) and whether you are inclined to be a thinker or a doer.

To determine writing size, measure the height of the baseline letters. Average handwriting size is about ⅛ inch, or 3 millimeters (Fig. 20).

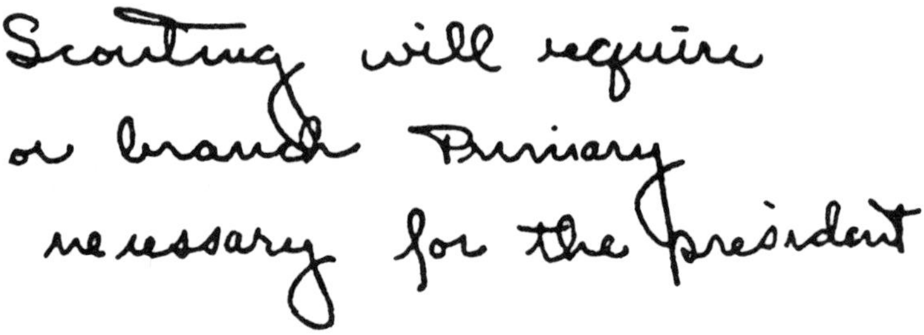

Scouting will require

a branch Primary

necessary for the president

Figure 20
Average handwriting size

Just as a tall person stands out in a crowd, so does the person who has larger-than-average handwriting. Large writers are social-minded, expressive, talkative, and active. They like movement and bustle in their lives, and need plenty of room in which to act out their restlessness. They are generally self-assured and bold (but check other writing signs to see how self-assured they really are). Their outlook on life is broad and expansive, allowing them to see the overall picture but usually not the details. As a rule, they are open-minded, tolerant, and willing to consider approaches other than their own. With negative signs, they can be pretentious and boastful in their need to be the center of attention, and they tend to lack attentiveness, focus, and self-discipline. Large writers are doers rather than thinkers (Fig. 21).

FIGURE 21
Large handwriting: Pearl Bailey, singer

Small writing, on the other hand, denotes modesty and humility. Small writers understate their importance and are reserved and introspective, except perhaps with close friends. Unlike large writers, these people are not the center of attention or the life of the party. They usually need little *physical* space in which to move about. Mental activity is their forte, and they are able to concentrate for long periods of time. Because of their strong attentiveness to details, they often do not see the forest for the trees. Their overall outlook on life is narrow, they tend to think small, and if their writing is tiny, they tend to feel inferior and to retreat into a small world. In some cases, small writers like Einstein and Gandhi had widespread influence as a result of their concentrated efforts. Small writers tend to be thinkers rather than doers (Fig. 22).

A

B

FIGURE 22
Small handwriting: (A) Albert Einstein, physicist;
(B) Mahatma Gandhi, Indian nationalist leader

Average-size writers establish a good compromise between thought and activity. They neither overestimate nor underestimate themselves and can be either social or reserved, depending on other characteristics. They are generally doers, but their good thought patterns enable them to focus on details.

Writing that changes in size from one writing session to another indicates a flexible outlook. In conjunction with positive indications, variable size is interpreted as versatility and an ability to see things from various perspectives. When variable size accompanies less positive characteristics, impulsiveness, indecision, and a lack of good emotional control are suggested.

Writing size that changes within one sample of writing implies an unsettled approach and a changeable self-image that is sometimes confident and sometimes modest, depending on how much the size varies. With a good formlevel such changeability indicates that the writer is able to roll with the punches. In a poor formlevel, however, it indicates uncertainty and indecisiveness.

SPACING

Like regularity or irregularity, the spacing of handwriting illustrates a great deal about overall thinking style and organization. When a writer sits down to a clean sheet of paper, the primary objective is to communicate. If the communication is clear and direct, lines, words, and letters are so spaced that the addressee is able to read the writing clearly. Even when writing space is limited, the clear-minded, communicative person allows for balanced spacing. The writing of the muddled thinker and poor communicator, on the other hand, will have uneven spacing, sometimes with tangled lines or words and letters that run together.

LINE SPACING

The careful and conscientious person writes with enough spacing between the lines so that no letters from one line tangle with those in the line above or the line below. Moderate spacing between lines (neither too wide nor too narrow) implies organization, clarity, and good judgment, especially when the spacing is consistent (as in the handwritings of Alexander Hamilton, Abraham Lincoln, and Henry Wadsworth Longfellow). Moderate spacing implies a mature approach to life, genuine spontaneity, and reasonableness in thoughts, feelings, and interaction with people, in conjunction with other signs, of course (Figs. 23, 24).

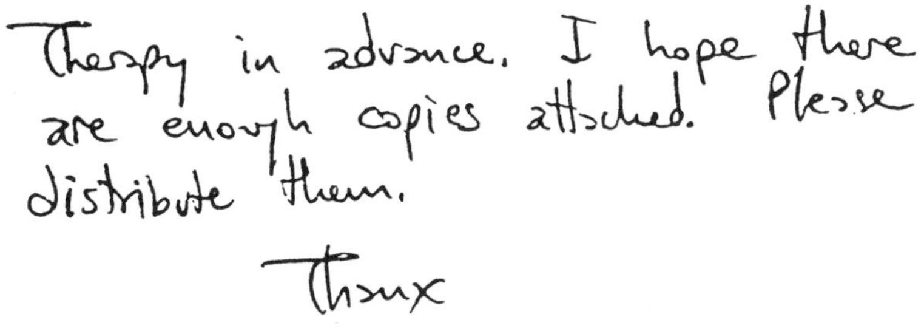

FIGURE 23
Moderate line spacing

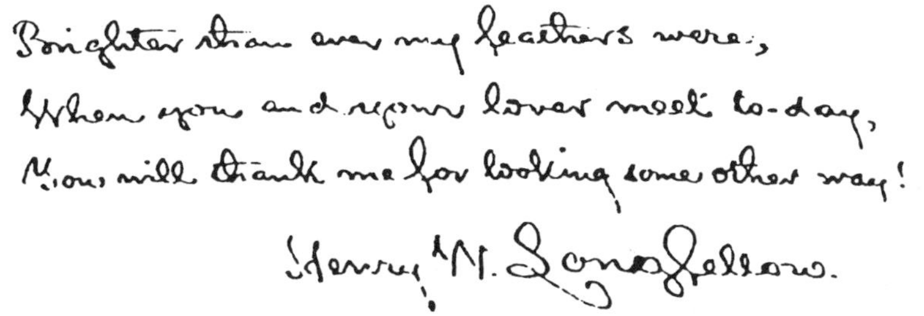

FIGURE 24
Consistent line spacing:
Henry Wadsworth Longfellow, American poet

Tangled lines are a sign of disorganized thinking and emotional or mental confusion. People who produce them tend to be impulsive, indecisive, or both. They are frequently busy (especially if the writing is large and expansive), and they find themselves unable to devote adequate time to any one of their many interests. The more tangled the lines, the more urge toward variety.

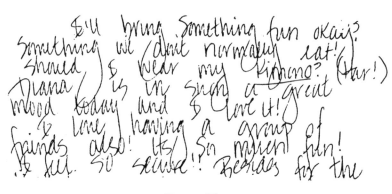

FIGURE 25
Tangled lines

When the lines overlap and are twisted together, the writer is very muddled and confused and has trouble separating fact from fiction. Thoughts and feelings are tangled together, and not knowing which impulse to act on, the person acts erratically and irresponsibly on all of them. This confusion also indicates that the writer does not understand social boundaries (Figs. 25, 26).

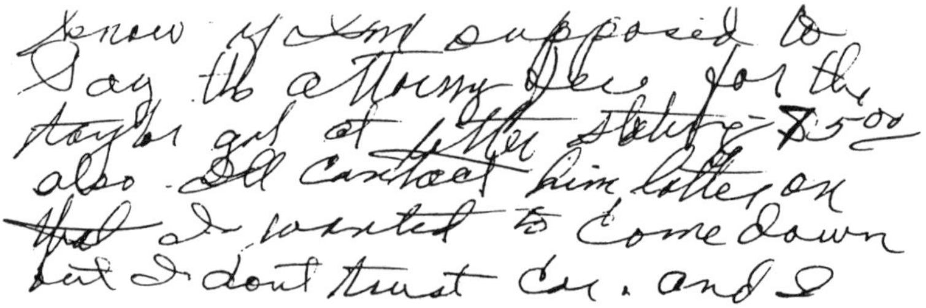

FIGURE 26
Overlapped lines

However, if some of the ascenders or descenders of one line reach into the line above or below but the spacing is even and the writing is legible, the writer is mentally active, probably in a positive way. He or she likes variety, needs a frequent change of pace, and is apt to be busy or to be interested in more than one sphere of activity (Fig. 27).

When the spacing between lines is exaggerated, the interpretation is unfavorable. This writer is either psychologically or socially isolated, is apt to have a cautious, blase approach to life, and prefers not to become involved. This is also an indication of extravagance (Fig. 28).

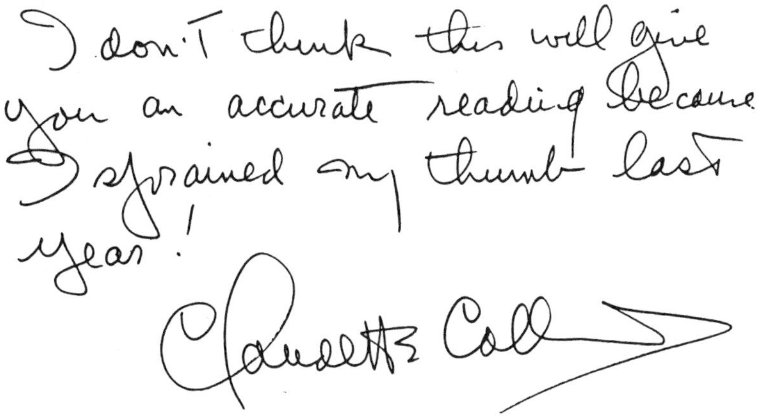

FIGURE 27

Lines contact with minimal tangling: Claudette Colbert, actress

FIGURE 28

Exaggerated line spacing: Louisa May Alcott, U.S. author

Narrow line spacing (without tangling or interference from lines above or below) represents caution, thrift, and economy (Fig. 29).

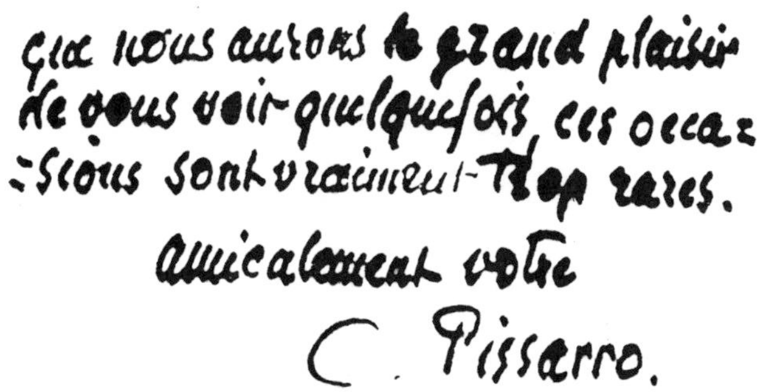

FIGURE 29

Narrow line spacing: Camille Pissarro, French impressionist painter

Changeable spacing—sometimes narrow, sometimes wide—shows variable feelings and responses, versatility, or both, depending on how changeable the spacing is. If it is erratic, the writer is likely to be unreliable, unpredictable, or even unstable (Fig. 30).

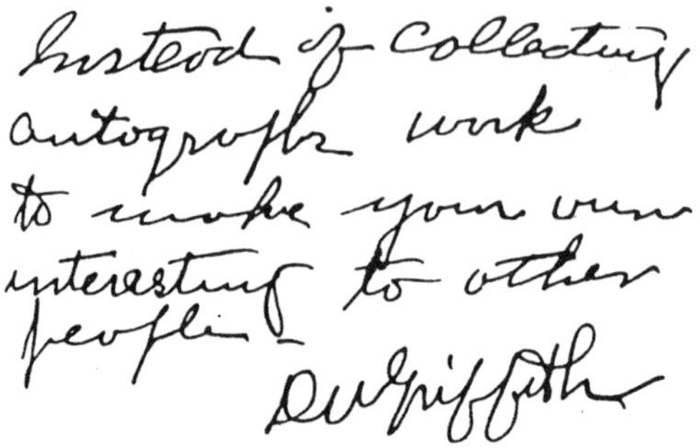

FIGURE 30
**Variable line spacing: D. W. Griffith, film producer
(originator of "close-ups")**

WORD SPACING

The amount of space left between words represents the amount of psychic and physical distance the writer needs to feel comfortable. Word spacing is one indication of an approach to other people. Even spacing shows respect for social boundaries and a consistent approach to social encounters. Even word spacing points toward stability and reliability with regard to relationships (Fig. 31).

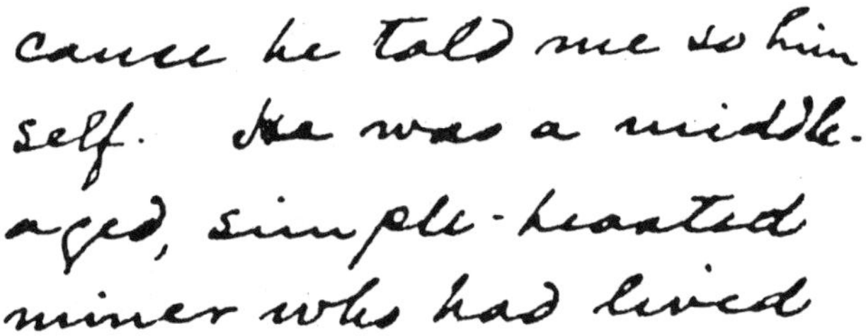

FIGURE 31
Consistent word spacing: Mark Twain, U.S. writer

Changeable or uneven spacing indicates an inconsistent approach to social encounters. Such writers want to be sometimes close, sometimes distant (Fig. 32).

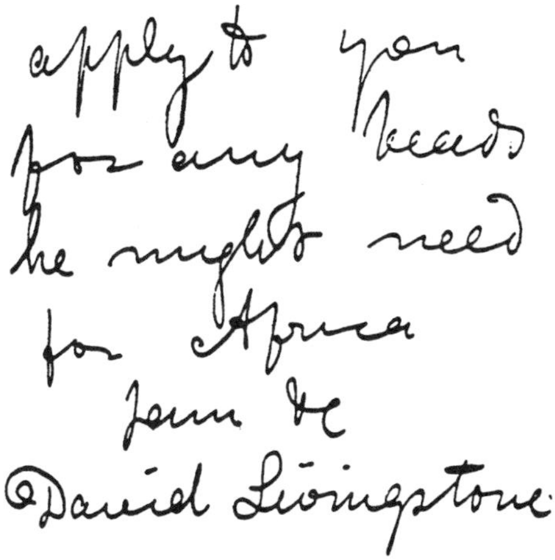

FIGURE 32
Inconsistent word spacing: David Livingstone, English explorer

Narrow word spacing suggests that the person needs little elbow room and can deal with people at close quarters without feeling uncomfortable. These writers may even prefer to be close to other people and, when the word spacing is extremely narrow, may be unable to allow them space. If the writing is also large and/or tangled, such writers can be dominating and overly talkative. Very narrow word spacing also implies that the writer fears independence.

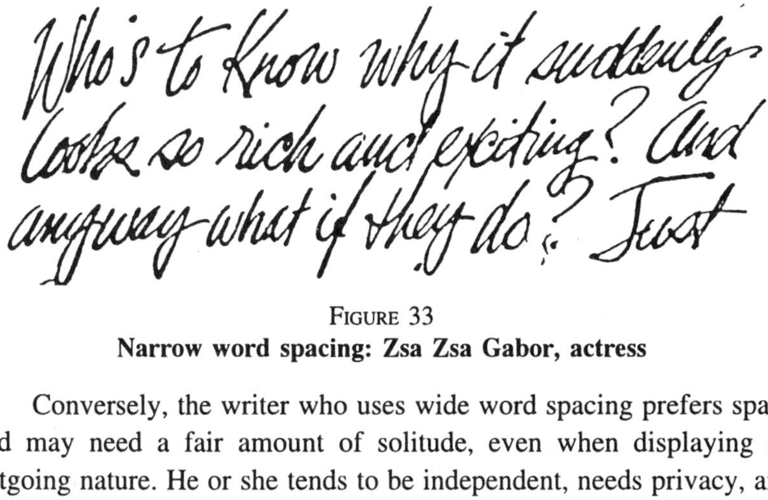

FIGURE 33
Narrow word spacing: Zsa Zsa Gabor, actress

Conversely, the writer who uses wide word spacing prefers space and may need a fair amount of solitude, even when displaying an outgoing nature. He or she tends to be independent, needs privacy, and may be isolated from people, either emotionally or literally. These writers sometimes dislike being touched, which they perceive as an encroachment on their personal space. Wide spacing is also an indication of caution, a "look before leaping" approach. Just as one may pause between words when talking, so this writer pauses for space between words before making the next stroke (Fig. 34).

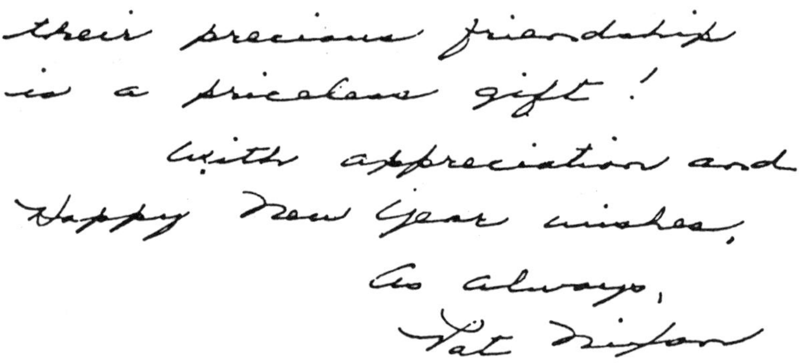

FIGURE 34
Wide word spacing: Pat Nixon, wife of president Richard Nixon

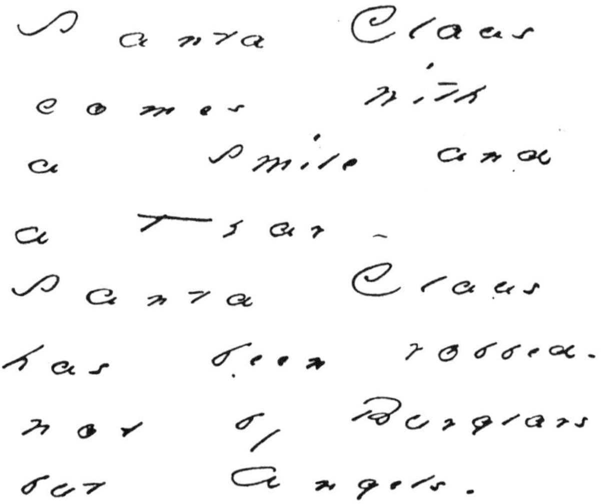

FIGURE 35
Extremely wide word spacing: Emily Dickinson, U.S. poet

Extremely wide spacing between words shows isolation, fear of contact or intimate communication, and difficulty establishing close relationships because of a fear of identity loss. This sign is also suggestive of paranoia (Fig. 35).

Ideal word spacing is somewhere between narrow and wide. Moderate, even word spacing reflects the writer's social maturity and mental health. Such writers are neither entirely dependent nor independent. They are able to be intimate without either invading others' space or fearing loss of identity.

LETTER SPACING

The width of individual letters reflects the writer's self-perception. If letters are very narrow, the writer is apt to feel narrow-minded or self-judging and can be expected to be self-conscious or uptight about personal feelings and self-expression. Tight letters show that the person habitually represses emotions and behaves in a cautious, conservative manner. They also signify that the writer, because feelings have been hidden for so long, does not have clear self-understanding (Fig. 36).

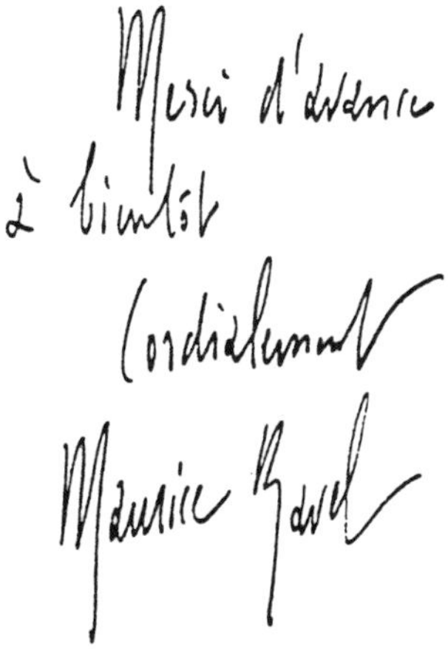

FIGURE 36
Narrow individual letters: Maurice Ravel, French composer

Wide individual letters indicate that the writer feels at ease and is likely to be less self-critical and more open to new and different experiences. Such a writer is usually broad-minded, able to accept inner feelings, and openly expressive (Fig. 37).

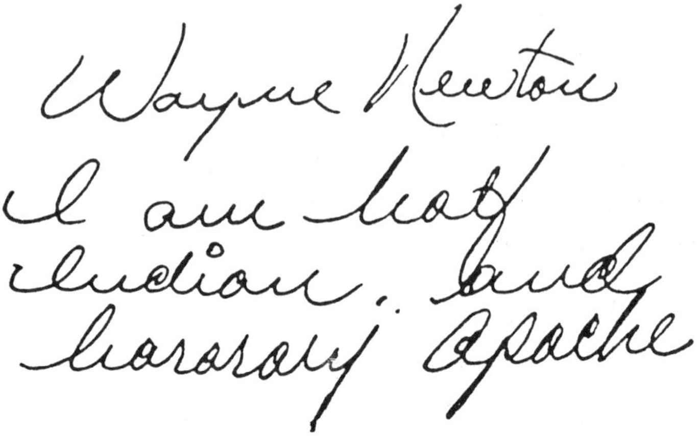

FIGURE 37
Wide individual letters:
Wayne Newton, entertainer

Spacing between letters, in addition to spacing between words, illustrates how the person shares himself or herself with other people. Moderate, consistent letter spacing reflects an extroverted writer (Fig. 38).

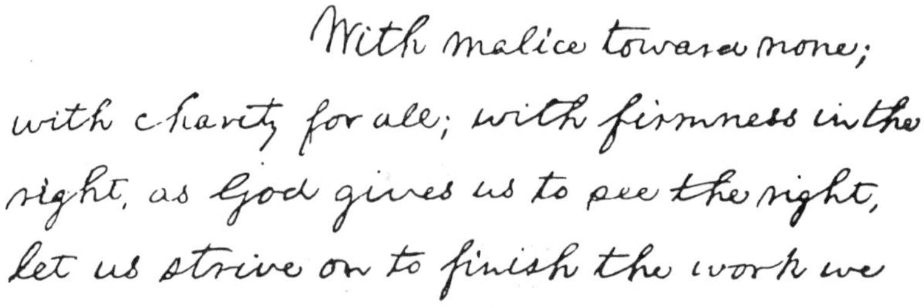

FIGURE 38
Moderate spacing between letters:
Abraham Lincoln, U.S. president

Narrow spaces between letters suggest tightness in the person's approach to people. He or she is apt to be introverted or cautious in approach or, in extreme cases, fearful. Exceptionally narrow letter spacing indicates that the writer is fearful of making contact (Fig. 39).

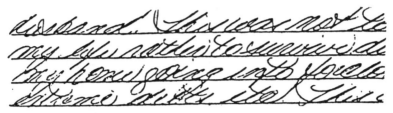

FIGURE 39
Narrow spacing between letters

Wide letter spacing belongs to people who are outgoing, expansive, generous, and people oriented. These writers feel at ease with themselves and are willing to share thoughts and feelings with others. Strong self-regulation is not their forte, and if other indications are present, they can be extravagant or impulsive (Fig. 40).

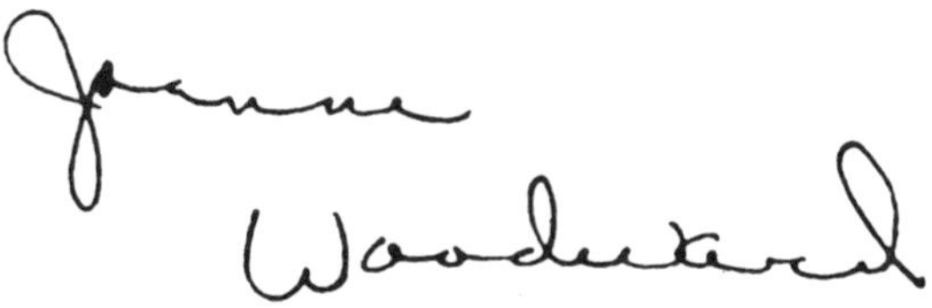

FIGURE 40
Wide spacing between letters: Joanne Woodward, actress

THE BASELINE

The baseline is the imaginary line on which we write. We usually start to write by positioning the pen or pencil at this line, and then move away from this point in creating a handwriting stroke (normally in an upward direction), followed by a stroke downward to complete the letter. By doing so, we have established a base for the letter and those that follow.

The baseline is not arbitrary but comes from your very nature and as such is one of the most important of all handwriting indicators. In fact, it is a strong indicator of the foundation on which your personality stands. It represents your sense of reality, your relationship to the here and now, and your way of integrating emotion into daily life. The baseline also represents the threshold of consciousness, the division between subconscious (below), and superconscious (above).

Everyone, guided by psychic and physical mechanisms, places letters on this imaginary line, although not consciously. Even on ruled paper there is a tendency to form one's own baseline and to ignore the actual line.* People who choose to write on lined paper usually like to have structure in their lives; those who prefer unlined paper tend to be more independent, more spontaneous, and less structured.

The baseline is like the ground on which the writer stands: When one walks or stands on level ground, one has good footing and is, therefore, secure and stable; uneven ground takes away from one's footing and makes for less stability. Extremely uneven ground may make it necessary to watch for sudden changes in the terrain in order to keep one's balance.

Likewise, a level or even baseline in handwriting reflects security and stability, whereas an uneven baseline points to lack of inner stability. Specifically, the ability to write on an even line indicates emotional stability: a person who is consistent, dependable, and reliable and has well-regulated emotional responses, inner security, and self-discipline (Fig. 41).

FIGURE 41
Consistent baseline: John D. Rockefeller, oil magnate and philanthropist

Writing that adheres rigidly to a straight baseline, however, is not generally a positive indication. Such an inflexible line suggests that the writer feels an unconscious need to carefully control the emotions. There is little real responsiveness, and reactions are predictable, monotonous, and even artificial, especially if the writing appears perfect (e.g., letters are all identical in size, spacing is exact, formations are very carefully written). Such rigid writers can hardly be called spontaneous or flexible.

---

*The writing sample should be on unlined paper to allow for more freedom of movement and a more personal baseline.

Therefore, some flexibility in the line of writing is a positive indication. A supple baseline (as long as it does not become erratic) implies flexibility in the writer's life, ability to adjust to situations that arouse feeling, willingness to experience emotion, and healthy spontaneity (Fig. 43).

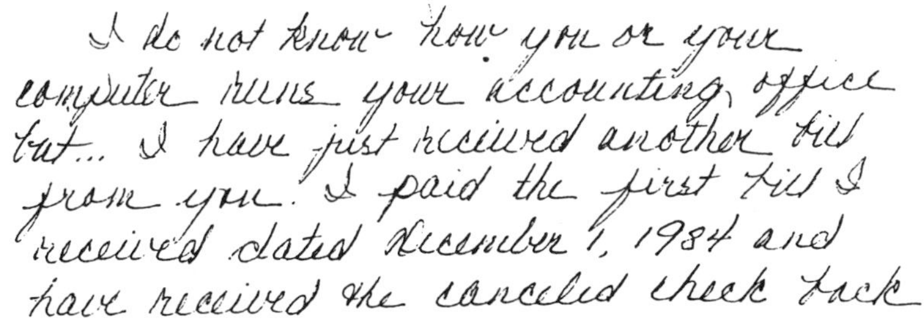

FIGURE 42
Rigid baseline

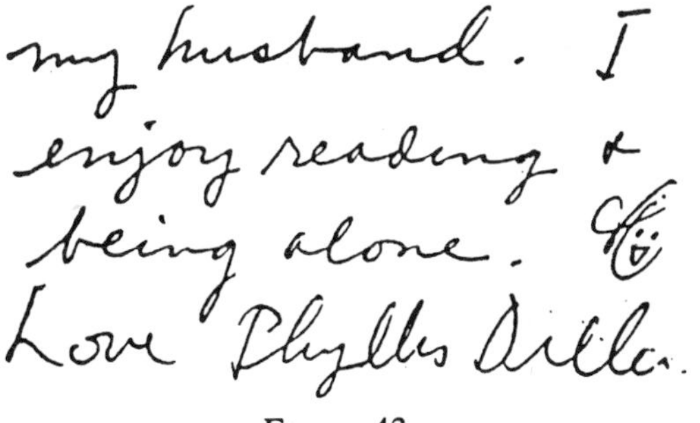

FIGURE 43
Flexible baseline: Phyllis Diller, comic

Too much variability in the line of writing points toward a person of very changeable or unstable emotions, someone whose footing is less than secure (Fig. 44). A wavering baseline indicates that the writer is sensitive to events and circumstances and is on an emotional roller coaster ride. Sometimes the person lacks positive or appropriate emotional control. A changeable baseline also suggests an inner moodiness and an unpredictable nature, although other writing indications need to be considered as well.

An exceptionally erratic baseline, when combined with other writing signs that indicate lack of control, may imply emotional or mental illness. It is very important to evaluate this possibility carefully by considering all other indications in the writing, as well as the writer's physical condition, which can sometimes create a wavy line (Fig. 45).

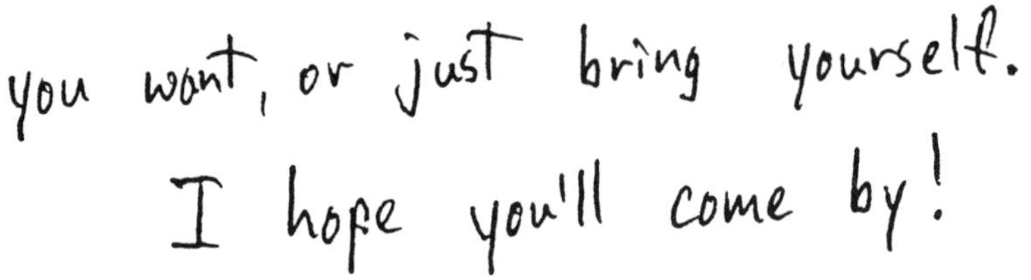

you wont, or just bring yourself.
I hope you'll come by!

FIGURE 44
Wandering baseline

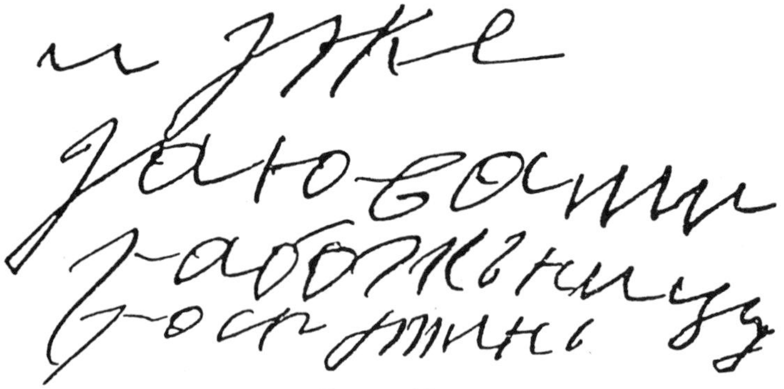

FIGURE 45
Erratic baseline: Gregori Rasputin, Russian mystic

LINE DIRECTION

The direction of the baseline, in addition to how well the writer adheres to it, is important in determining his or her overall attitude toward life. The direction can change according to the individual's mood at the time of writing, so it is important to examine more than one sample of writing before drawing a conclusion.

Writing lines that ascend slightly show that the writer is hopeful, optimistic, and cheerful. He or she has a healthy and positive outlook that usually results in enthusiasm (especially if the writing is large), a pleasant demeanor (if there are no negative indications such as sarcasm or aggressiveness), and an energetic approach (if the writing is bold or if capital letters are large compared with lowercase letters).

FIGURE 46
Ascending lines: Maxwell Maltz, author of *Psycho Cybernetics*

If the lines ascend wildly, the writer is overly optimistic and lacks a solid sense of realism. This sign sometimes points toward manic activity. He or she may be mentally "in the clouds."

Lines that descend belong to the person who is less hopeful and tends to have a negative approach to life (Fig. 47). Descending lines may also result from temporary fatigue, illness, or depression, or may suggest a pervasive despondency, which is borne out by checking more than one sample and other indications in the writing. People whose writing lines descend are likely to be somber, troubled, unenthusiastic, or pessimistic. They often find something wrong with an idea or situation even when nothing is wrong. (Note: Descending lines are *not* indicative of suicidal tendencies.)

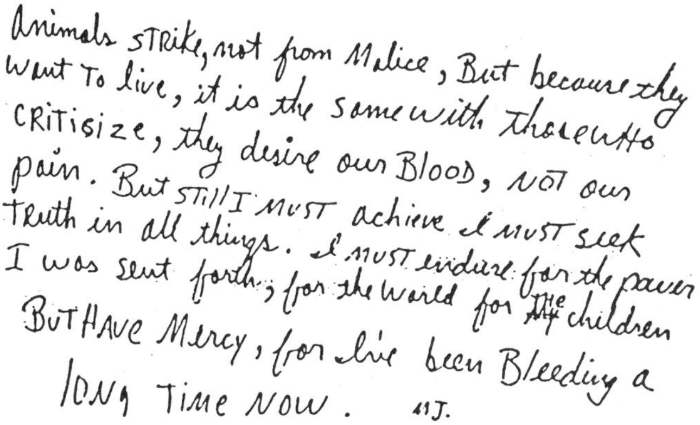

FIGURE 47
Descending lines: Michael Jackson, rock star

Sometimes this downward trend happens only at the end of the line. In such cases the line goes straight across the page and then takes a sudden downward motion, indicating that the writer goes along for a while on an even keel and then suddenly becomes discouraged.

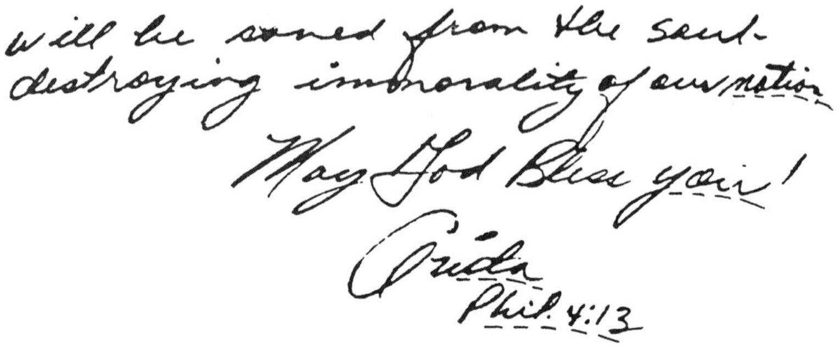

FIGURE 48
Lines descending at end: Anita Bryant, singer

If the lines go straight across the page, indications are that the writer is well-balanced and steadfast in purpose. He or she is emotionally stable and can deal effectively with day-to-day situations. However, since this is the normal way to write, these indications must be validated elsewhere in the writing.

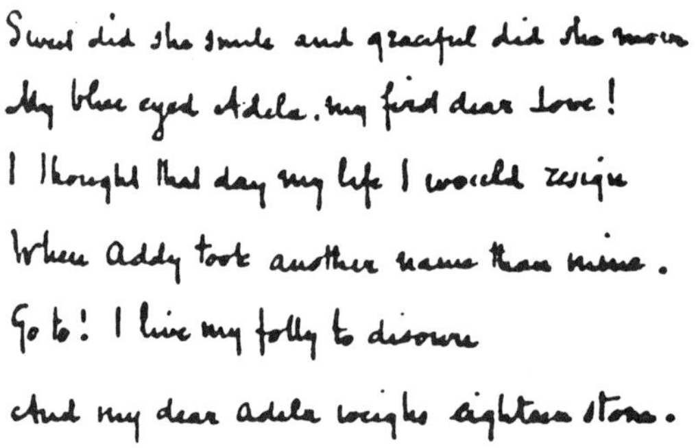

FIGURE 49
Lines straight across page: William M. Thackeray, English author

When the baseline slopes up and then down, forming an arch, the writer is initially hopeful, enthusiastic, and energetic but then becomes more practical, serious, and less energetic. The downward end suggests discouragement, depression, or defeat (Fig. 50).

FIGURE 50

Arched lines: Rudolph Hess, Nazi official and Hitler's secretary

Lines sloping down, then up, resulting in a concave formation, show that the writer is initially unenthusiastic or negative but becomes more hopeful and energetic with time (Fig. 51).

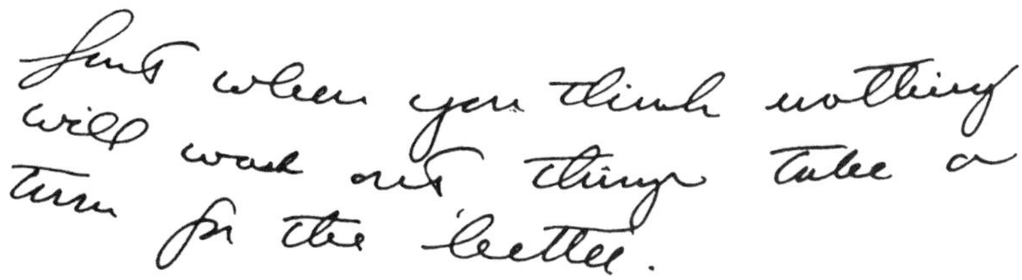

FIGURE 51

Concave lines

HANDWRITING FORM

The form of the writing relates to the writer's general disposition. Generally speaking, soft writing suggests a compliant, relaxed person, whereas strong or angular writing indicates one who is resistant and rigid.

In this section we consider the four primary stroke formations, which illustrate four different outlooks on life: Arcades, angles, garlands, and threads. Later, we will look more closely at these formations and relate them to how people think.

ARCADES

Arcades are slowly written arches that resemble palms turned downward. These are the formations most of us learned to write. Adults who continue to use arched letters tend to be conforming and conventional, especially if the writing lacks original structures. Arcade writers are careful and methodical in their approach to people and tend to be secretive and self-protective. They are comfortable with the familiar and generally do not like to threaten the status quo; they like to follow the rules and what they were taught was correct. Arcade writers express their emotions carefully.

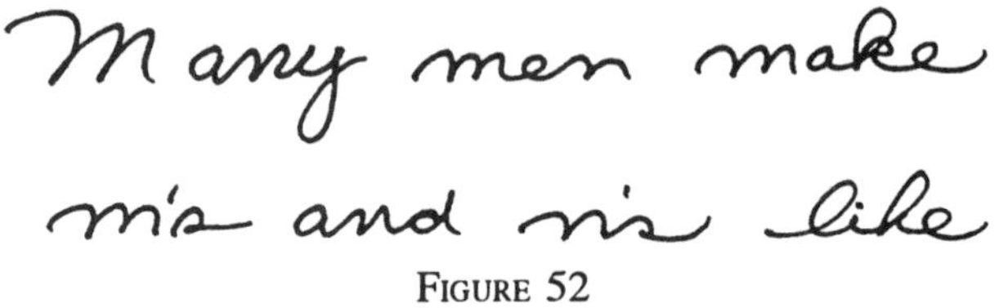

FIGURE 52
Arcade formations

ANGLES

Angular structures point toward firmness of purpose. Angular writers are more intellectual and factual than emotional. As a result, they sometimes do not show their real feelings, or they find a way to quantify them. Very strong angles mean that the person can be rigid and inflexible. The angular writer's strong function is thinking.

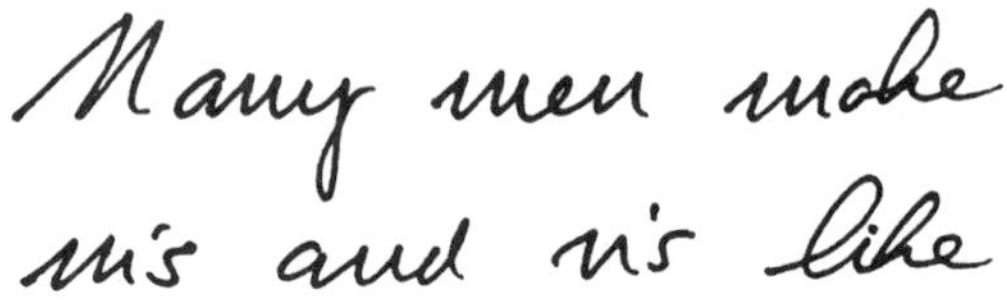

FIGURE 53
Angular formations

GARLANDS

Garland formations are shaped like basins or upturned palms and are curved, soft, flowing, and smooth. They reveal the person who is amiable, kind, receptive, and generous and are usually written by people who like people. Garland writers are cooperative, flexible, and compliant (Fig. 54).

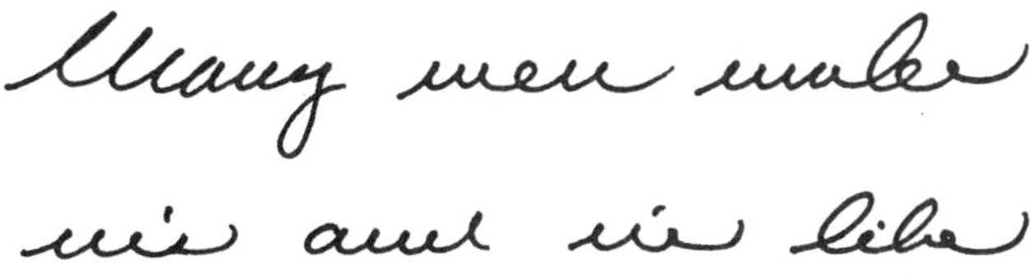

FIGURE 54
Garland formations

THREADS

Thready handwriting is characterized by indistinct formations. Thread writers tend to have a come-what-may approach. They are neither strongly decisive nor opinionated and, because they can often see both sides to a story, are usually tactful and diplomatic. They tend to be indecisive and somewhat irresponsible, although you should check other writing signs to be certain. They ease their way through life, get along with a variety of people, and frequently act spontaneously.

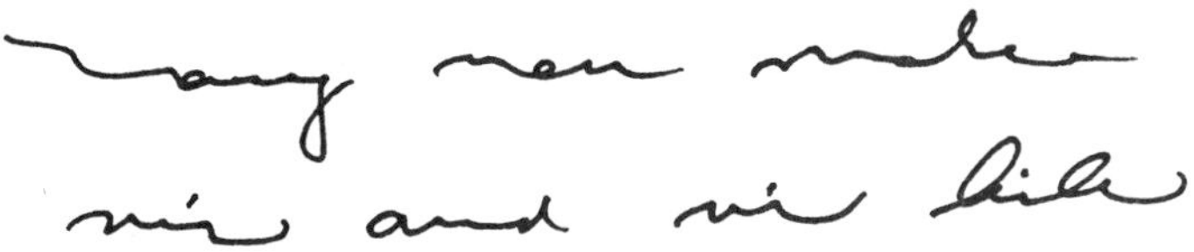

FIGURE 55
Thread formations

4
ZONAL
DISTRIBUTION AND
DIRECTIONAL
TRENDS

Handwriting is divided into three primary zones, each of which represents a different area of the writer's personality. The upper zone contains the upper loops, upward extensions, and capital letters; the middle zone is made up of lowercase letters (e.g., *a*, *c*, *e*, *i*, *m*, *n*, *o*); and the lower zone contains the lower loops and downward extensions.

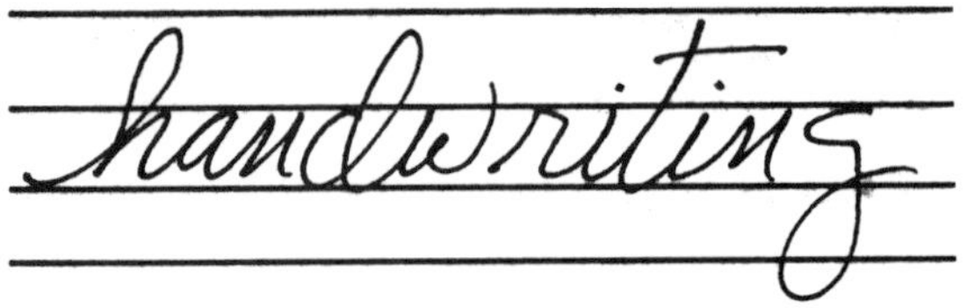

UPPER ZONE

MIDDLE ZONE

LOWER ZONE

FIGURE 56
The three handwriting zones

The three zones correspond to the division of the personality into mind, soul, and body (or superego, ego, and id, to use Freud's terminology). The zones can also be likened to a tree: The trunk is the main structure, the branches reach upward, and the roots lend support and nourishment. Most peoples of the world conceive of the spiritual or divine as above, of the demonic as below, and of humanity as in between the two, which is another analogy for the division of writing into three separate areas.

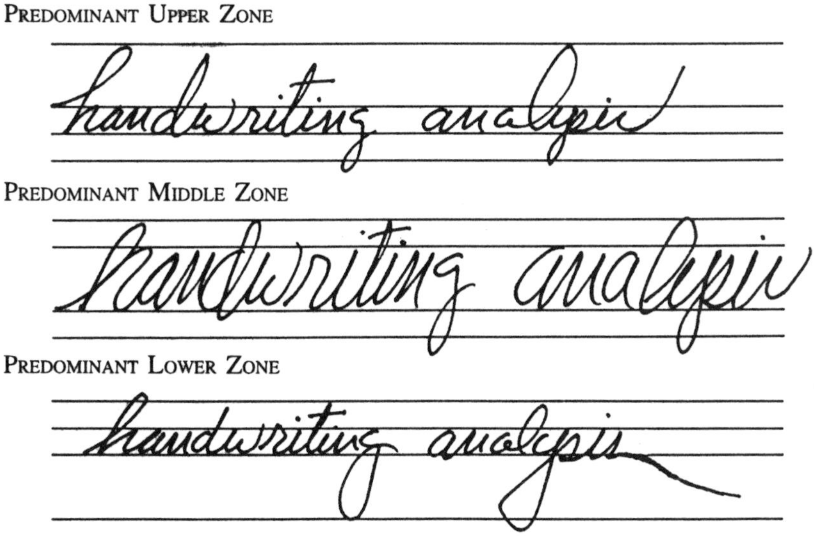

PREDOMINANT UPPER ZONE

PREDOMINANT MIDDLE ZONE

PREDOMINANT LOWER ZONE

FIGURE 57
Predominant zones

The upper zone, therefore, represents the abstract (i.e., mental pursuits, imagination, ideas, and fantasy). It portrays the writer's morals or code of ethics, spiritual needs, and philosophy and also indicates the writer's ambition—what he or she reaches for.

The middle zone is a reflection of reality and practical concerns. It represents the present, the here and now, and also reveals the writer's ego, thought and communication styles, and social involvement.

The lower zone is the materialistic area, where biological demands and the physical are revealed. It reflects the writer's unconscious, instinctual urges, and socio-sexual needs. It is the action area of the writing. In addition, it suggests the writer's degree of resourcefulness.

For overall personality balance the three zones should be equally represented. When the three areas are well balanced, the personality is stable and the ego has an inner equilibrium enhanced by both material and spiritual needs.

When one of the areas is predominant, it is at the expense of the other two. If the upper zone is emphasized, the writer lives in the abstract or the ideal, placing importance on mental pursuits and perhaps ignoring social or physical needs. If the middle zone is emphasized, the writer is socially inclined and deals well with day-to-day concerns but may have little interest in either the abstract or the physical. When the lower zone predominates, the physical is given more emphasis than the social or the mental.

MIDDLE ZONE

The zones are all relative to the baseline on which the lowercase letters rest. The middle zone, or baseline, letters represent everyday life, the here and now. In this area are found clues to how the writer thinks, communicates, responds emotionally, and feels about those responses in relation to society. This area, called the mundane area by many graphologists, is the zone that integrates the spiritual (upper zone) and the material (lower zone).

When the structures of the middle zone are adequate in size (neither extremely small nor overly developed) and the letters are clearly written, the writer has self-confidence, clear communication skills, and a practical outlook on life. If letter size and formation are consistent, these positive qualities are emphasized.

When the writing of the middle zone is emphasized at the expense of the upper and lower zones, the writer lives in the here and now, has down-to-earth interests, and is concerned with practical, everyday matters and what is happening at the moment. The person may have little interest in intellectual or philosophical matters and tends to be primarily concerned with his or her own feelings.

Usually, middle zone writers are seemingly self-confident and social-minded, although their self-confident approach is often a pretense. The writer of an exaggerated middle zone is sometimes boastful and is nearly always concerned with his or her looks, and looks in general. An overly emphasized middle zone suggests immaturity and difficulty in connecting the past with the present.

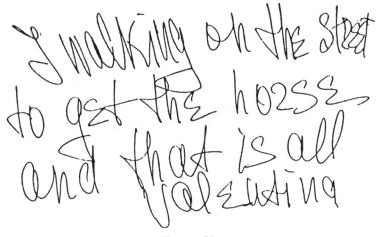

FIGURE 58
Large middle zone: "Valentina," clothes designer

A very small middle zone, on the other hand, generally indicates a lack of self-confidence. Small middle zone writers are often not in touch with their true feelings and are generally unexpressive of emotions. They choose to lead independent lives, sometimes concentrating on their own small world and ignoring what goes on around them. This can indicate that the writer neglects everyday matters (when baseline letters are poorly formed, for example). When the middle zone is small, the meanings of either the upper or lower zone (or both) are given added emphasis. If the middle area is dwarfed by the upper or lower areas, the writer probably attempts to compensate for a lack of confidence through mental activity or a search for the ideal (upper zone) or through materialistic pursuits (lower zone).

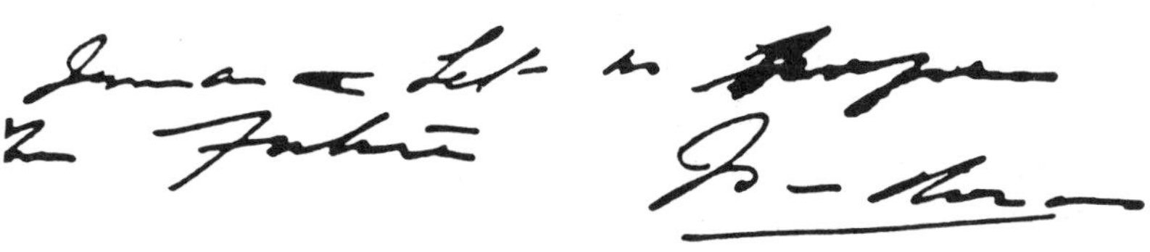

FIGURE 59
Small middle zone: Isadora Duncan, innovative dancer

UPPER ZONE

In the upper zone we encounter the writer's relationship to abstract concepts. Mental pursuits, imagination, ideas, and fantasy are all indicated by this area, as are the writer's code of ethics, morals, spiritual needs, and overall philosophy.

A normal upper zone is one in which the loops are about two times taller than the middle zone letters. Balanced upper zone letters are rounded and moderate in width and imply a healthy philosophical outlook—a personal code by which the writer lives his or her life. If the upper zone loops are not exaggerated (either in height or width, or by the presence of extraneous marks), the writer is likely to have conventional standards and to follow societal expectations.

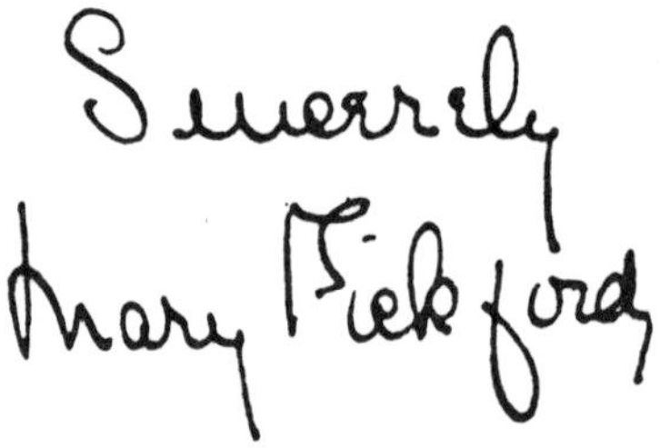

FIGURE 60
**Balanced upper zone: Mary Pickford, U.S. actress
("America's Sweetheart")**

A neglected or stunted upper zone implies that the writer is more concerned with daily living and practical considerations than with ideas or philosophy. He or she tends to take little interest in intellectual matters and may lack imagination (Fig. 61). In extreme cases, where there are *no* upper loops, or tiny ones, the writer may lack a strong sense of morals or ethics (see Bruno Hauptmann, Fig. 93). This is especially true when the overall organization of the writing is poor and there are indications of deceit, materialism, or uncontrolled sensuality.

Narrow loops in the upper zone point out a practical, workable value system. The writer has a personal code of ethics to which he or she remains loyal. Although not especially philosophical or spiritual, he or she nevertheless follows conservative personal guidelines. Robert Frost's writing indicates a down-to-earth philosophy (Fig. 62).

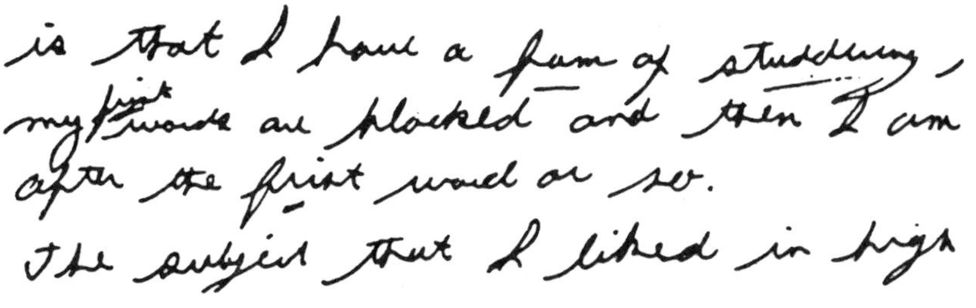

FIGURE 61
Neglected upper zone

FIGURE 62
Narrow upper loops: Robert Frost, U.S. poet

Retraced loops in the upper zone reveal inhibitions in the intellectual sphere. A retrace occurs when the writer makes a normal upstroke and then follows down the same stroke instead of forming a loop. The imagination is repressed and the writer does not allow room for ideas. If the retraced loops are also tall, the person has a narrow, perhaps strict, code of ethics that does not allow for other ways of thinking. If the retraced loops are short, the upper zone is considered to be neglected, as discussed earlier.

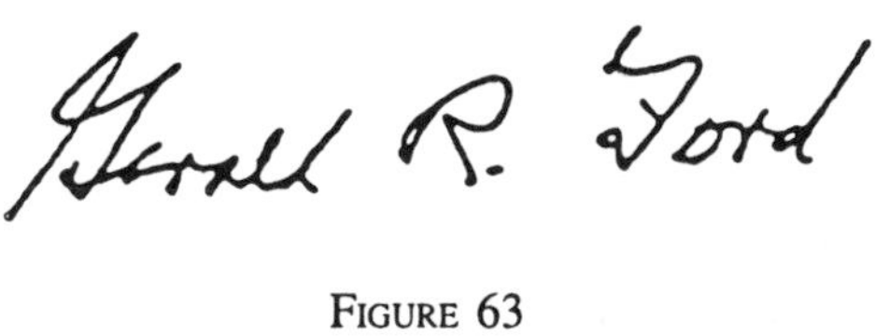

FIGURE 63
Retraced upper zone: Gerald Ford, U.S. president

Sticklike formations in the upper area (not retraced but coming directly down from above) imply a practical, workable code of ethics.

These writers are more concerned with facts than ideas and are direct and to the point. Generally, they are independent in their thinking, unlikely to be concerned with custom or convention, and intellectually inclined.

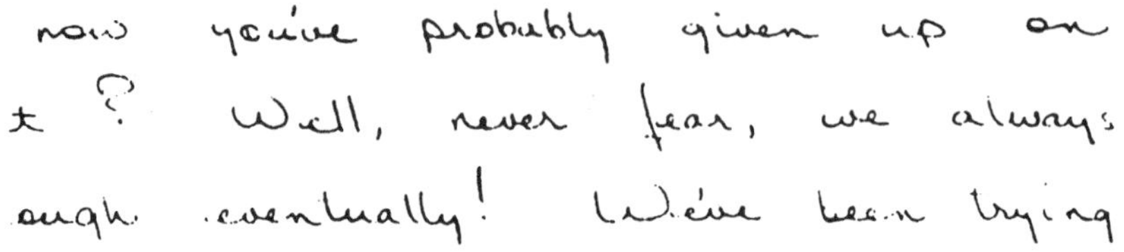

FIGURE 64
Sticklike upper zone

Wide upper loops show imagination and openness to ideas and possibilities. They indicate writers who are morally tolerant and are usually willing to give others the benefit of the doubt; they are also tolerant with themselves, thinking and doing things that a more narrow-looped writer might not (Fig. 65).

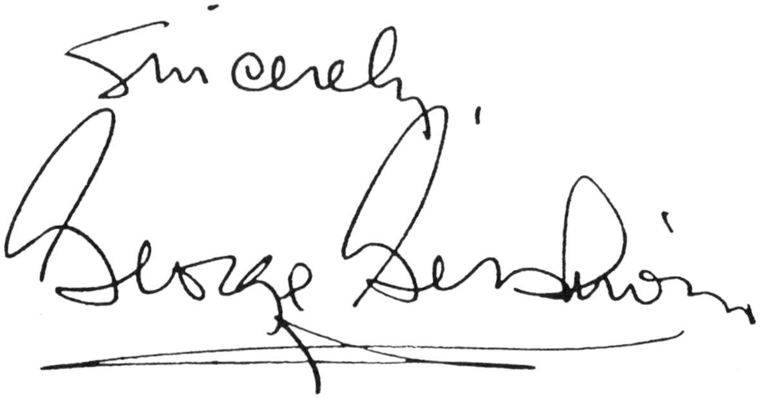

FIGURE 65
Wide upper loops: George Gershwin, American composer

Exaggerated upper loops show an overly broad-minded attitude and a tolerance of many approaches, none of which the writer totally embraces. Extreme upper loop writers are highly imaginative, especially when the loops are wide as well as tall: they are keen on ideas, philosophies, and intangibles, but may be carried away with their ideas. If their upper loops are not balanced by the other two zones, they lack a sense of practicality and may have difficulty using the ideas that come through the imagination. The dreamer, the idealist, and the seeker of Utopia fit into this category. When *t* crosses float into this area, the writer has "way out" goals and may not have the inner resources to reach those dreams. An exaggerated upper zone also suggests that the writer needs attention and recognition for supposedly great ideas, wants you to know he or she is smart, and may boast so that you will not underrate his or her importance. Exceptionally inflated upper loops indicate that the person may feel intellectually inferior, and may compensate by bragging about a supposedly wide range of knowledge, or maintaining an over-rated personal philosophy.

FIGURE 66
**Exaggerated upper zone: (A) Joan Collins, actress;
(B) L. Ron Hubbard, founder of Dianetics/Scientology**

LOWER ZONE

The lower zone is below the baseline. It contains the lower loops and any extensions that come down from the middle zone. This area, because it rests below the baseline (reality) represents the unconscious and an individual's instinctual drives; it contains graphic indications of the writer's approach to materialism and sexuality as well as the amount of emotion behind social encounters.*

"Normal" lower loops are about two or two-and-a-half times longer than middle zone letters. They are smoothly rounded and neither pro-portionately too large nor too small, although they are usually a bit larger

---

*See *Handwriting: Its Socio-Sexual Implications,* by Reed C. Hayes, for a more thorough discussion of the lower zone.

than the upper loops. A well-balanced lower zone reflects a "normal" and healthy attitude toward social encounters and biological urges. For these writers sex is a normal part of everyday life, neither a threat nor an obsession. They gain satisfaction from sex, view social encounters as enjoyable, and have an adequate amount of resourcefulness to meet everyday situations.

The handwriting of actress Loretta Swit contains well-formed, proportionate lower loops that illustrate (along with regularity, good spacing, clarity, and straight baseline) a positive, healthy approach to life.

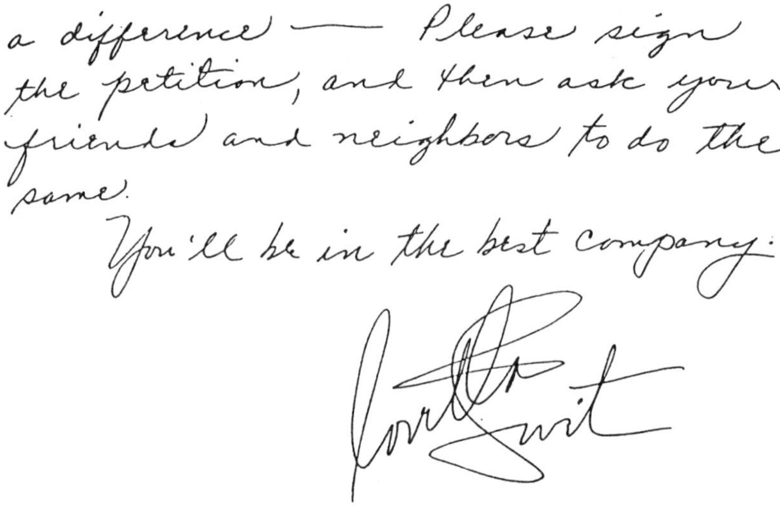

FIGURE 67
Normal lower zone: Loretta Swit, star of *M*A*S*H*

A stunted or neglected lower zone implies lack of interest in both social and sexual encounters. Although they may occasionally appear to be the life of the party, these writers need solitude and often prefer to work by themselves. They sometimes avoid intimate contact, perhaps because of unconscious inhibitions. These writers tend to be socially or sexually immature and are not adequately equipped with a sense of ingenuity. More emphasis on the middle or upper zones, or both, shows that the writer places more importance on everyday activities and mental concerns than on the fulfillment of instinctual urges (Fig. 68).

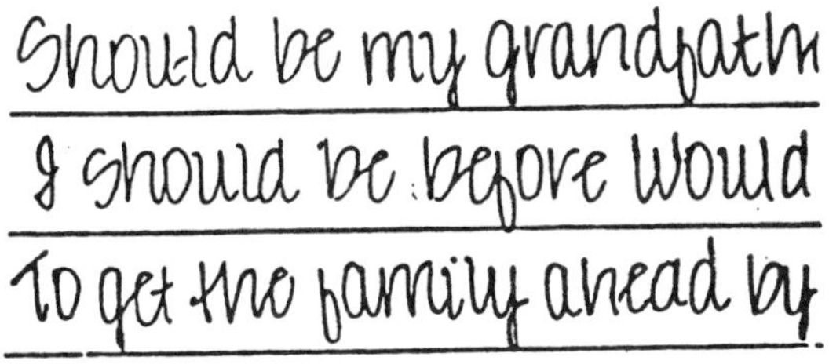

Should be my grandfath
I should be before would
To get the family ahead by

FIGURE 68
Neglected lower zone

Repressed (squeezed) strokes in this area imply that the writer is out of touch with his or her instinctual nature. Repressed strokes are those in which the downstroke is covered by the upstroke. These writers fear closeness in social or sexual encounters and have trouble opening up to people because of childhood influences that convinced them that sex was bad. Repressing these unpleasant memories, the writer avoids close contact and does not have to face potential loss of energy to the ego by being vulnerable (Fig. 69).

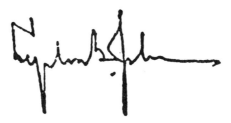

FIGURE 69
Repressed lower loops: Lyndon B. Johnson, U.S. President

Sticklike lower zone strokes, which come down from the baseline and do not form complete loops, show that the writer is self-sufficient and independent although seldom materialistic. He or she is factual rather than imaginative, practical instead of romantic. These writers are not inclined to emotional expression but look instead at practicalities. If the sticklike strokes are also short, the writer does not derive much pleasure from either sex or social activities. Long, straight, lower zone strokes, like those of President Jimmy Carter (Fig. 70-A), show consistent and determined efforts. When these strokes are made as clubs (growing steadily heavier and ending in a blob of ink) the person is capable of relentless determination, sometimes negatively so.

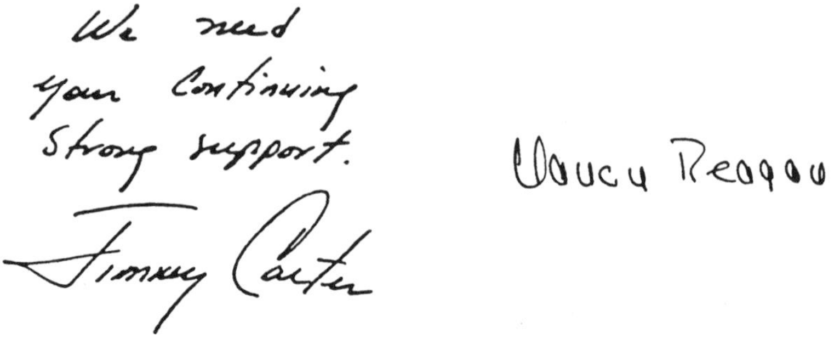

FIGURE 70
Sticklike lower zone: (A) Jimmy Carter, U.S. president;
(B) Nancy Reagan, wife of U.S. president Ronald Reagan

Wide lower zone structures place emphasis on the physical because of an active imagination. These writers seek material comfort and social contacts and have healthy sexual appetites as measured by the relative size of the formations. They want variety and activity in their lives, both socially and sexually, and are inclined to be romantic and emotionally expressive (Fig. 71).

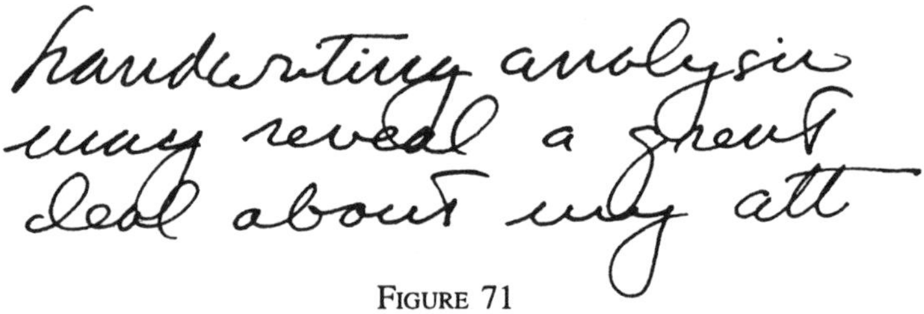

FIGURE 71
Wide lower zone structures

When the lower loops are exaggerated, however, the urge for social and sexual variety may be intense. The writer of very large lower loops is restless because of an active emotional life, needs frequent variety and activity, and may be constantly on the move, especially when the loops tangle with the next line below. Such people have trouble settling down to one relationship and, if sexually loyal to one person, need a lot of social variety. These writers often feel that a new job or a new relationship will satisfy an inner uncertainty: In essence, they are running from themselves. Whether the upper or middle zone balances this area is important.

FIGURE 72
Exaggerated lower zone:
Marilyn Monroe, actress (signed "Norma Jean," her birth name)

DIRECTIONAL TRENDS

The instant the pen touches the paper, a dot is formed. This point represents where you are at that moment. If you lift the pen and leave only a dot, you are leaving evidence that you have been there. As soon as you alter the dot in any way, there is motion. The motion may be only enough to elongate the dot, or the movement may result in an elaborate series of formations. Whatever the result of the pen's movement, the written gesture shows a directional trend, either upward, downward, backward, or forward. The direction of such movements is important in understanding the "direction" of the writer's personality and in discovering more accurately how he or she expresses character traits.

With the exception of handwriting based on non-Latin alphabets (Hebrew and Arabic, for example) writing proceeds from left to right. We place pen to paper and then move forward into new and unseen territory. We move from where we are to where we are going; we shift away from the present and into the future. Therefore, writing movements that go rightward indicate forward thinking, advancement, and progress. As the writer moves away from self and toward other people, so does a rightward trend suggest extroversion. The right also represents the father (not always literally) and masculinity.

However, if the pen moves leftward from the starting point or turns leftward after beginning in a forward direction, the person is moving away from the present and into the past. How far leftward the movement goes indicates the degree of hesitation or regression. Leftward-directed strokes imply introversion. The writer who pulls to the left expresses a desire to return to the past, to the mother, or to the nurturing qualities that the mother represents.

INNER WORLD	OUTER WORLD
REGRESSION	PROGRESSION
PAST ⟵————— **PRESENT** —————⟶ **FUTURE**	
MOTHER	FATHER
FEMININITY	MASCULINITY

FIGURE 73
Indications of rightward and leftward directional trends

These principles can be applied to handwriting slant. A rightward trend indicates a leaning toward other people and a willingness to take part in the world, whereas a leftward slant represents an emotional pull away from the world and a desire to remain stable by reaching for past security (see the next chapter for a more detailed explanation of slant characteristics).

Movements to the right or left can, of course, be located in any of the three zones. Rightward movements in the upper zone reflect a progressive mentality and a concern for the future. In the middle zone they indicate that the writer reaches out to others (soft forward movements) or pushes toward others (harsh, straight movements). In the lower zone they reveal aggressiveness and strong urges toward physical activity.

| UPPER ZONE | MIDDLE ZONE | LOWER ZONE |

FIGURE 74
Rightward movements in the three zones

Likewise, leftward movements can be found in any of the zones. In the upper zone, a leftward trend shows a philosophy strongly tied to past experiences and a reluctance to move ahead to new ways of thinking. In the middle zone, such strokes imply introversion and an unwillingness to reach out emotionally. In the lower zone, these movements reveal emotional dependency, immature sexuality (especially for men), and regressive behavior.

| UPPER ZONE | MIDDLE ZONE | LOWER ZONE |

FIGURE 75
Leftward movements in the three zones

The implications of the various handwriting areas will take on fuller meaning when we discuss handwriting slant and as we delve into individual stroke interpretations.

5

YOUR SLANT

ON LIFE

EMOTIONAL RESPONSIVENESS

Handwriting slant is a highly significant sign that indicates the degree of emotional responsiveness. Emotions are vital in understanding personality, as they are at the base of everything we think, say, and do. Emotions cause us to respond to people and to life in general. Through emotions we express happiness or sadness, confidence or insecurity, warmth, coolness, anger, love, and a host of other feelings. Our emotions are an essential link between our inner and outer worlds.

When we meet people for the first time, our impressions of those people are based on how we react to them emotionally. When we hear a heart-rending story or see an especially moving play, we respond according to our individual propensity for emotional reaction. The foundation for whatever we do is the feeling below the surface.

The general graphological rule about emotions is that the more the writing slants away from vertical (either to the right or left), the more emotionally responsive the writer is, and the more feelings affect his or her thoughts and actions. The feelings may or may not be lasting, and

56

the writer may or may not express them outwardly, depending on other characteristics, but slanted writing always indicates inner responsiveness.

To determine how emotionally responsive you are, compare your writing with the following gauge.

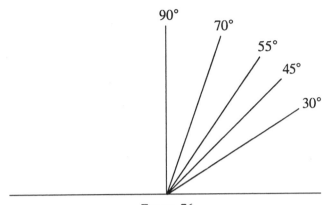

Figure 76
Handwriting slant gauge

To be certain of the writer's "slant on life," you can actually measure the handwriting strokes. This is a simple procedure that I recommend for the beginning stages of handwriting analysis. It gives a more accurate reading on the slant and, at the same time, allows a closer look at the structures of the handwriting. First, draw a line under a few words of the writing; then, draw slant lines through several of the *up*strokes of letters, as shown in Fig. 77. Using a protractor, you can now readily see which slant area(s) the writing fits into.

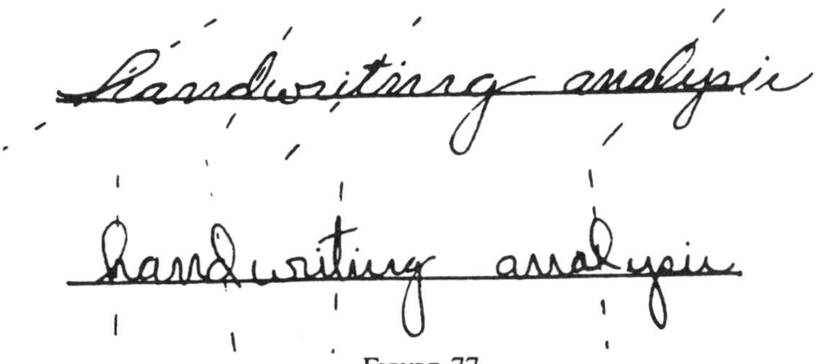

Figure 77
Slant measurements

Vertical or near-vertical writing shows reserved emotions. The vertical writer is usually cool, calm, and collected and seldom allows feelings to enter into decisions and actions. The vertical writer considers the possibilities before moving ahead and asks, Is it wise?, Will it pay?, or What will be the consequences? He or she makes decisions based on logic, tends to be self-sufficient or independent, and is often indifferent to other people. Vertical writers usually do not express their feelings (unless the writing is large, or heavy and angular, or has enlarged loops). Nonslanted writing does not mean that the writer is cold or unfeeling but that he or she controls emotions and their expression.

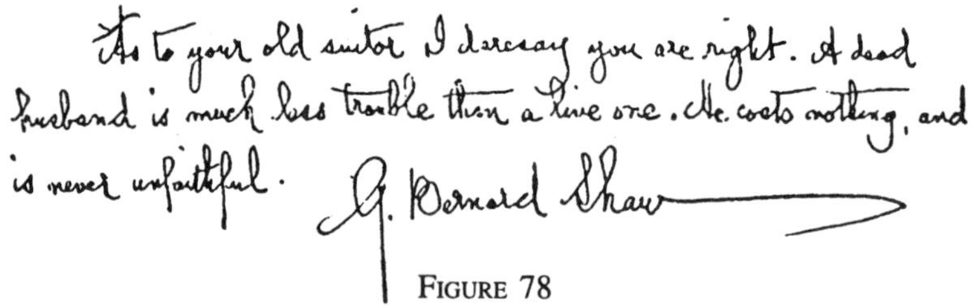
As to your old suitor I daresay you are right. A dead husband is much less trouble than a live one. He costs nothing, and is never unfaithful. G. Bernard Shaw

FIGURE 78

Vertical writing: George Bernard Shaw, British author and socialist

Handwriting slightly inclined to the right indicates that the person is mildly reactive to people, situations, and events. He or she is apt to initially feel emotion and then to step back and take a second look to avoid any impulsive moves. Sometimes caught between logic and feeling, these writers often do not know whether to act on emotion or good common sense, and can therefore be indecisive. They are generally friendly and sympathetic, and can see both the logical and human sides of any situation.

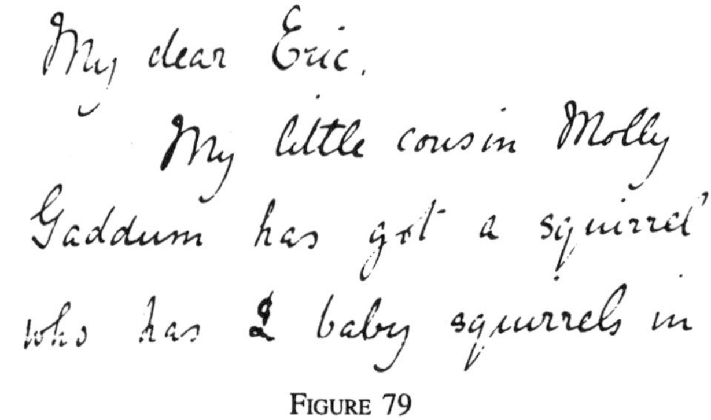
My dear Eric,
My little cousin Molly Gaddum has got a squirrel who has 2 baby squirrels in

FIGURE 79

Slightly inclined writing: Beatrix Potter,
British children's writer and illustrator; creator of *Peter Rabbit*

Most of us, because we are socially inclined and interrelational, fall into the next category to the right. Rightward slant reveals quick inner reactions, a tendency to lean toward people, and quick involvement with people and situations based on inner responses. Actions and decisions are based primarily on feelings rather than thought, although other signs modify this. With a lack of self-regulating factors, rightward slant indicates impulsivity; with other social traits, it is the basis for friendliness.

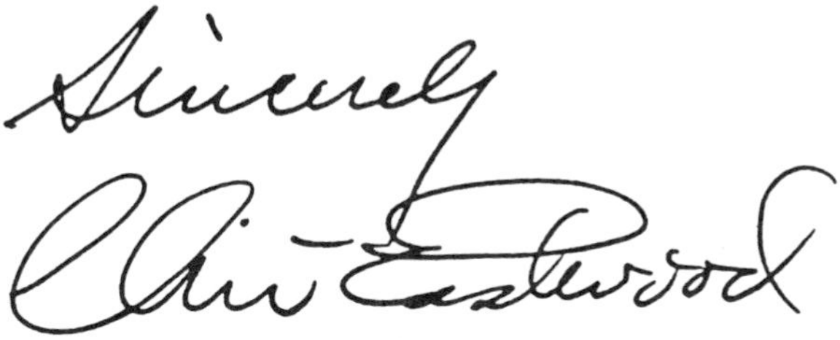

FIGURE 80
Rightward slant: Clint Eastwood, actor

A far rightward slant discloses intense and extreme emotional responses. These writers react strongly to both inner and outer stimuli and therefore find it difficult to be objective. They have a strong tendency to be impulsive and to act on whatever feelings prevail at the moment. These writers are emotional whirlwinds—up one minute and down the next. Their moods, which are usually extreme, can change quickly and without notice. Such intensity of feeling results in periodic emotional burnout and requires that the writer get away occasionally to recharge the emotional batteries.

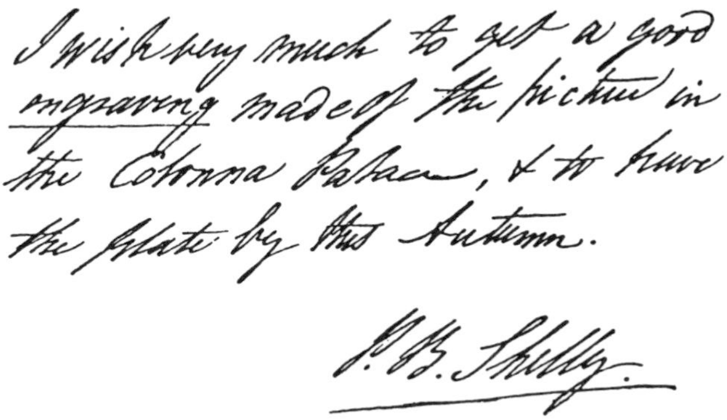

FIGURE 81
Far forward slant: Percy B. Shelley, British romantic poet

Far forward writers need emotional feedback to feel secure and balanced. They tend to wear their hearts on their sleeves and lean toward emotional dependency. They need to be liked. Because they are so intense in their reactions, they are sensitive to the needs and feelings of those around them and often do well as writers, actors, salesmen, or speakers, because these are areas in which they can effectively express themselves with sensitivity and intensity. If the writing is also heavy, the person becomes impassioned about his or her interests. Far forward writers include Percy B. Shelley, Romantic poet (Fig. 81); Isadora Duncan, innovative and controversial dancer (Fig. 59); and Adolph Hitler, dictator (Fig. 240).

Backhand writing, which is a bit more difficult to interpret, implies that the writer withdraws emotionally. He or she still responds to emotion, as shown by movement away from the vertical, but the feelings are turned inward. Self-absorbed and self-protective, backhand writers are concerned with their own inner feelings and security needs. They are careful in approach and are inclined to ask "How will this benefit *me*?" before taking action. Leftward slant in itself is not a sign of selfishness; it should not be considered negative before other writing signs are studied.

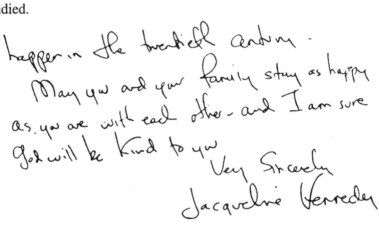

FIGURE 82
Backhand writing: Jacqueline Kennedy Onassis

However, leftward writing is a suggestion that the writer thinks or acts contrary to the norm and habitually does things in an unconventional way, whether out of defiance, fear, or egotism.

Teenagers frequently adopt this slant, which reflects a time of emotional uncertainty. (This is often true of girls, while the writing of teenage boys tends to become more heavy and angular, suggesting a more aggressive approach.) Often the person remains in the emotional retreat into adulthood. Sometimes the person is able to work out of the self-imposed shell, at which point the handwriting takes a more forward direction.

Writing that leans far backward (reclined) reveals inner fears and strong emotional withdrawal. The person represses emotions and natural expression out of unconscious fear and a strong need for security.

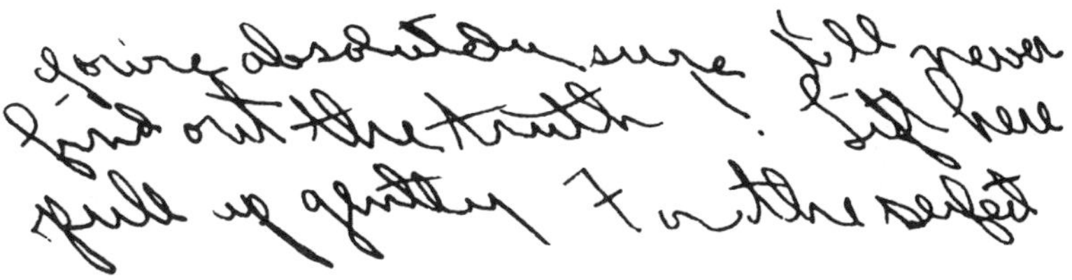

FIGURE 83
Extremely reclined writing

Students and clients frequently ask how left-handedness affects writing slant. Contrary to popular belief, most left-handed writers do not write in a backhand fashion. Many left-handed writers have far forward writing, and there are right-handed writers whose writing slants leftward. If the writer, whether right-handed or left-handed, is strong on emotional response to people, his or her writing will slant forward.*

Consistency of slant suggests emotional stability and an unfluctuating approach to people and situations (if the baseline is also unwavering and if the writing is regular overall). When writing strokes are consistently vertical, the writer is systematic and logical; if the writing slants far forward in a consistent manner, the writer is invariable in emotional responsiveness; and if the writing slants consistently leftward, the person is routinely withdrawn.

_____

*However, it is good to know if the writer is left-handed, as some left-handers have a tendency to make their *t* crosses from right to left, in which case the indications of that stroke are given less importance. See discussion of this stroke in Chapter 11 on the letter *t*.

However, few handwritings are so regular that they fall entirely into any one of the slant areas. Most people are pliable and willing to roll with the punches where feelings are concerned, and the slant of their writing strokes varies accordingly.

With strong slant variability the interpretation is negative. Inconsistent slant reflects emotional fluctuation and uncertainty. Writers of changing slant can sometimes be cool and collected and at other times more emotional, according to how much the slant varies. Variable slant implies indecisiveness, unpredictability, unreliability, impulsiveness, or flightiness, especially when the writing strokes are light and when there are other variations in the script. Extreme variability reveals an erratic, unstable person (Fig. 84).

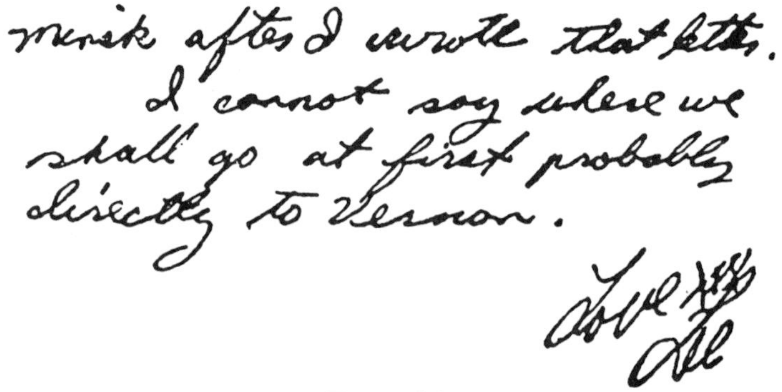

FIGURE 84
Inconsistent slant: Lee Harvey Oswald, assassin of John F. Kennedy

EMOTIONAL PERMANENCE

Handwriting pressure is also significant in determining the writer's emotional makeup.

As with the other basic signs, consistency of pressure reveals emotional balance and suggests that the writer deals with situations in a steady and reliable way. Erratic pressure, of course, shows inconsistent emotions and, in the extreme, emotional imbalance.

Intensity or permanence of feeling is represented by the heaviness of the writing strokes, which shows the degree to which a person absorbs and remembers feeling. If heavy pressure is applied to the writing instrument, the person's feelings are strong and lasting, whereas light pressure suggests temporary, even flighty emotions. Heavy pressure shows emotional stability, whereas light pressure indicates that the writer is more sensitive and easily influenced.

Moderate pressure is the norm and indicates that the person has sufficient energy and holds onto feelings appropriately but does not become absorbed or biased by them (Fig. 85).

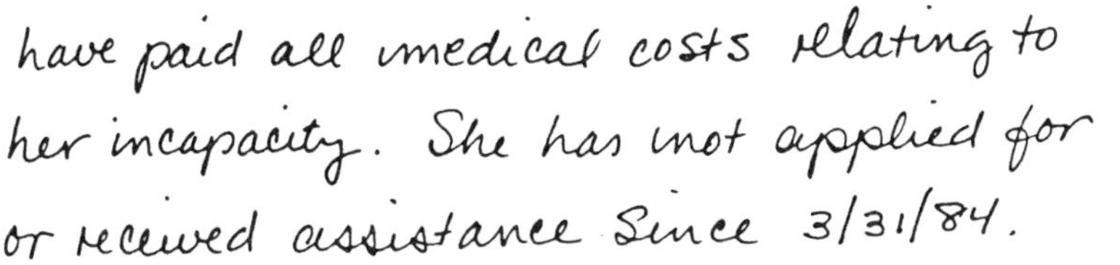

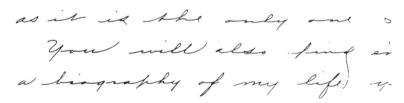

FIGURE 85
Moderate pressure

Temporary feeling shows in the lightness of the strokes in Fig. 86. The writer feels immediately and is highly reactive, as indicated by the far rightward slant, but the feelings do not last; by tomorrow (or perhaps an hour from now) they will have changed.

FIGURE 86
Light pressure

People who use little pressure on the pen or pencil tend to be more concerned with mental or spiritual aspects of life or both, and less concerned with sensory impressions. They are sensitive to the environment and are sometimes easily influenced by situations and events. On the positive side, they are usually sensitive to people's feelings. Less positively, they have little "depth" of feeling; and they often have to relive each situation as it comes up anew.

Very light pressure that hardly adheres to the paper reveals the writer with little built-in emotional stamina, who is supersensitive to events and circumstances but casts off experiences almost as soon as they happen. Extremely light script usually shows a lack of vitality and the need for lots of rest.

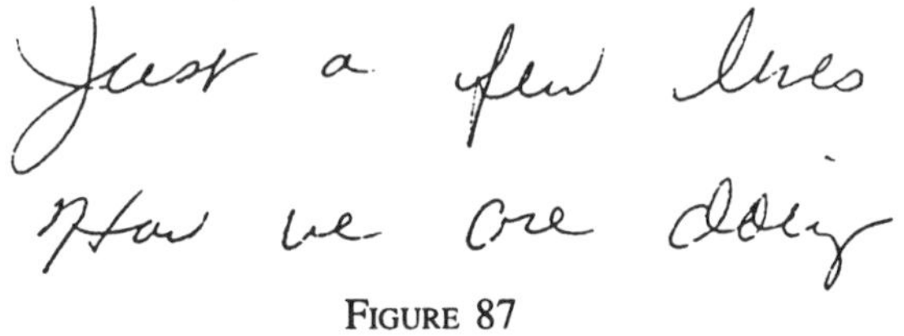

Figure 87
Very light pressure

Consistent, heavy pressure, like that of Los Angeles mayor Tom Bradley, shows deep, strong, and lasting feelings. Because of the lasting quality of the emotions, the writer is strongly influenced by past exeriences and involvements. Heavy writers are concerned with sensory impressions and tend to like the good life. As a rule, they are energetic, mentally or physically or both, and if the writing is very heavy, they have a strong sense of color, taste, or smell. Their personality texture is rich, for they absorb feeling as a sponge absorbs water. They need spice in their lives. On the negative side, these people can be insensitive to others' feelings and tend to be prejudiced by past situations.

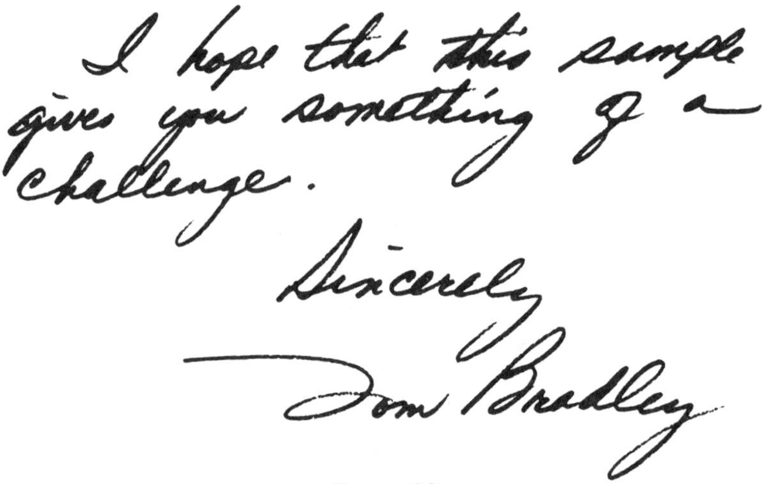

Figure 88
Heavy pressure: Tom Bradley, mayor of Los Angeles, CA

With very heavy pressure, feelings are especially strong and the writer is biased by feelings from the past. Heavy writers both love and hate with intensity and have very strong opinions. These writers are sensuous and energetic, and they possess driving power that can be used either positively or negatively. With exceptionally heavy pressure, the handwriting strokes are sometimes fuzzy or inky and the interpretation leans toward the negative. (Note that even though Tom Bradley's writing is heavy, the edges of letters are sharp and clearly defined and the pressure is not intense, as indicated by the light upstrokes.)

Handwriting is muddy when curves and circles are ink-filled and strokes seem to swell. Muddy writing is different from heavy-pressured writing in that it looks blotched or unclean; the outer edges of the strokes are not as sharp nor clearly defined as in merely heavy pressured script, and the "mud patches" are often sporadic. (In evaluating muddy strokes, be certain that the muddiness is not the result of a bad pen.) This sign denotes sensuality, uncontrolled passions, strong physical needs, and a tendency toward excesses. Muddy writers are inclined to take part in the unrefined side of life (unlike the heavy writer who likes food and drink but is more refined and less prone to excess). If the writing appears clean overall but has sudden blotches of ink dispersed throughout, the writer has periodic bouts with excessive living. Muddy writing is never a positive sign, especially when combined with irregularity, indications of deceit, aggressiveness, anger, sarcasm, unclear thinking, defiance, and so forth (Fig. 89).

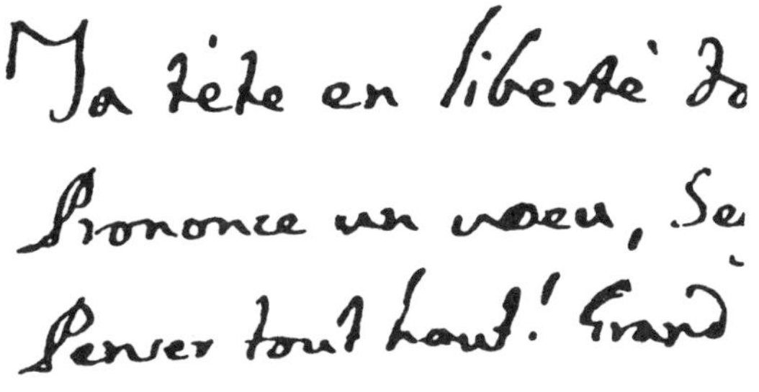

FIGURE 89
Muddy, ink-filled handwriting: Giovanni Casanova,
Italian lover and adventurer

Determination of handwriting pressure can be confusing, especially for the beginning handwriting analyst, although this uncertainty dispels with experience. Ballpoint pen writing is particularly hard to decipher in this respect, because ballpoint pens are designed to deposit only a certain amount of ink on the paper. Feeling the underside of the paper will help you to decide how heavily the writer pressed on the pen. A magnifying glass will also provide a closer look at how much ink has been deposited in the writing trail.

6
HOW
YOU THINK

The regularity and overall rhythm of your handwriting are primary indicators of how you think. If the writing as a whole is inconsistent, poorly spaced, uneven, or changeable, your thinking will be adversely affected. But when the writing is harmonious, consistent, evenly spaced, and regular, your thinking processes are enhanced.

The speed of the handwriting is also an important clue to thinking style. The more active one's thinking, the more quickly the desire to express ideas. Quick, lively writing shows rapid thinking and the ability to perceive readily; it also suggests spontaneity and a tendency to act instinctively (see John F. Kennedy and Albert Einstein, Fig. 90).

Careful evaluation of other characteristics is important. If fast writing is also poorly formed and lacks organization and good rhythm, the writer is apt to be impulsive, indecisive, reactive, and unsettled. The presence of regulatory traits and those indicating self-discipline help fast writers to make positive use of their quick thinking style.

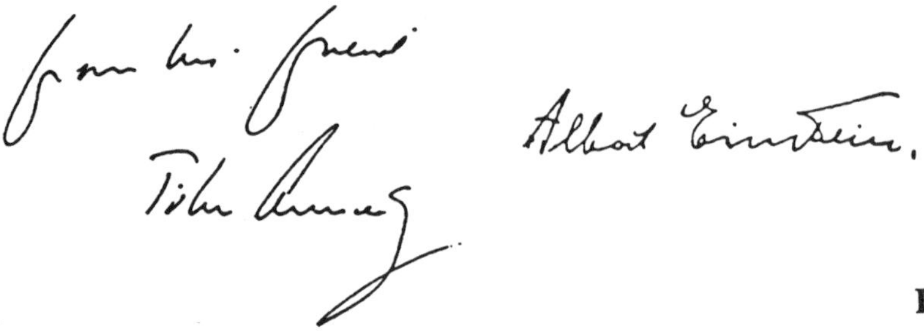

A

B

FIGURE 90
**Fast writing: (A) John F. Kennedy, U.S. president;
(B) Albert Einstein, physicist**

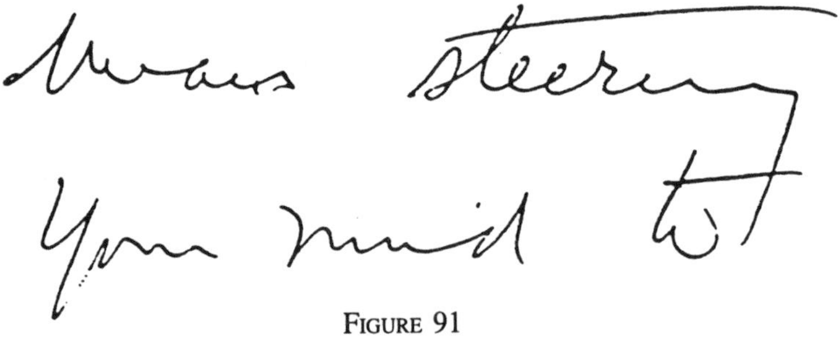

FIGURE 91
Fast, poorly formed writing

Slowly written strokes indicate the slow and deliberate thinker. These people like to take one step at a time, acting with caution and carefully considering the angles before they move deliberately toward their aims. They tend to be traditional, conservative, and restrained, and generally express emotions carefully.

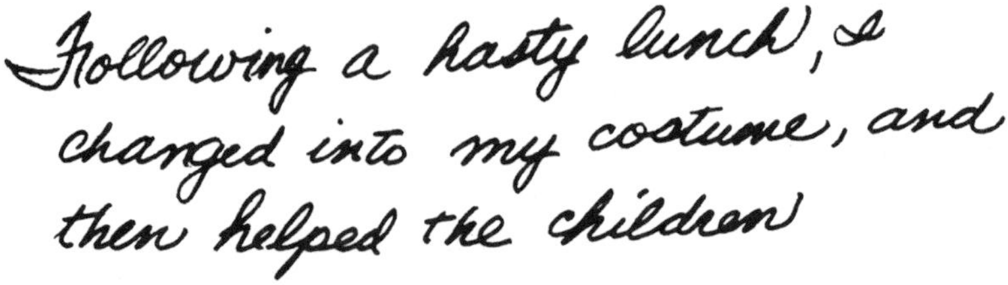

FIGURE 92
Slow handwriting

The extremely slow writer may be immature or lacking in education. This can be determined by considering the overall organization and consistency of the writing, as well as by checking for gross spelling errors and frequent corrections. Sometimes exceptionally slow writing is used as a cover-up or an attempt to hide one's true identity, as in the case of Bruno Hauptmann, kidnapper of the Lindberghs' baby. Hauptmann's ransom note (Fig. 93-A) is very deliberate compared to his normal writing (Fig. 93-B), which is faster and more forward.

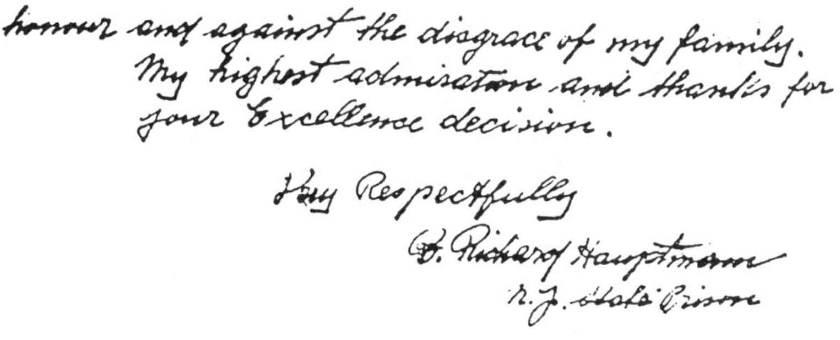

FIGURE 93
**(A) Bruno Hauptmann's deliberately slow, vertical writing
of the ransom note: an attempt to cover his true nature
(B) Bruno Hauptmann's normal writing: faster and more forward
than the writing of the ransom note**

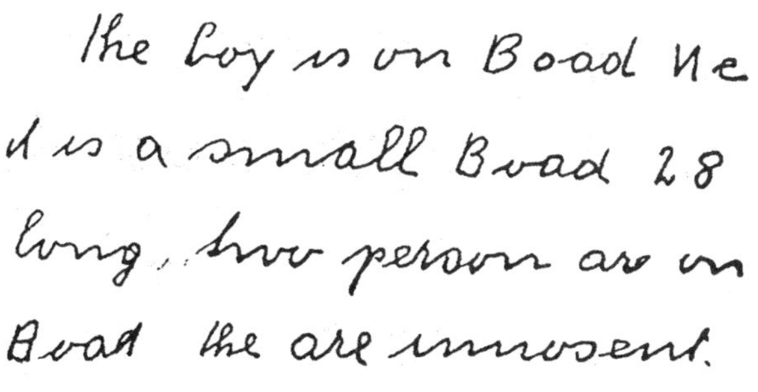

The age of the writer is also important, as it is natural for an immature youngster to write slowly (see Fig. 94).

Most handwriting falls between very slow and very fast, indicating good overall intelligence and responsiveness. Other writing signs give further clues to the thinking and reaction speed of moderately fast writers.

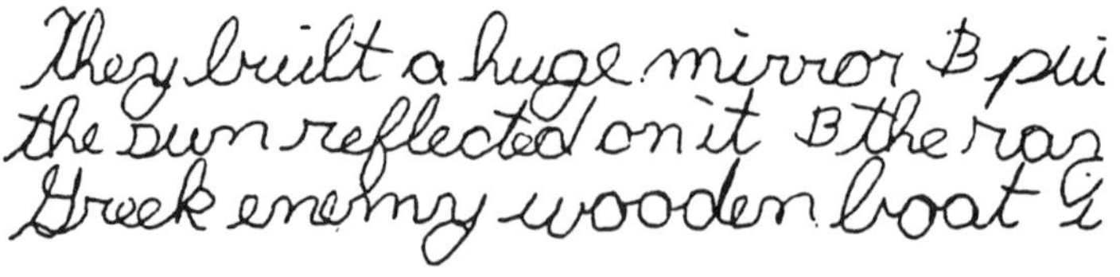

FIGURE 94
Very slow writing: Nine-year-old boy

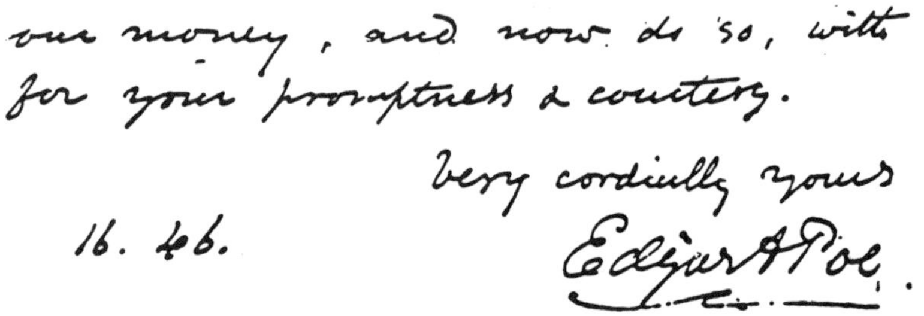

FIGURE 95
Handwriting of moderate speed: Edgar Allan Poe, U.S. writer

Determination of writing speed can be tricky, especially if you do not watch the person write. If you are uncertain of this feature, trace over the script with a dry pen to get a feel for the writer's movements.

Fast writing has these characteristics:

- Fluid, connected, unbroken strokes
- Simplified letters (no lead-in strokes)
- *i* dots and *t* crosses placed to the right
- *i* dots made as dashes
- Rightward slant
- Ascending lines
- Wide, open, expansive writing
- No corrections or adjustments
- Lively or fluid end strokes
- Sometimes, increasing width of left margin
- Garland formations (see Figs. 102, 103)

Slow handwriting has these characteristics:

- Artificial writing that shows marked carefulness
- Leftward to upright slant or leftward formations
- *i* dots and *t* crosses to the left of the letter or carefully placed
- Circle *i* dots
- Superfluous ornamentation
- Descending lines
- Long lead-in strokes
- Corrections
- Alterations of direction, slant, or flow
- Arcade formations (see Figs. 96, 97))

In addition to handwriting speed, the basic handwriting formations covered in Chapter 3 (garlands, arcades, angles, and threads) represent four different thinking styles. These movements may be used to form individual letters and to connect letters together. Although any one of these strokes may predominate in a handwriting, usually two or more are combined, suggesting variable thinking patterns and a versatile disposition. To discover which thinking style predominates, look primarily at the letters *m* and *n*, as well as *h*, *r* and *s*, recalling that no one of these thinking styles is any more positive than another until you have looked at the writing as a whole. Careful observation and common sense will guide you in evaluating the writer's thinking style.

THE METHODICAL THINKER

A careful thinking style is shown by arcades—the slowly written arches taught in penmanship classes. Arcade writers are careful, methodical thinkers who tend to look at things from a conventional standpoint, are comfortable with the familiar, and generally do not like to threaten the status quo by trying new and different things. Seldom are they impulsive (note that arcade writing is usually slowly written). They carefully weigh facts and possibilities step-by-step, taking time to come up with final conclusions. They learn deliberately (sometimes slowly) and by repetition, and when they "have" it, they have it. They accumulate information bit by bit, much as a bricklayer builds a wall. When all the bricks are in place, the wall is complete and the person remembers the position of each brick—the steps taken to arrive at that conclusion.

Usually sociable and conforming, they are nevertheless self-protective and secretive (the arcade is a sort of covering stroke like an overturned basin, an umbrella, or a downward palm). Arcade writers are often seen in volunteer positions and charitable organizations. They frequently have good manual skills.

Ambition, Imagination, and

17 hours work day

Thomas A Edison

FIGURE 96
Arcade writer: Thomas Edison, U.S. inventor

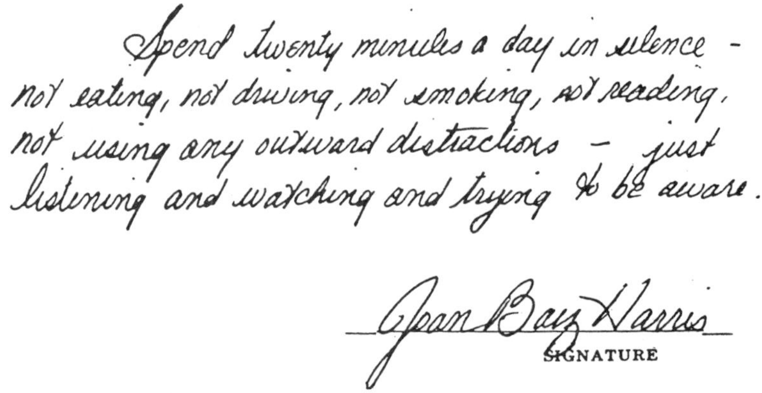

Spend twenty minutes a day in silence –
not eating, not driving, not smoking, not reading,
not using any outward distractions – just
listening and watching and trying to be aware.

Joan Baez Harris
SIGNATURE

FIGURE 97
**Arcade formations: Joan Baez Harris, U.S. folk singer and
founder of the Institute for the Study of Nonviolence**

Few writers create arcades with the precision of Thomas Edison (see Fig. 96). More often, we find arcades like those in the *m*'s and *n*'s of Joan Baez's writing (see Fig. 97), which is rounded but not as broad as Edison's. Her thinking style is careful and methodical but less disciplined and deliberate than that of Edison.

THE INVESTIGATIVE–ANALYTICAL THINKER

As a person becomes more certain of his or her own thinking, school-book style may be abandoned, allowing rounded formations to give way to a more angular style. Writers of angular formations are willing to challenge tradition: These are the investigative–analytical thinkers. They are mentally energetic, questioning and evaluating at every turn, and planning strategy for the next move ahead. Because the writer must stop momentarily to change direction at the bottom and top of each angle, the implication is one of tension, as opposed to garlands or arcades, which are much softer and more relaxed. Angular writers are investigative thinkers and will go to great lengths to satisfy their need to know how and why. The bottom line is important to them. Writers of strong angular formations can be tense, aggressive, and forward-moving; they can be very decisive, even stubborn, and are often critical, but their forte is sifting and sorting information. They often excel at research or technical work.

Two types of angles are common in handwriting—those that point upward (as in the humps of *m*'s, *n*'s, *h*'s or upper loop structures) and those that point downward (as between the humps of *m*'s, *n*'s, *h*'s and at the bottom of lower zone structures).

Upward pointed angles that are strong and that penetrate into the abstract area show exploratory thinking—an urge to delve into the unknown and a willingness to go to the source of the information. Less pronounced and shallow angles that point upward (usually at the baseline) indicate investigative thinking—the urge to uncover information and the willingness to accept second-hand information rather than to go to the source. Pronounced angles, when found in the upper zone, show that the writer goes to great lengths to find out what is not yet known. David Livingstone's writing shows exploratory thinking in the two *p*'s of "apply," the *f* and *b* of line 2, and the *A* and *f* of "Africa."

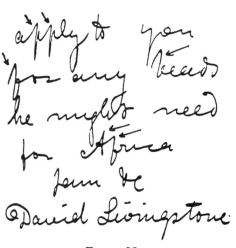

FIGURE 98
Upward-pointed angles: David Livingstone, British explorer

Downward pointed angles show analytical skill—the ability to mentally separate the chaff from the wheat and to scrutinize essentials. (Think of the downward angle as a funnel through which the person filters information.)

FIGURE 99
Downward pointed angles

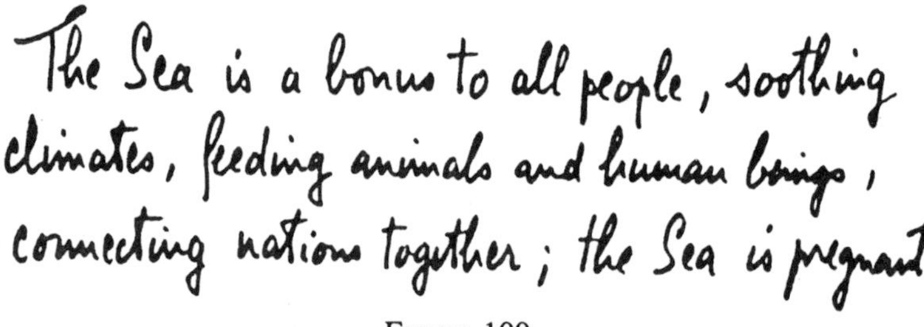

FIGURE 100
Angular formations: Jacques Cousteau, French marine explorer

The angular writing of Jacques Cousteau shows him to be a person who questions and evaluates information. The upward pointed angles of the baseline letters portray an investigative mind and a natural curiosity, whereas the downward pointed angles show his ability to evaluate whatever he uncovers.

Sincerely,

Donald J. Trump
Dinner Chairman

FIGURE 101
Donald Trump, U.S. entrepreneur

In Donald Trump's signature we see relentless scrutiny in the rigidly formed angles that have no give. Note his strong exploration into the unknown, indicated by upward pointed angles in upper zone formations, and his ability to dissect knowledge, shown by baseline angles. "Glassy" or sharp-edged angles like these point to cool emotions, criticism, and harshness as well as aggressive forward movement. His strong thinking style is no doubt responsible for his success in the business world.

THE PERCEPTIVE THINKER

Perceptive thinking is characterized by garland formations, which are shaped like basins or upturned palms, and are curved, soft, flowing, and smooth. They reveal quick thinking, amiability, kindness, receptivity, and generosity; they are usually written by people who like people. Garland writers are generally cooperative, flexible, and compliant.

True garlands are firm, definite u-shaped structures that indicate, in addition to those traits mentioned above, a perceptive thinking style. This is especially so when the letters *m* and *n* are written so they resemble the letters *u* and *w*. If the needlepoint formations at the top of these letters are sharp, incisive mental penetration is revealed. (However, if the garlands are placed tightly together (*ww w*) the writer is also narrow-minded and unwilling to accept what is perceived.) Writers of sharply defined garlands are quick to understand people and situations and, therefore, are able to make snap decisions. They need little explanation for anything and they are acutely aware of both people and surroundings (see John F. Kennedy, Fig. 90).

A   **B**

FIGURE 102
Clearly defined garland formations:
(A) Wayne Newton, entertainer; (B) Jerry Lewis, actor

Shallow garlands, which are not as well defined, show surface understanding. They are written by people who make quick but superficial or incorrect impressions. As seekers of pleasure and luxury, these writers are easy-going and sometimes lazy; they often have indefinite opinions and sometimes find it hard to say no or to stand up for their feelings (Fig. 103).

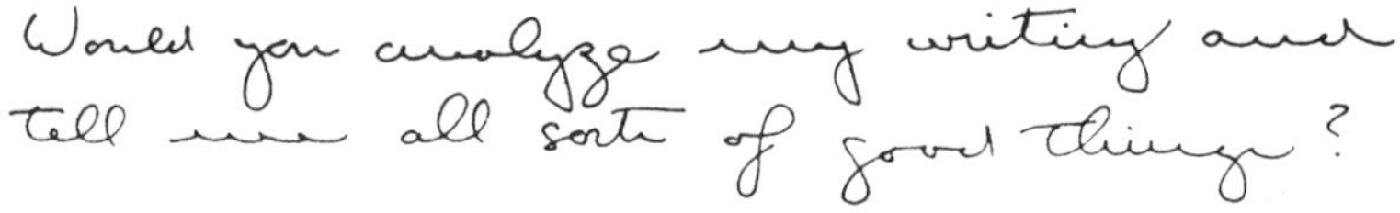

FIGURE 103
Shallow garland formations

THE ADAPTABLE THINKER

Threadlike formations (so called because they resemble threads) are a sign of adaptable thinking. Thready writing is a bit difficult to analyze accurately, and care must be taken to consider the overall writing before drawing a conclusion.

Threadlike writing lacks definition for one of two reasons: the writer is either a quick and adaptable thinker or an indefinite, uncertain thinker. To determine which interpretation fits, consider the writing's rhythm, regularity, and consistency and any "strong" traits (e.g., decisiveness, determination, persistence, organizational abilities, and lasting feelings). Also take into account the conditions at the time of writing (e.g., whether the writer was in a hurry, as when taking notes). The person's profession should also be noted. Physicians are often rushed, causing them to leave an illegible trail of writing, and executives, having many things to deal with, may not take time to write carefully. To become a physician or the president of a large organization requires the ability to think clearly and it would be a mistake to say that they are nonthinkers based solely on their thready writing. Instead, we might say that they know their professions and are able to think quickly based on the knowledge and experience they have acquired. They may also be able to delegate details to someone else.

For example, the writing of John F. Kennedy (Fig. 90-A) and of Henry Kissinger (Fig. 104) show thready formations. Given the positions of these two men, we would interpret their threadiness as a sign of speedy thought and of the ability to make quick decisions based on accumulated knowledge and experience.

FIGURE 104
Henry Kissinger, U.S. diplomat

A positive variation of thready writing is the tapering of successive letters. This is often seen in the letter *m* and it indicates the ability to be tactful and diplomatic. Such writers feel out people and situations and are able to deal with people effectively. They are discreet, prefer peaceful solutions to any situation, and can make a point without arousing antagonism. These traits are enhanced if the letters maintain their legibility as they diminish in size (Fig. 105).

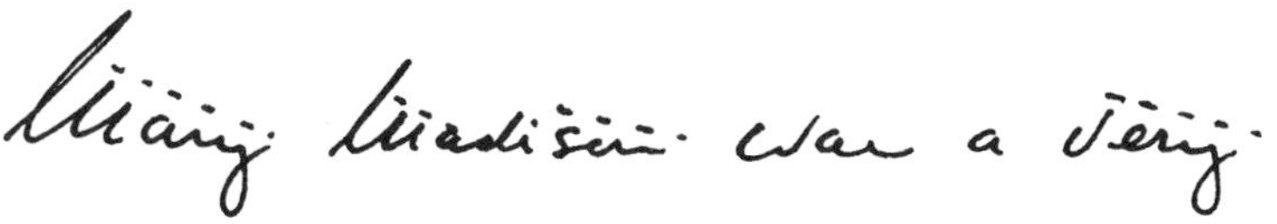

FIGURE 105
Tapering letters: Diplomacy

Thready formations, when found in irregular, undisciplined, indecisive hands, are the result of limp garlands, poorly formed arcades, or ill-defined angles. They suggest the "could have been" or the "might have been" where thinking is concerned. These writers tend to be indecisive about practical, everyday matters but are often adept at social intercourse. They do not like to be tied down and tend to skim the surface of life, neither investigating a subject thoroughly nor taking a definite stand on issues. Their tendency is to be impulsive and opportunistic; with signs of deception they can be slick and crafty. Again, consider the whole personality before making a negative interpretation of the thready writer.

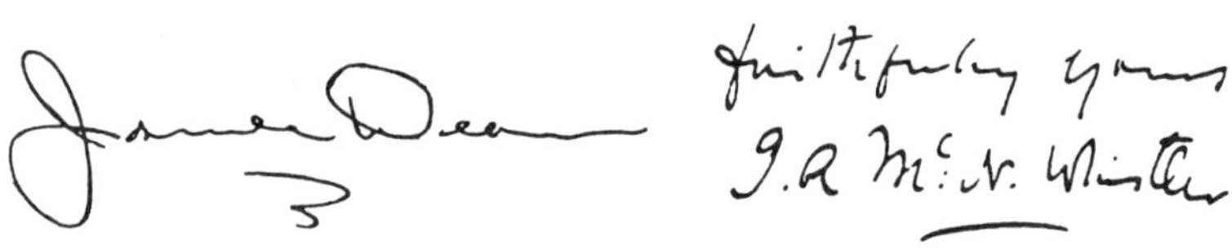

A   B

FIGURE 106
**Threadlike formations: (A) James Dean, actor;
(B) James McNeill Whistler, artist**

Any of the above formations can be found in various combinations in any given script. Usually a combination of two or more thinking styles is beneficial, giving the person various ways of looking at situations and dealing with everyday life, whereas a singular style gives a more one-sided approach. A clear picture of the writer's thought processes can be obtained only by consideration of individual combinations of stroke formations, as well as evaluation of other handwriting signs that will enhance or detract from mental skills.

The handwriting of writer Gore Vidal (Fig. 107) is primarily a garland script, showing a quickness of thought and a basically pleasant disposition. His garland formations are soft, adding flexibility to the already easy, spontaneous style and the desire to follow his own impulses without influence from convention. However, slightly angular formations (as in the *m*'s and *n*'s of "wonder" and "make" and the *o-r* of "Gore") show a curious and questioning mind. With this combination he investigates somewhat superficially, makes quick decisions as he goes and stops to analyze when he feels it necessary.

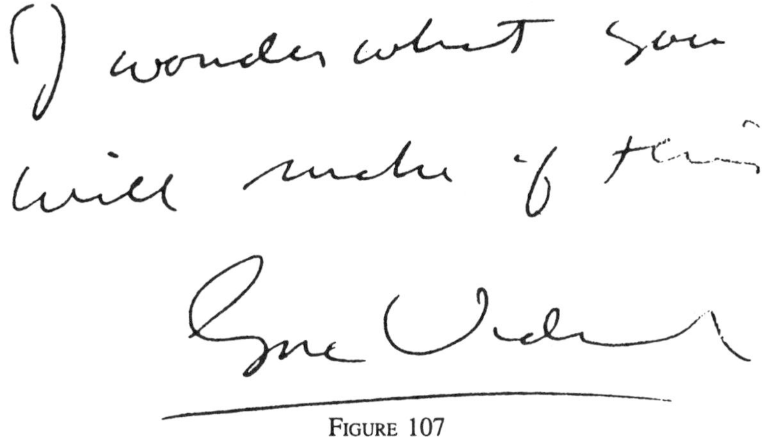

FIGURE 107
Gore Vidal, writer

In the signature of Isaac Asimov we see a combination of angles and garlands. The downward-pointed angles in the *m* express a strongly analytical mind, whereas the top of the *m* structure is sharp and penetrating, evidence that he readily grasps whatever subject he investigates.

FIGURE 108
Isaac Asimov, science fiction writer

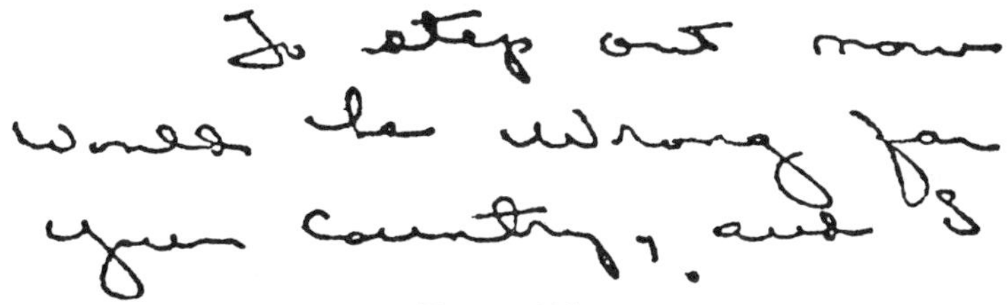

FIGURE 109
Lady Bird Johnson, wife of U.S. president Lyndon Johnson

Fig. 109 combines arcade structures in a basically thready handwriting. The writer is careful and methodical (arcades) when she chooses to be, although the thread formations detract from in-depth involvement or strong mental effort. However, we must consider that the line and word spacing are consistent. Also, the upright to backhand slant shows that reason dominates feeling.

IS THE WRITER
LOGICAL OR INTUITIVE?

When letters are connected, the writer is able to write more quickly and fluently than when letters are disconnected. Some writers say they print because it is faster than cursive writing, but this is a misperception because there is a stop-and-start motion between printed letters that detracts from writing speed.

Connected letters (four or more in succession) indicate logical, step-by-step thought processes. Such people are systematic in their thinking and are able to follow a logical train of reasoning (depending on other traits, of course). If the connections are smooth (not jerky), fluid thinking is enhanced.

A   **B**

FIGURE 110
Connected letters:
(A) General Westmoreland, U.S. military officer;
(B) Alexander Graham Bell, U.S. inventor

When words are connected to each other, logic and fluidity are even stronger. These writers are very fluid in their thinking or communication, or both, always with one-half of the brain on the next step ahead. They are adaptable and flexible and can come up with quick alternatives that help enable them to carry ideas to completion (see Fig. 111).

Disconnected letters reveal intuition. Such breaks between letters represent pauses in thinking that allow thoughts to come from "nowhere." These writers act on hunches or a sixth sense, so they can often see the outcome of a situation ahead of time. Whether the intuitive flashes are accurate or not depends on other traits (see Fig. 112).

Figure 111
Connected words

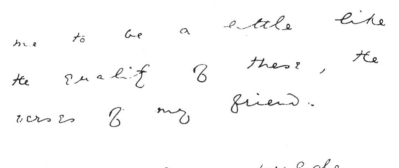

Figure 112
Disconnected letters: Oscar Wilde, Irish playwright and satirist

When breaks and connected letters both appear (as in the handwriting of Carol Burnett) the writer has a good balance between intuition and logic and can take advantage of intuitive flashes by applying ideas logically.

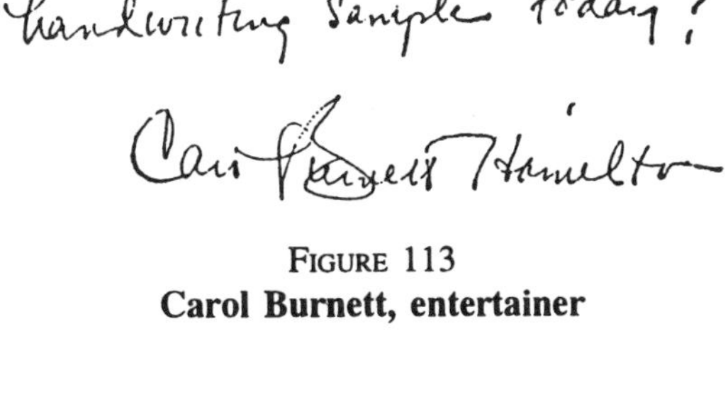

Figure 113
Carol Burnett, entertainer

TRAITS THAT REVEAL
CLEAR THINKING

SIMPLIFICATION

Clear thinking is enhanced when the writer is able to simplify letter structures, which is accomplished by omitting any strokes that are unnecessary to the legibility of letters. Initial strokes are dropped and capital letters are printed or made with few strokes, the writing lacks ornamentation and straight strokes may replace loops.

> This is to show you the different ways I write.
> try interested in this subject because one time
> e did a quickie look at my writing and said
> it was very "positive." Well, whatever that

FIGURE 114
Simplified writing

With simplified writing, the person is direct, to the point, and thinks in a straight line; he or she is efficient and therefore eliminates anything that does not relate to the subject at hand. Time and effort are saved and communication is enhanced by getting to the heart of the matter. As one person with simplified writing said, "Why take a suitcase when an overnighter will do?"

Overly embellished writing points to the person who is unable to deal with situations directly. These writers talk around a subject and collect anything and everything that remotely resembles the subject. Their thinking is crowded with extraneous information that distorts communication and is a waste of time and effort.

> Although a complete analysis requires more.
> and a good deal of evaluation, copying these
> paragraphs will give you a good indication.
> - major traits that make you who you are.

FIGURE 115
Overly embellished writing

Attention to Detail

Detail orientation is an obvious plus where thinking is concerned: It indicates that the person notices even the smallest of matters and that the parts of an object or idea are as important as the whole. The writer with an eye for details is also likely to have a good memory. Detail mindedness shows in closely dotted *i*'s and carefully crossed *t*'s, as well as in small writing, careful spacing and punctuation, and good organization of the writing on the page.

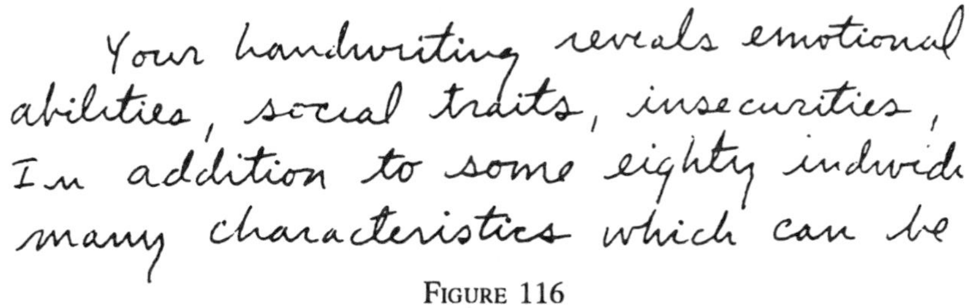

Your handwriting reveals emotional abilities, social traits, insecurities, In addition to some eighty individual many characteristics which can be

Figure 116
Detail orientation

However, too much concern with details has a negative implication. Overly precise writing in which every *i* dot and *t* cross is exact reflects the perfectionist, the person who always feels things could be better. These writers are the nitpickers who seem unable to find satisfaction.

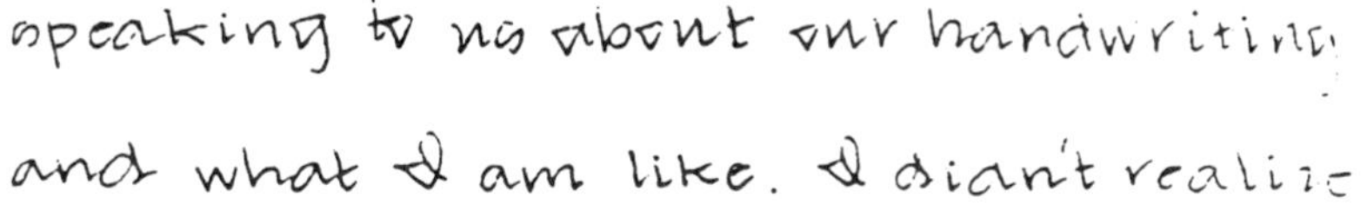

speaking to us about our handwriting and what I am like. I didn't realize

Figure 117
Overly detailed writing

Concentration

People who concentrate are able to focus their energy and attention: They apply themselves singlemindedly to any project, idea, or situation that catches their attention, often ignoring everything around them. People with concentration are capable of working for long time periods on one project and their forte is dealing with details. With negative signs, there may be a tendency for them to see the parts and not the whole and a propensity to become so focused that they retreat into their own little worlds.

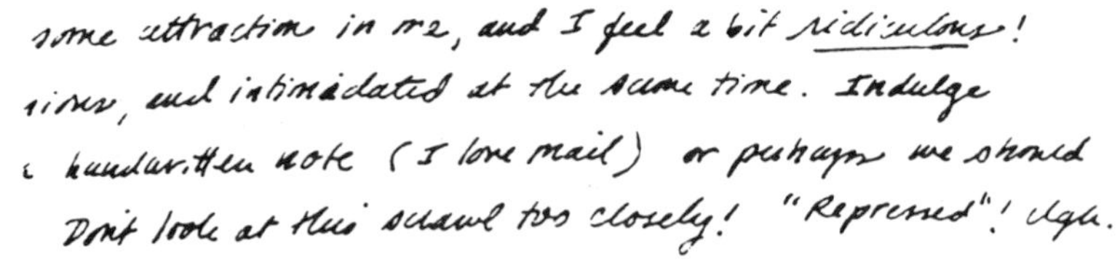

FIGURE 118
Small writing: Concentration

Concentration is shown by small writing (¹⁄₁₆" or smaller). To better understand the effects of this trait, write a short sentence in your normal writing. Now write the same sentence slightly smaller. Repeat this again and again until you can no longer reduce the size of your writing. You can now appreciate the focus of people such as Albert Einstein (Fig. 22-A) and Mahatma Gandhi (Fig. 22-B).

7
YOUR SIGNATURE:
THE FACE
YOU SHOW THE WORLD

Signatures have always been recognized as unique and personally expressive. Your signature indicates your public identity—the image you want other people to see. It can be considered your persona, as it is the face you show the world.

As an individualized symbol, your signature is a very personal trademark; it can be recognized as yours alone, whether affixed to a check, a driver's license, a credit card, or a legal document. The word signature comes from a Latin word meaning "to seal." By signing your name you declare yourself accountable for what you have signed. One's signature is legally binding because no one else can successfully duplicate it in all of its nuances.

As no prescribed standards govern signatures, you have unlimited freedom in creating your mark. Your signature may be clear and concise, legible or illegible, ornate or simple, underlined, or followed by a dash, dot, or paraph.

Whatever stroke formations constitute the signature, it must never be analyzed apart from the text of the writing, which reinforces or modifies the signature's indications. Evaluation of the signature calls for the same principles that generally apply to handwriting and also the awareness that this is how the writer wishes to be *seen*, not necessarily who he or she really *is*. Zonal emphasis, stroke direction, slant, pressure, spacing, and so forth all apply, as they do to other writing.

Perhaps the best-known signature in the United States is that of John Hancock, who said as he signed the Declaration of Independence, "King George can read that clear across the sea." To emphasize his statement, he added a bold, confident, somewhat showy paraph under his name (Fig. 119).

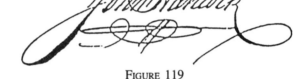

FIGURE 119
John Hancock, statesman of the U.S. revolutionary era

A primary consideration is the clarity of the signature. If legible, it reveals straightforward communication based on a healthy self-concept. The writer of a clear signature does not need to make a pretentious display (unless deliberately exaggerating, like John Hancock) because he or she feels at ease with the self, and does not make a chore or a guessing game out of reading his or her name or personality. A clear signature implies frankness and a consideration for others. The writer who is socially conscious writes a legible signature.

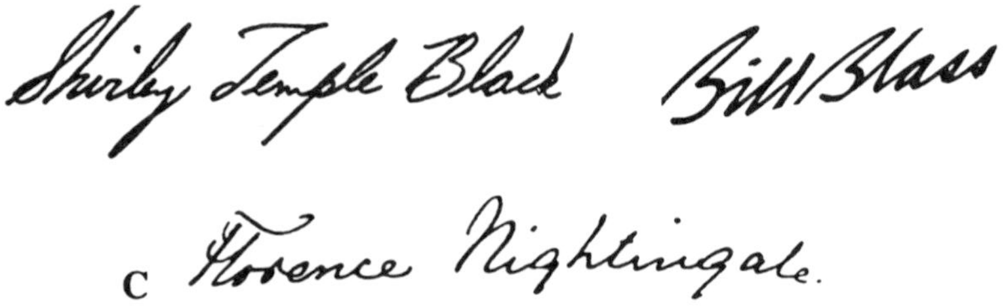

A   B

C

FIGURE 120
Clear signatures: (A) Shirley Temple Black, sometime child actress and U.S. ambassador to Ghana; (B) Bill Blass, designer; (C) Florence Nightingale, English nurse and philanthropist

After seeing their signatures, one would hardly expect Shirley Temple Black, Florence Nightingale, or Bill Blass to be anything but clear and honest.

When unclear, or overly embellished with curlicues, loops, and exaggerated capital letters, the signature shows an attempt to compensate for hidden feelings of inadequacy. The writer is a showperson, someone who wants you to notice that he or she has been there. An ostentatious signature reflects an ostentatious, arrogant attitude.

FIGURE 121
Overly embellished signature

The signature that is simply and tastefully decorated with mild flourishes implies social demeanor, good taste, confidence, and a healthy and expressive ego.

FIGURE 122
Moderately embellished signature: Basil Rathbone, actor

Relatively few people leave a legible signature behind. An illegible signature can be the result of an unwillingness to communicate clearly, an attempt to cover true thoughts and feelings, a belief that an embellished or bizarre signature is less likely to be forged, or a desire to impress. It is also important to consider whether the writer is required to sign his or her name many times a day and has therefore developed an expedient, indecipherable way of doing so.

If the signature is illegible by neglect, the writer fails to communicate. He or she may be unclear in speech, or may leave part of the details out when talking or writing. (See Richard Nixon, Fig. 123.)

FIGURE 123
Illegible by neglect: Richard Nixon, U.S. president
(written at the height of the Watergate scandal)

The "tricky" and illegible signature of "S.M.F." implies subversive motives and activity, which is fitting for the writer's career as a private investigator.

Sincerely,

S   M. F

FIGURE 124
Signature of a private investigator

Most graphologists agree that whatever the reason behind an unreadable signature, the writer either consciously or unconsciously wishes not to be open but rather to maintain distance and remain anonymous. Checking the text accompanying the signature clarifies this issue. Signs of secrecy or dishonesty in the text or an attempt to hide are iterated, whereas clarity and honesty in the script along with an illegible signature indicate that the person's public and private lives are quite different.

When the signature and text are similar in style, size, spacing, slant, and zonal distribution, the writer's outward expressions reflect inner attitudes. Such writers are unpretentious and have no need to hide or mask their true natures.

When the signature and text are different, conflicts are suggested; the writer projects one thing but feels another. If the body of writing is small he or she may hide behind the facade of a strong, bold signature to impress others with a show of confidence which may actually be a compensation for low self-esteem.

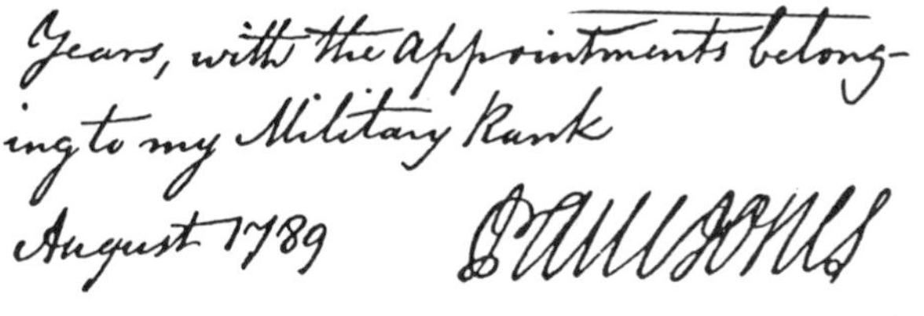

FIGURE 125
Signature larger than text:
John Paul Jones, Scottish-born U.S. sailor

A small signature attached to larger text implies that the writer projects less self-importance than he or she really feels. The person is confident and self-reliant inside but modest on the surface—perhaps even self-effacing if the signature is much smaller than the text—as in the case of this shy ten-year-old boy (Fig. 126).

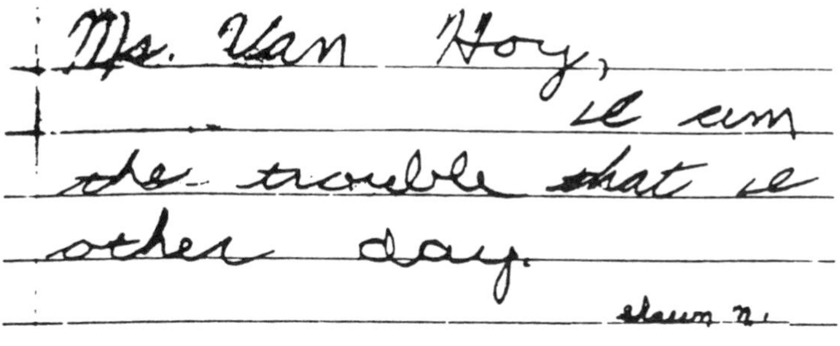

FIGURE 126
Signature smaller than text

A difference in slant shows the desire to create a false impression. A slanted signature affixed to vertical writing indicates that the writer likes to be seen as warm-hearted, social, and expressive whereas in reality he or she is cool, calm, and independent. A vertical signature at the bottom of slanted script reveals a cool exterior that belies a more emotional interior.

FIGURE 127
Slant of signature and text differ

The placement of the signature is also revealing. Positioned toward the left, it signifies withdrawal, caution, inhibition, or avoidance of the future. (In a block-style business letter, a left-placed signature is of course less important.) A right-placed signature implies a progressive and self-assured person who reaches out to other people or who is, at least, not socially inhibited. This quality will be further evaluated by consideration of the writing size and spacing.

Signatures are composed of up to four separate components: first name, middle name, last name, and an underscore or paraph, which may all be executed in one movement or separated. The person may write only first and last names, omitting the middle name and paraph; use only initials for first and middle names and write out the surname; or write the first name clearly and turn the last name into a blur or squiggle. Whatever the preference, it expresses the writer's feelings about self and family.

The first name relates to the writer's ego and to feelings about self carried over from childhood. Therefore, when the first name is larger, clearer, or otherwise more emphasized than the surname, the writer is independent of family or tradition, giving more importance to a feeling of individuality. This usually indicates self-reliance and a de-emphasis of prestige or social standing. The writer of an exaggerated first name may want to remain childlike or hold onto childish ways and ignore social considerations. An overly embellished first name reveals a craving for personal recognition beneath which may be a narcissistic attitude.

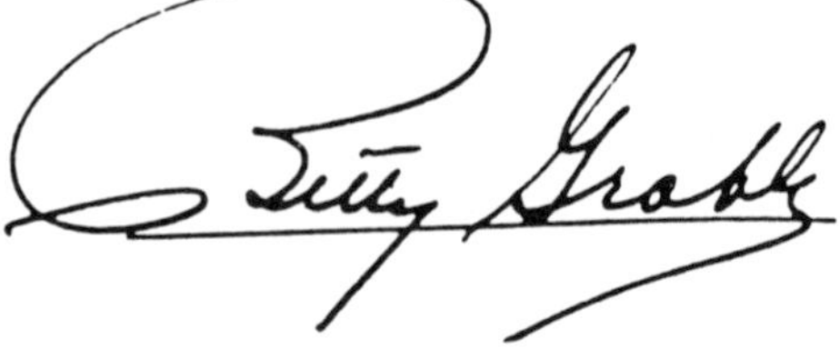

FIGURE 128
First name emphasized: Betty Grable, actress

When the family name is emphasized, the person is dependent on status, family values, heritage, and tradition. The writer may sacrifice the private, inner life to social prestige, power, or business. A woman who writes her married name bolder or larger than her first name is likely to be secure with her husband and perhaps dependent on him. She likes being connected to his name and may even write "Mrs. John Smith" instead of "Jane Smith."

FIGURE 129
Surname emphasized

Sigmund Freud's modest self-concept is revealed in the absence of a first name and the uncapitalized surname.

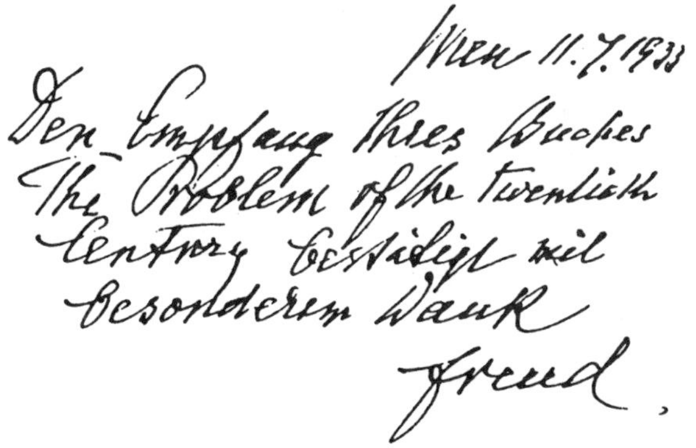

FIGURE 130
Sigmund Freud, Austrian psychiatrist and founder of psychoanalysis

A signature underlined either by a continuation of the final stroke or by a separate line reveals independence, courage, self-worth, and self-reliance. Such a writer believes in the self and personal accomplishment (if signs in the text also indicate confidence). The underscored signature is common to people who have achieved notoriety, as it is one sign that the person wishes to do something important (see Fig. 131). Sometimes this is expressed as a "but Mother I'd rather do it myself" attitude.

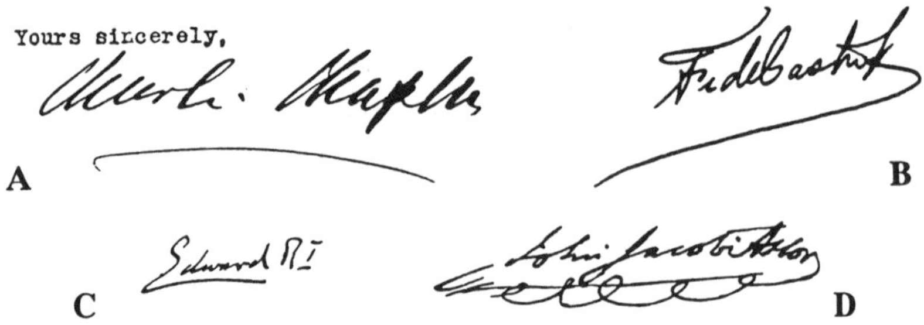

Yours sincerely,

FIGURE 131
**Underscored signatures: (A) Charlie Chaplin, silent film actor;
(B) Fidel Castro, Cuban premier;
(C) Edward VIII, king of Great Britain, January to December 1936;
(D) John Jacob Astor, American fur trader**

The degree of importance the person places on the self is indicated by the formation and style of the underscore. If straight, forward-moving, and heavy, the underscore strongly emphasizes the writer's self-image, whereas a curved, light underscore reveals more of a wish to be self-confident. A series of strong underlines portrays even greater strength, whereas an embellished, curly addition calls out that the writer wants recognition (perhaps for an illusive self-confidence).

Though a firm underscore might seem to be a positive component of any signature, it must be carefully evaluated in conjunction with other handwriting personality traits. For example, the signature in Fig. 132 has an underscore so strong and heavy that it becomes clublike at the end. By itself the underline shows courage, strength of will, and a self-reliant approach that increases in the face of obstacles. However, the extreme rightward slant (immediate emotional reactions) and the heavy blotched strokes (intense and deep feelings, sensuality), coupled with very narrow and tall letters (inhibitions and repressed emotions)—along with other negatives to be discussed later—belong to an introverted man with very intense but blocked inner feelings. The clublike ending allows for periodic aggressive outbursts of charged emotions. The signature is that of Dr. Hawley H. Crippen, an amiable and insignificant little man convicted of poisoning his wife and dismembering the body.

Occasionally, a signature is partially or completely enclosed in a circle. This self-protective movement guards one's family status or the individual's own personal image or reputation, depending on which part of the signature is enveloped. The writer, by closing himself off, prefers to remain a mystery and does not want his privacy to be penetrated. Actor Don Johnson (Fig. 133) has encircled much of his given name with the circle part of the *J* of "Johnson." Judy Garland also created a large circle around her name (Fig. 134). Embellished, encircled, and illegible, the signature of William B. Camp, U.S. comptroller of the currency, makes one wonder what he might have been hiding (Fig. 135).

FIGURE 132
Hawley H. Crippen, poisoner

FIGURE 133
Don Johnson, actor

FIGURE 134
Judy Garland, actress

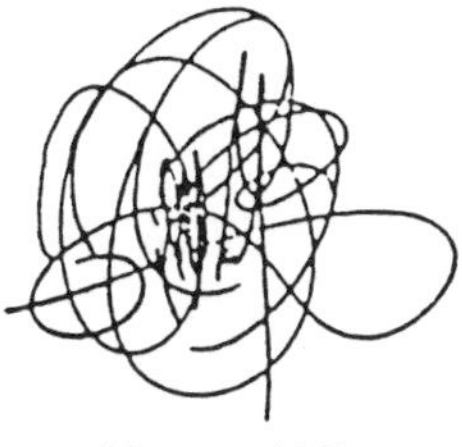

FIGURE 135
William B. Camp, U.S. comptroller of the currency, 1966–1973

Signatures that are crossed out reveal that the writer is not happy with his or her own status quo or that of the family. The crossing out reveals an unconscious dislike for how things are and a desire to make a major change in life. This can also be an indication that the writer is self-driven and pushes him or herself. You often hear these writers say "I should" or "I shouldn't." (Notice the whiplike motion used by Herbert W. Armstrong as he drives back, then strongly forward.)

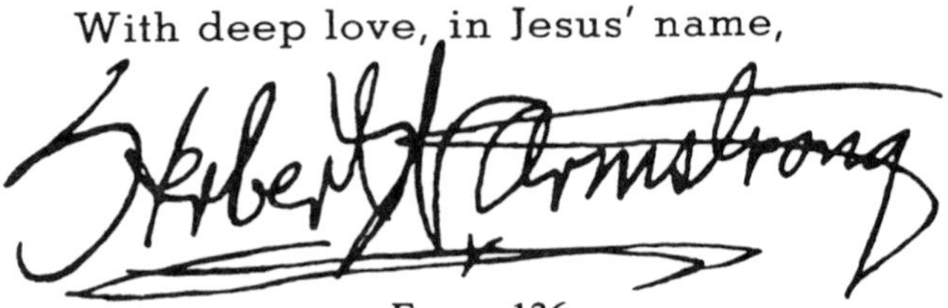

With deep love, in Jesus' name,

FIGURE 136
Surname crossed out: Herbert W. Armstrong, evangelist

Patched letters in the person's name show inner anxiety and an uncertain self-concept. The writer, wanting to be seen as perfect, goes back to make repairs on the signature—the image the public sees. Patching may show that the writer dislikes and is trying to "fix" the self or how he or she is perceived (Fig. 137).

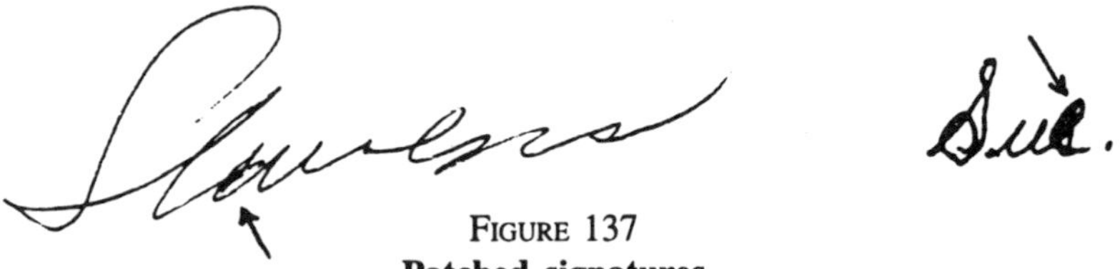

FIGURE 137
Patched signatures

FIGURE 138
Liberace, pianist

Signatures are frequently graphic indications of what the writer identifies with—a profession or perhaps a special interest. Liberace, for example, signed his name with the drawing of a grand piano, candelabra *in situ* (Fig. 138).

Cartoonist Chester Gould likes to be known as the creator of Dick Tracy.

FIGURE 139
Chester Gould, cartoonist

Fra Bernardino de Sahagún, Franciscan missionary in the time of Cortez, surrounded himself with the symbols of his religion.

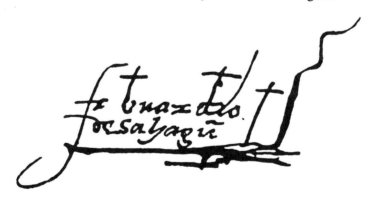

FIGURE 140
Fra Bernardino de Sahagún, Franciscan missionary

Other interesting signatures are those of Maxfield Parrish and of Walt Disney, which could only belong to artists, and of Anton Mesmer, with its mesmerizing movements.

FIGURE 141
Maxfield Parrish, U.S. artist

FIGURE 142
Walt Disney, cartoonist

FIGURE 143
Friedrich Anton Mesmer, German physician
who did early work with hypnosis

8

PREPARATION

FOR HANDWRITING
ANALYSIS

Once familiar with the information in this book, you will be armed with a valuable tool that tells you about people and what makes them tick. Already you are acquainted with enough graphology to create a thumbnail sketch of a writer's personality. If you are serious about studying people through handwriting, you probably have already started observing and collecting handwriting samples. Any writing, whether a grocery list, a letter, a short note, or a signature, is interesting and informative.

To prepare an objective and accurate analysis, you should follow some guidelines in collecting handwriting specimens.

The sample(s) you collect for the analysis should be as close to the person's natural writing as possible. The best sample is spontaneous, not copied from a book or written specifically for analysis. A personal letter is ideal, as the writer is likely to express true thoughts and feelings. The writing should be prose, not poetry, as the stylized arrangement of poetry greatly influences how the writing is organized on the page.

Several pages written over a few months give a more accurate overview of the personality than does a single page, and also covers changes in mood and health as well as any environmental influences.

Regular-sized, unlined paper allows the writer more spontaneity and freedom of expression than lined paper, and also provides a more reliable look at line spacing as well as whether the lines ascend, descend, or go straight across the page. Handwriting on postcards or other small papers is not good for analysis, as the small size is likely to "cramp the writer's style."

The writing instrument is also important. The writer should use his or her usual pen or choose one that feels comfortable. Felt-tip pen or pencil writing is not acceptable for analysis, as they greatly influence the pressure of the script. Photocopies, if they are of high quality and if originals are not available, are acceptable. However, with photocopies it is sometimes difficult to determine pressure patterns.

The writing sample must include at least one signature, because the signature is a trademark the writer has developed. It represents how the writer wants to be seen, and it may be different from how he or she really is.

If the writer claims to use different writing styles, ask for at least one page of each. Most people say their handwriting changes from one day to another, but what they usually mean is that they feel different from day to day and their writing therefore feels different. In the final analysis, these "different" writing styles usually turn out to be essentially the same. In special cases, people do have more than one style of writing. For example, some teachers use a very conventional schoolroom style for clarity and abandon it once they leave work. Architects, engineers, and accountants generally have special writing associated with their professions, which may or may not stay with them off the job. Again, ask for plenty of writing samples.

If the person prints exclusively, that is his or her normal writing. Printing can and does reveal personality although it is more difficult to analyze because the connecting strokes are absent and the letters are usually composed of two or more separated strokes rather than of one continuous movement. Ask the person to *write* at least a few lines as well, remembering that because the written sample is not in his or her normal style, the overall rhythm may be adversely affected. Therefore, pay more attention to the general organization, rhythm, and continuity of the printed sample.*

Likewise, if the writer uses a special style of writing (calligraphy, for example), find out if it is used exclusively. If not, obtain some of the person's "real" writing. If the special style is normal for the individual, analyze it like any other writing, keeping in mind that it *is* stylized and may be a facade, a pretentious effort to hide the real personality. Again, knowing when the writer adopted such a style tells you something about his or her past.

HOW TO LOOK
AT HANDWRITING

Now that the handwriting sample is in front of you, how do you go about analyzing it? The ideal approach is objectivity. Look at all characteristics as neutral and consider how any trait might be used in either a positive or a negative way. You will prepare a more realistic and useful analysis if you do not allow yourself to be prejudiced about the writer.

Before you start the analysis, be informed of the writer's age, sex, and any physical problems or limitations. It is also useful to know if the writer is taking any medication or other drugs.

When you initially look at a handwriting, respond to its overall impression, its gestalt. The writing is first viewed from arm's length, as it were, and the analyst determines the amount of regularity, overall organization, size, spacing, line direction, and so forth. The characteristics shown in these elements of the writing sample serve as a foundation for the traits that will be uncovered on closer examination.

Often, one or two aspects of the writing immediately stand out. These signs represent the strong traits, the ones on which the writer automatically operates and that are likely to have the most impact on the

---

*Ask the writer when he or she stopped using script and started printing. This date usually indicates a major change in the person's life, since printing suggests a cutoff from feeling and a strong urge to control inner emotions.

personality and the analysis. Make note of any such dominant traits, put them for the moment in the back of your mind, and start listing the other characteristics you find. Following the same logical sequence for each analysis helps train you to look at each writing systematically. You may want to follow the writing through each of the chapters of this book, looking at the basic structure of the handwriting first and then working toward the details. To help organize your findings, use the work sheet at the end of the book, which follows the order of material presented.

The details of handwriting are covered in subsequent chapters. As you read the remaining chapters you should work with a magnifying glass for a more in-depth look. Which aspects of the writing catch your attention now? The traits that attract your attention at this point also have a strong influence on the writer's personality as a whole. Look next at each letter of each word, starting with the first word. Make a note of each trait as you discover it. To qualify as a personality indicator, a handwriting feature must appear more than once, so every time you find the same trait again, put a check mark beside it. By the time you reach the bottom of the page you will have a fairly extensive list of traits and will be able to see, by the number of check marks, which influences are dominant and which are minor.

After you have looked over the handwriting thoroughly, transfer your findings to the work sheet. Score each finding on a 1 to 5 scale: 1 for a low score, 5 for a high score. Note that any exaggerated characteristic or a trait that scores very high usually results in a negative evaluation. Traits that are overdone imply that the writer is compensating for something else, sometimes the very opposite of the trait in question. With experience, you will learn how to interpret such characteristics.

To get the feel of the writing, you may wish to trace over the writing strokes with a dry pen or a blunt instrument: This allows you to feel changes in direction, formation, and so forth, and gives you a better sense of who the writer is.

As you identify the various signs, you begin to see the uniqueness of the personality unfold. You will find that all people are composed of various and sometimes conflicting personality traits. This should come as no surprise, given that people sometimes smile even during deep depression or are capable of loving and hating at the same time. Two opposing features in the same writing do not negate each other but indicate that the writer has conflicting traits. It is up to the graphologist to determine when each trait operates.

You may then choose to arrange in order the dominant traits, those found less often, and those that show up infrequently. When you have compiled the list, sort it according to category (e.g., thinking style, emotional makeup, social traits, fears, defenses, tastes, aptitudes), keeping in mind that some traits will fall into more than one category. As you do so, you will begin synthesizing what you have uncovered by deciding how the various traits modify one another within their respective areas. You will then be prepared to give a meaningful and cohesive report based on your logical deductions.

We now examine three handwritings using this approach (note that the information provided is based solely on the handwriting and not on individual biographies).

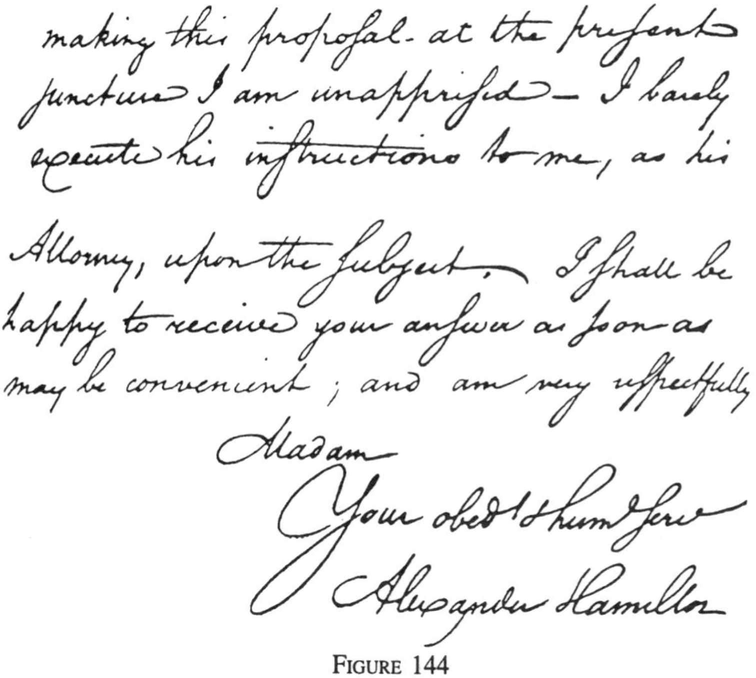

FIGURE 144
Alexander Hamilton, U.S. statesman

Regularity
Very regular; consistent (balanced, stable, consistent thoughts and efforts; integrity and positive overall character).

Size

Moderate (good balance between thought and activity).

Line Spacing

Moderate to wide; consistent (good judgement; consistently conscientious and organized).

Word Spacing

Moderate to wide; consistent (balanced approach to people; some elbow room and separation from people needed).

Letter Size and Spacing

Consistent size; moderately close spacing that is fairly consistent (moderately extroverted; fairly consistent in social contacts).

Baseline

Consistent; straight across page (emotional control and consistency, grounded; realistic attitude).

Formations

Primary: angles; secondary: arcades (ability to investigate, analyze; decisive thinker; careful, methodical thinker; things taken one step at a time).

Zonal Distribution

Good balance; moderate to strongly emphasized lower zone (good balance between spiritual, emotional, and physical, with some emphasis on the physical).

Directional Trend

Impression is of a rightward trend, but several strokes (especially initial strokes) remain leftward and some finals pull to left (forward moving and progressive in appearance, but rather strong inner tie to the past). Reflective; forward movement guided by past experiences.

Slant

Forward (responsive to people, feelings, situations; emotional influence on thoughts and actions).

Pressure

Moderate to moderately heavy (adequate reserves of energy; moderate to firm drive and intensity; feelings tend to last).

Thinking Style

Angles and arcades (investigative and analytical; evaluates information methodically; clear thinking reflected by regularity and consistency and by simplified yet original letter formations; occasionally attentive to detail [*i* dots]; sometimes forgetful [uncrossed *t*'s]).

Signature

Clear; consistent; similar to text (clear, open, honest expression; consistent, disciplined, confident; good taste).

The Analysis

The general balance of Alexander Hamilton's writing points to a stable, consistent, reliable person; his personality had a good foundation in the well-formed, consistent letters. The signature, which is similar to the text in organization, spacing, formations, and so forth, tells us that his expressions were an accurate reflection of his inner feelings; he was confident, unpretentious, and clear in his communication.

The writing shows a balanced approach to people and situations, a feeling for people (rightward slant), and moderate extroversion (moderate word spacing) that sometimes required solitude (occasional wide spaces between words).

Hamilton's writing also shows a quick responsiveness to people, situations, and events, and consistent moods and feelings. The straight baseline suggests that his emotions were regulated and that even though his responsiveness was strong, he would not be impulsive. Feelings left moderate to moderately strong impressions.

The combination of angles and arcades reveal a man who could carefully investigate and analyze any situation. Hamilton's curious and inquiring mind was often not satisfied with the information at hand. His methodical thinking style (arcades), added to logic (connected letters) and organization (straight baseline and consistencies), allowed him to reach accurate and firm conclusions. As a fluid thinker he connected ideas well (note connections in "obedient & humble servant") even though he was occasionally forgetful, as seen in missing *t* crosses.

Hamilton's writing is fairly well balanced between the three zones, with some emphasis on the lower area. His everyday life was therefore balanced between the spiritual and the material. Although he had rather strong materialistic urges, he was also able to consider abstract concepts and moral issues. Hamilton had many interests and needed frequent change and movement, as shown by some lower loops reaching almost to the next line down, but changes would be regulated due to the consistency of the writing as a whole.

Hamilton was progressive in his thinking and activity (rightward trend). However, he had very strong ties to the past, as indicated by initial letters pulling leftward ("Madam," "Your," "Alexander") and by final strokes that move forward, then back ("present," "unapprised," "juncture").

His strong points, according to the knowledge we have thus far, were regular self-discipline and clear, consistent thought processes, both enhanced by warm but regulated responsiveness.

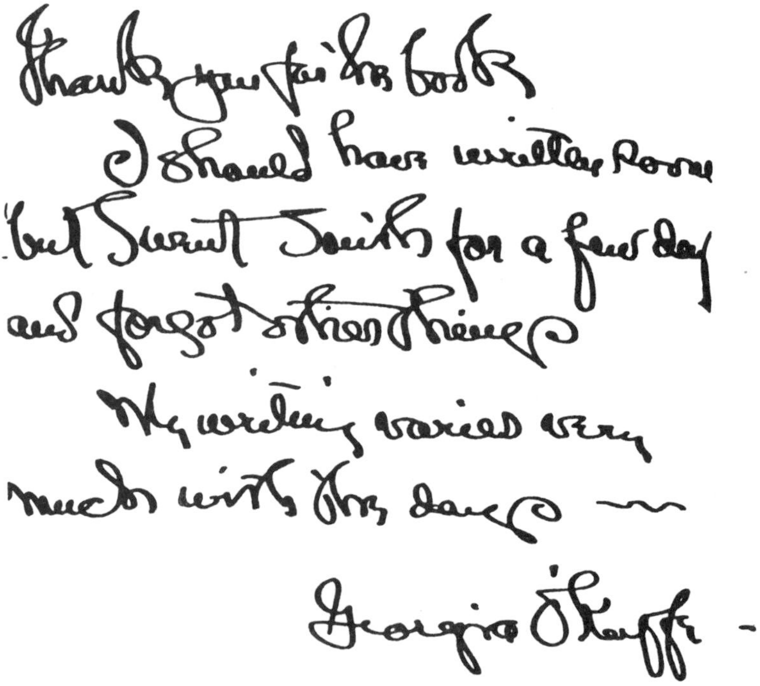

FIGURE 145
Georgia O'Keeffe, U.S. artist

Regularity
Regular, but with changeable letter size and flexible baselines (balanced and stable, flexible, tends toward flexibility).

Size
Moderately large (active, outgoing, expressive, recognition needed).

Line Spacing
Moderate to wide; consistent (good judgement, conscientious, moderately well-organized).

Word Spacing
Moderate (balanced approach to people and social situations).

Letter Size and Spacing
Wide letters; close, fairly consistent spacing (self-assured, mildly introverted, somewhat cautious approach).

Baseline
Flexible; basically straight but sometimes downward at word endings (emotional flexibility, some inconsistency, occasional negative attitude).

Formations
Arcades with occasional garlands (careful, methodical thinker; ideas built one step at a time; pleasantness).

Zonal Distribution
Good balance; moderate to strongly emphasized middle zone (good balance between spiritual, emotional, and physical, with some emphasis on the practical, everyday aspects of life).

Directional Trend
Moderate leftward trend (strong inner ties to the past, consideration of past in relation to present).

Slant
Vertical to backhand (thoughts and actions based on logic and self-concern; calculated expressions, cautious).

Pressure
Variable; moderate, but light in places; heavy downstrokes (variable energy and drive; feelings moderate in depth, some more lasting than others).

Thinking Style
Arcades (careful, methodical thinker, ideas built step by step; information absorbed slowly and thoroughly; overall picture [large size] and details attended to when necessary (occasionally close-dotted *i*).

Signature

Similar to text (energetic, confident expression; no desire to conceal inner thoughts and feelings).

The Analysis

The initial impression of Georgia O'Keeffe's writing is one of heavy pressure. The writer chose a wide-nibbed pen, which accounts for the thickness of most of the letters. However, note that in many places the writing strokes are light, almost leaving the paper (top of *o* in "you," *o-o* connection in "book," *i-n-g* connections in "things"). These light strokes indicate that the "pressure" we see is due to the pen itself, not the writer bearing down on the pen. The variable stroke pressure shows that Georgia O'Keeffe was a woman of variable emotions; some feelings were lasting; others were almost fleeting.

The regularity of the writing is also somewhat variable, especially regarding letter size and baselines. It is sufficiently regular to indicate stability but in general is one of flexibility (note that O'Keeffe admits that her writing "varies very much with the days.")

The somewhat large size indicates that O'Keeffe was active, energetic, and social-minded; the size suggests an urge for recognition. Adaptability is further implied by the flexible baseline. Movement and activity were deliberate (slow writing speed).

Moderate to wide line spacing shows adequate good judgment and organization, which are supported by connected letters (logic). Her organization and judgment are both flexible (versatile baseline and letter size) and deliberate (slow, rounded script).

O'Keeffe's mildly introverted nature (close letter spacing) corresponds to her emotional stance—the cool, calm and logical attitude shown in vertical strokes, and the backhand tendency, which reveals independence and mild emotional withdrawal. However, she would not *appear* introverted owing to the large and expressive writing size.

Primarily arcade in structure, the writing points to a careful, methodical thinker, someone who puts ideas carefully in place before coming up with a final conclusion. This is enhanced by the verticality of the writing and the logical connections. The occasional garland formations (*n*'s in "written," "went," "and," and "things") reveal a pleasant approach to people and add to her adaptability. The arcade structures, original stroke formations, fluid connections (as in *s-h* of "should"), and choice of a pen which would leave a trail of sensuousness and color, reveal her artistic nature.

Like her baseline and overall regularity, zonal distribution is somewhat variable. The three zones are rather equally represented, with some emphasis on the middle zone—the here and now—and some strokes that pull toward the left. The writer, therefore, deals well with the moment, has somewhat strong ties to the past, and balances her life between the real and the ideal. Leftward strokes, combined with arcade structures, imply a careful consideration of past efforts before moving ahead.

Georgia O'Keeffe's signature and text are congruent, illustrating straightforward expression of thoughts and feelings: What you see is what you get.

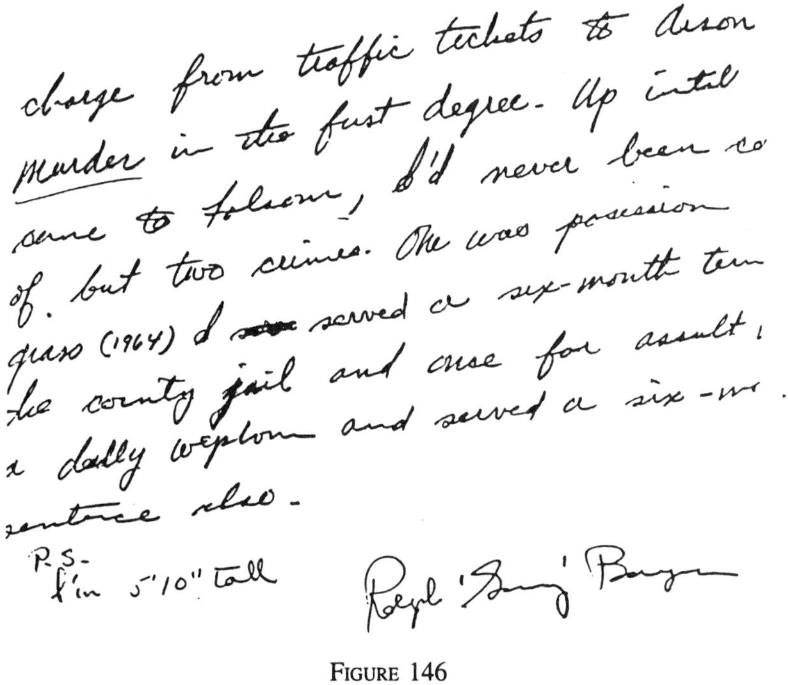

FIGURE 146
Ralph "Sonny" Barger, originator of Hell's Angels Club

Regularity
Irregular (balance and inner stability lacking; changeable, inconsistent).

Size

Moderate (no meaning by itself, must be evaluated with other signs). Note: writing sample in Fig. 146 was reduced 38%.

Line Spacing

Moderate; somewhat inconsistent (moderately conscientious but inconsistent in thought and organization).

Word Spacing

Wide (mentally or actually separates self from people and social situations).

Letter Size and Spacing

Inconsistent (changeable attitudes about self and relationships).

Baseline

Flexible, exaggerated upward direction (except drooping signature). Emotional flexibility and inconsistency; overly optimistic and ambitious; manic and energetic.

Formations

Inconsistent formations; poorly formed angles, occasional threads (poor thinking habits; "could have been"; indecisive, impulsive).

Zonal Distribution

Moderate balance, but distortions in all three areas (poor spiritual, emotional, and physical balance).

Directional Trend

Rightward trend (forward moving; concerned with the future).

Slant

Variable, mostly rightward (thoughts and actions based on changeable emotional responses; impulsive, reactive).

Pressure

Heavy, spotty, variable (variable energy and drive but usually intense; strong feelings and biases; drawn to sensual pursuits and excessive living).

Thinking Style

Poorly formed angles; threads (poor thinking skills; surface thinker who grasps only enough information and analyzes just deeply enough to get by; blotches and inconsistencies suggest erratic thinking and add to impulsiveness).

Signature

Nearly illegible, relatively straight line that droops instead of ascending, indicating negative attitudes and expressions; thready, large capitals (not communicative; omits details; dislikes being known; wants to be seen as level-headed; initally appears confident [large capitals]).

The Analysis

The initial impression of Barger's writing is one of manic activity (wildly ascending lines). The irregularity of the writing shows itself in changeable letter size and spacing, inconsistent formations, some variability in line spacing, and slant fluctuation. The already negative signs are augmented by the unclean look and the muddy spots of ink.

Based on the signature, we see a face untrue to the real character inside. He wants to be seen as level-headed (signature baseline level as opposed to ascending like the text) but he gives way to depression or a negative attitude (drooping tendency of signature). He appears confident and forward moving (large captials and rightward movements). However, the illegible signature reveals that he communicates poorly, leaves out information, and shows us the face he wants us to see.

Barger separates himself from people (wide spaces between words) and has a variable opinion of himself (changing letter size and inconsistent formations). His thoughts, activities, and relationships are influenced by emotional reactions that are not under the regulation of a solid personality base. His sense of reality is poor (middle zone distortions and poorly formed m's and n's), and he is full of anxiety (patches, especially "jail"); therefore, he is reactive and impulsive.

He is driven by sensuality (mud spots), biases (strong pressure), and inconsistent emotions (changeable pressure). Although concerned with the future and ambitious (forward movements, uphill baseline), he lacks the self-direction, the thinking habits, and the interpersonal skills necessary to succeed in the "real" world. For him, the world of crime was an easier one.

9
STROKE
BASICS

A stroke is any single handwriting movement that does not abruptly change direction. As soon as the pen lifts from the paper or makes a sudden change in direction, a new stroke is formed. There are many basic writing strokes, some of which are described at this point; innumerable combinations of strokes can join together to form individual letters, some of which will be interpreted later.

Primary strokes are straight or curved and may go upward, downward, forward, or leftward. Strokes may be heavy, light, very heavy, pasty, jerky, smooth, broken, firm, brittle, simple, or complicated. Strokes may end abruptly or come to knifelike points. A curved stroke may finish as a completed circle or loop. Some strokes are at once straight, heavy, and forward moving; others are curved, smooth, light, and leftward moving, and so on.

As suggested in an earlier chapter, any stroke combination may be found in any area of the writing, thereby giving added meaning as to the way it is expressed or used by the writer. Remember that none of the stroke basics can be interpreted without consideration of other indications in the writing as well.

Straight strokes are direct, strong, firm, unyielding, and "masculine."

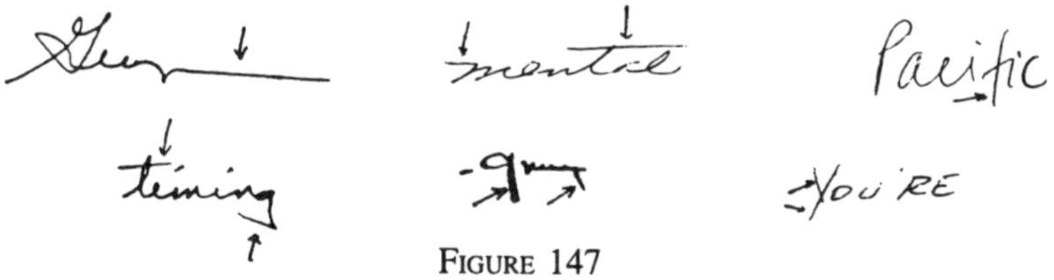

FIGURE 147
Straight strokes

Curved strokes are pliable, yielding, giving, less strong and direct, and "feminine."

FIGURE 148
Curved strokes

The pressure or heaviness of the handwriting stroke indicates how much energy is directed into its movement and therefore into the psychological trait indicated by that particular stroke. Generally speaking, the heavier a writing stroke, the more mental energy is associated with its meaning(s). (See also Chapter 5 for more information about handwriting pressure.)

Heavy-pressured strokes show healthy energy, strong and lasting feelings, intensity, strength, and deep emotions. Heavy stroke writers are sensuous; they relate to the physical aspects of life and are generally practical and grounded.

FIGURE 149
Heavy-pressured strokes

Light-pressured strokes indicate less energy, lack of intensity, superficial emotions, and sensitivity of feeling. Light stroke writers relate to the mental aspects of life and are inclined to be aesthetic and sensitive.

FIGURE 150
Light-pressured strokes

Moderate-pressured strokes (the norm) reveal sufficient mental and emotional energy and vitality. Moderate stroke writers can relate to both the physical and mental aspects of life (but check other indications).

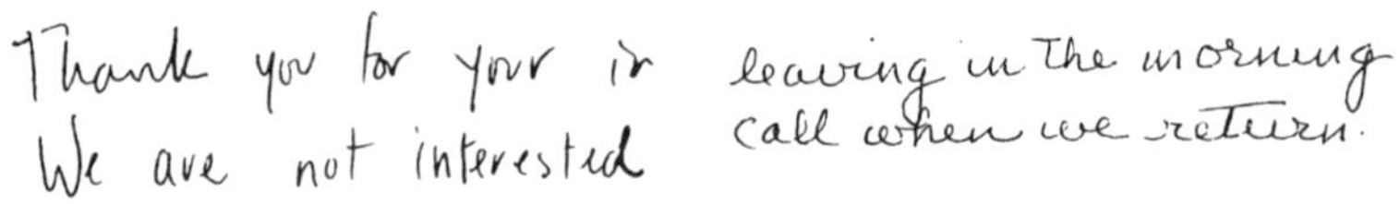

FIGURE 151
Moderate-pressured strokes

Very light strokes show lack of energy, oversensitivity to the environment, and flighty emotions. There is little relation to the physical and more relation to spiritual or otherworldly matters.

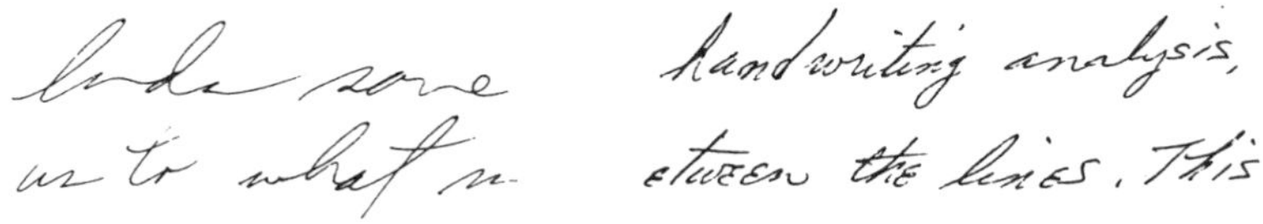

FIGURE 152
Very light strokes

FIGURE 153
Very heavy strokes

Very heavy strokes with sharp edges (look with a magnifying glass) suggest intense energy, very deep feelings, biases, strong influence from the past, and driving power. Very heavy stroke writers relate to the sensuous but refined aspects of life.

Muddy or pasty strokes belong to writers who are driven by passion. They are sensual, have strong physical desires, and are prone to excess. Muddy writers relate to the sensate, unrefined aspects of life.

FIGURE 154
Muddy strokes

Consistent stroke pressure adds to stability and predictability, whereas inconsistent pressure takes away from stability and predictability.

When the handwriting stroke carries the same weight from start to finish, the energy related to the personality trait indicated by that stroke is consistent. If the stroke edges are smooth, consistency is enhanced. When the pressure fades in and out or is spotty, energies are inconsistent, changeable, or unstable.

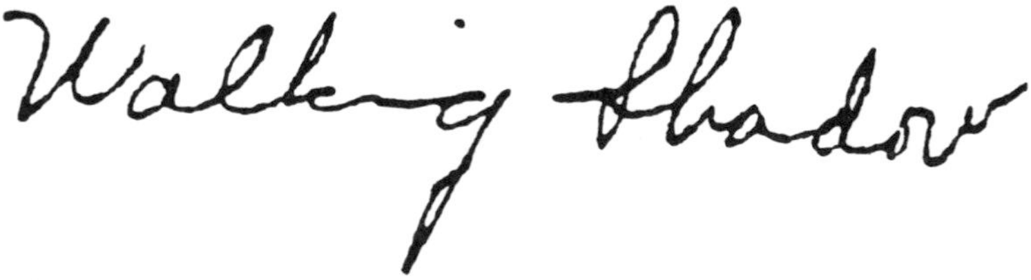

FIGURE 155
Spotty pressure: From a murderer's ransom note

If the weight suddenly fades at the end of the stroke, so does the energy. When the pressure lightens gradually to form a knifelike edge, it is evidence of sarcasm, wit, criticism, or aggression, depending on where the stroke is located and how it is evaluated with other signs. With light, soft writing it can indicate good repartee, but with heavy writing, it shows aggression.

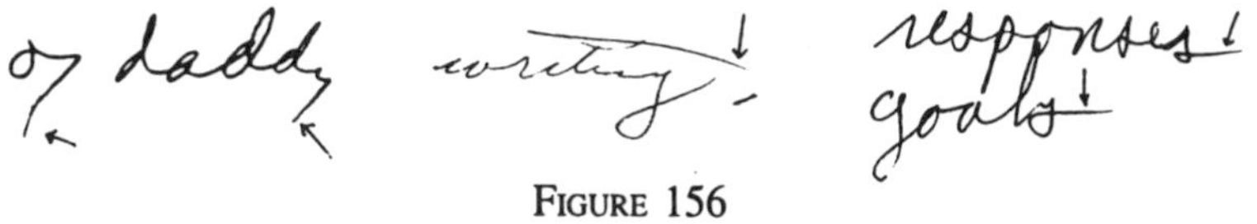

FIGURE 156
Fading pressure

10
BEGINNING
AND ENDING
STROKES

Whatever we intend to do, we must first have a starting point. In handwriting, the initial letter represents this starting point, whereas the final stroke or word ending illustrates the manner in which we finish things up.

Initial handwriting strokes and letters illustrate how people initiate action in their everyday lives. The first letter of a word (especially capital letters and signature initials) show us a self-representation of the writer. This is how the person wishes to be seen, how he or she wants to (or does not want to) impress.

Initial letters can be likened to the way in which the person enters a room. If these letters are firm and well proportioned or bold and heavy without being exaggerated, the writer has a confident approach; he or she arrives with self-assurance (Fig. 157).

Small or neglected initial strokes or capitals indicate a less noticeable entry and a tendency toward humility (Fig. 158).

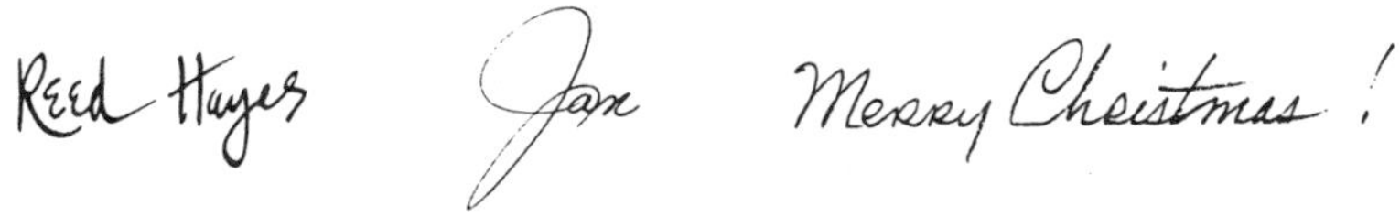

FIGURE 157
Capitals showing confidence

FIGURE 158
Small capitals

Beginning capitals that are very large or overly embellished present the writer as showy, ostentatious, or vain (the person who arrives with dash and flair or coarse bravado, depending on other characteristics). The show of confidence is sometimes an act to conceal an underlying lack of confidence.

FIGURE 159
Very large/overly embellished capitals

The style of capital letters suggests the person's taste. When capitals are simplified or printed, the writer is efficient, practical, and purposeful. Taste in clothing, furniture, food, and so forth lean toward the simple and useful. These writers want no clutter in their lives and they present themselves accordingly.

FIGURE 160
Simplified capitals

Moderate flourishes that appear in good taste belong to writers who add a bit of flair to their presentation. They are somewhat showy and seek recognition, but they do so in a tasteful, nonoffensive way.

FIGURE 161
Moderately flourished capitals

Capitals overly embellished with loops, curlicues, exaggerated movements, and distortions reveal the person who is egotistical. Such people are prone to be pretentious and want you to notice them. They enter rooms loudly or boisterously. They crave anything that brings them attention or feeds their hunger for recognition—gaudy jewelry, extra frills, elaborate meals, lavish cars, the best and the most showy of everything. With other more positive signs in the writing, embellishments can demonstrate artistic expression, but these writers generally offend rather than delight.

FIGURE 162
Overly embellished capitals

Mature people generally write simplified capital letters and omit lead-in strokes as a reflection of their efficiency of thought and their separation from the past. An absence of lead-ins shows that the person is a direct communicator. These people are mentally stripped for action, and they make straight and direct movements to achieve their aims.

FIGURE 163
Omitted lead-ins

Those people who retain the lead-in strokes learned in penmanship classes hold to childhood memories and are strongly influenced by the past. They are comfortable doing things as they always have—with a bit of forethought, caution, and an eye to tradition.

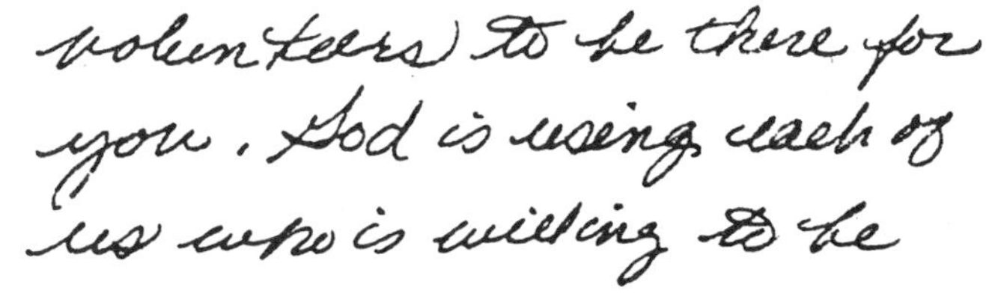

FIGURE 164
Lead-in strokes retained

Very long lead-in strokes tie the person to the past and indicate some difficulty initiating forward movement. These writers hesitate before taking action, holding back until they are certain of what might lie ahead. In communication they tend to be indirect and sometimes talk around a subject rather than getting to the point.

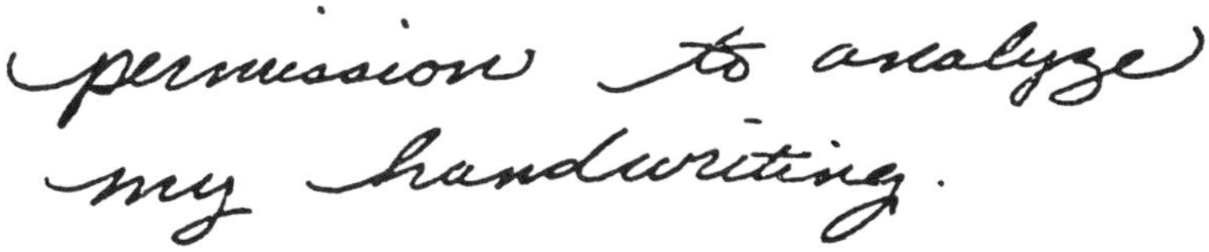

FIGURE 165
Very long lead-ins

When the first letter of a word (especially a capital letter) is attached to the next letter (without a break between) indications are that the writer does not pause between the inception of an idea and taking action. Thoughts flow smoothly toward results.

FIGURE 166
Initial letter attached to next letter

When a break separates the first letter from the next, the writer pauses between the idea and its implementation (Fig. 167).

Take care. Idaho. baby squirrels

FIGURE 167
Initial letter separated from next letter

Other initial stroke indications are as follows.

Initial hooks: acquisitiveness; urge to acquire; the need to have things; size of hook indicates the importance placed on what is desired: large hooks catch big fish, small hooks catch little fish.

Wavy lead-ins: humor, gaiety, flirtatious approach, comes on with a sense of humor or a happy-go-lucky attitude.

Initial spirals or curlicues: pretense, hypocrisy, mistrust, camouflages true feelings by putting on a show, bad taste.

Large, reversed loop: desire for responsibility, wants to do something important, ambitious, group oriented, caretaking.

Small, reversed loop: competitiveness; wants to get ahead; sees others as rivals; wants to be number one; jealous; wants to be important, but to one person only; may feel rejected.

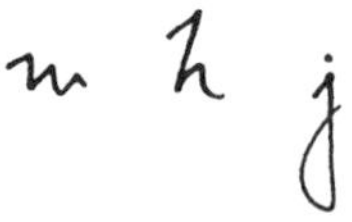

Initial "tic" or barb: if light, irritability and frustration; if heavy, temper or anger; easily "ticked off"; anger is often hidden; approach can be negative and offensive.

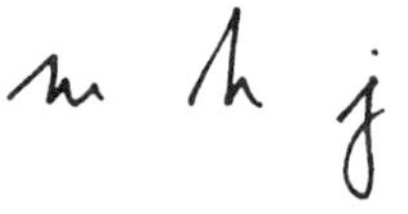

Initial brace stroke: resentment, anger carried for an extended time period, holds grudges, guarded, resistant.

Strong initial brace stroke—variation of above: surging resentment, strong anger (especially if heavy) related to past situation(s)

has resulted in a chip-on-the-shoulder approach, mistrust ("I've been burned and I will not be burned again!"), fears being taken advantage of, does not want to be intruded upon.

Final strokes show how the writer completes projects, what sort of decisions are made, how the person is seen as opposed to how she or he wants to be seen, whether the writer reaches out to other people, or how he or she delivers what was promised in the initial strokes. Terminal strokes show the outcome of the writer's intentions—how the person leaves the room, so to speak.

Various decision-making methods are shown in the following endings:

Final stroke comes to a firm stop (look with a magnifying glass): decisiveness. The writer uses an extra bit of energy (pressure) showing that this is it, the decision has been reached; this allows the person to think and act with certainty and to feel that the right choice has been made.

Very strong ending: very firm decisiveness; stubbornness. The person has made a decision and will defend it; she knows she's right.

Ending in a blob of ink or a clublike structure: willfulness; obstinacy; stubbornly sticks with ideas even when given a better choice; forceful; may be brutal.

Finals fade out: indecisiveness; vacillation between one possibility and another; the person makes a decision only to change later on; not always negative, if stronger traits are also indicated.

Finals do not come down to the baseline: very indecisive; ideas are left hanging; too many possibilities or options; tendency not to trust one's own judgment; even after seeming to come to a decision, will question whether the right choice was made.

Thready endings: fading willpower or loss of interest as a project or situation progresses; may become impatient with final details.

Gradually tapered endings: tact, diplomacy, understanding of people that allows for subtle influence.

Letters gradually increase in size: childlike understanding of people and social situations; naïveté; lack of tact; social blunders, especially in script of poor formlevel.

Final letter suddenly larger: strong and sudden final decision, defiance, takes a strong stand in spite of what others think and even if he or she is not convinced.

Terminals extend straight down below the baseline: the person carries through with ideas, decisions and projects, according to how heavily the stroke finishes; also implies a need to be right and to prove oneself.

Final extends below the baseline and to the right: hidden aggression; strong, forceful decisions if stroke is heavy; if clublike, can be brutal; if sharp-pointed, can be mean and sarcastic; if weak, may be passive–aggressive.

Final strokes also show how (or if) the writer reaches out to people.

Curtailed finals that end at the baseline: efficiency and conservatism relating to people and when tying things up; conservative with resources (usually not generous), since the final stroke does not waste any effort and does not reach out toward people; tends to terminate relationships abruptly.

Terminals reach outward and slightly upward: generosity; expansiveness; like outstretched hands, these finals seem to say, "Take it, it's yours"; a sign of consideration for others and an urge to share whatever is felt to be of value.

Finals reach far outward—variation of above: extravagance; an inability to conserve one's resources; gives very freely and in excess; spends money readily; if also talkative, sometimes follows you from room to room, not knowing when to stop speaking.

Terminal stroke reaches upward and back to the left: desire for attention added to generosity; may give for recognition; craves appreciation; needs to be needed; these strokes are like hands waving in the air saying, "Look at me, I give you nice things and I'm wonderful."

Other final stroke indications are these:

Stroke reaches straight upward: active optimism, actively reaching for the future and for good times ahead, idealism, concern with ethics and morals, mild play for attention.

Stroke curves upward: passive optimism; belief in a higher power, religion, or a spiritual realm: God or the universe will make everything come out right.

Final reaches straight out: caution; at the last minute the writer puts on the brakes in order to reconsider; curbs impulsiveness and sometimes delays final action; if heavy, the caution will be more effective than if light or if the stroke fades out.

Final hooks: tenacity; holding on to what the

person owns; may hold on to material possessions or ideas, beliefs, or feelings; adds to
persistence.

Drooping finals: despondency; feels sad or
disheartened; life is difficult; may use a "poor
little me" attitude, especially if in combination with desire-for-attention strokes (page
121); drooping *y*'s, *g*'s, *or j*'s show depression about one's relationship(s) or sex life.

Firm downstroke for lower zone structures:
determination, decisiveness carried into action, good follow-through, heaviness and
length of the stroke shows the intensity of the
determination.

Lower zone downstroke fades: fading determination; the person is not decisive enough
to carry ideas through to completed action;
gives up easily unless willpower, persistence,
or tenacity are indicated.

11
YOUR WRITING
FITS YOU

TO A *T*

You can learn more about yourself and others from the lowercase *t* than from any other single letter. The lowercase *d* is also very revealing and is included in this chapter because some of the rules about *t*'s also apply to *d*'s.

The lowercase *t* can be written in many different ways, allowing for a variety of personal expressions. The *t* stem may be tall or short, slightly looped, exaggeratedly looped, or retraced. The *t* cross can also take on many variations (in length, heaviness, and placement on the stem) or a tie stroke may be formed instead of an actual *t* bar. The letter *t* is associated with your goals, plans, accomplishments, and intentions.

The stem of the *d* can also be proportionately tall or short and retraced, looped, or exaggerated in size. The letter *d* relates to your feelings about personal matters such as dress, mannerisms, and personal tastes.

First, consider the height of the *t* stem in relationship to the baseline letters. The normal height of the *t* stem is about two and one-half to three times that of the middle zone letters. This height implies a healthy sense of pride where goals and accomplishments are concerned. Writers of tall *t*'s feel as though they "measure up." They stand tall with pride, knowing that other people's eyes may be on the results of their efforts. They feel good about what they have done or wish to do, and their intentions are measured against a yardstick of personal standards.

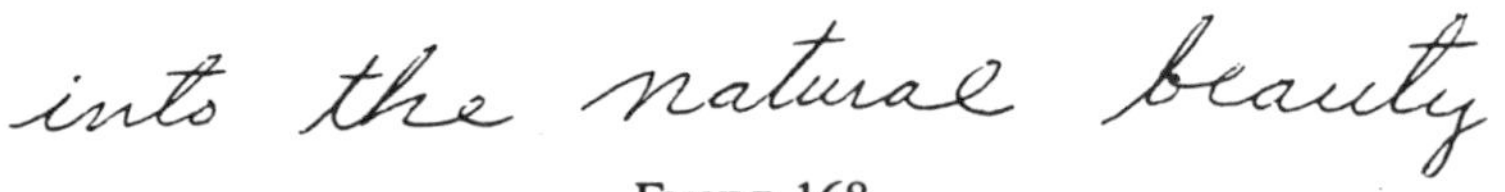

FIGURE 168
Tall *t*'s: Pride in work and accomplishment

Tall *d*'s are also a sign of pride, but the pride is more personal. The person feels self-respect or self-esteem where individual tastes are concerned. Such writers want to create a good impression and are conscious of how people see them. As a standard of conduct, pride helps to curb the expression of feelings that might look negative to other people. Proud people are generally concerned with custom and convention, morals, or standing in the community.

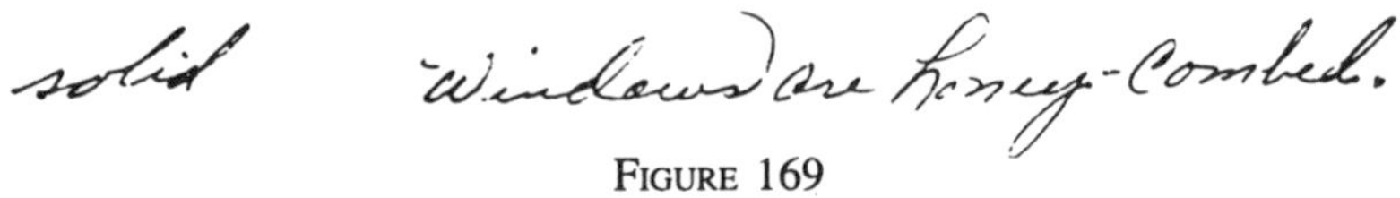

FIGURE 169
Tall *d*'s–Pride in one's standards

Montesquieu said, "It is pride which, by virtue of possessing us, prevents us from possessing ourselves." That pride is illustrated by exceptionally tall *t*'s and *d*'s (more than three times the height of baseline letters). These letters suggest pride that has gone to seed. In an exaggeration of self, the writer has adopted vanity, an attempt to defend the ego and to compensate for inner feelings of inferiority. Although normal pride seeks approval, vanity demands it. When others do not approve, the vain person supplies the approval. Vain people are overly concerned with their images and afraid they will not measure up, so they overestimate their self-worth (*d*'s) and/or their ability to perform (*t*'s). Vanity is accentuated when other upper loop letters are also very tall.

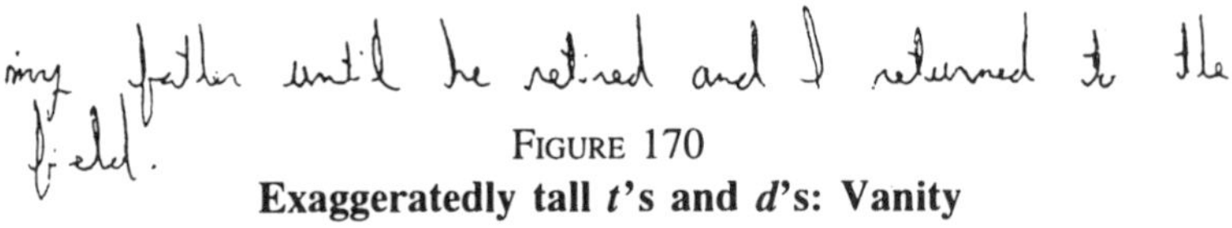

FIGURE 170
Exaggeratedly tall *t*'s and *d*'s: Vanity

Vanity often does not show on the surface, and the writer may be socially aloof, or even withdrawn, while inwardly suffering from rejection and an unfulfilled need of true acceptance and approval (in fact, the repression frequently seen in combination with vanity is such that the person is not always aware of his or her own self-possession.) Expressed vanity (ostentation) is indicated by such signs as exaggerated and overly embellished writing, very large writing, exaggerated capitals, very strong pressure, and strongly angular and forward-moving writing.

At the other extreme are very short *t* and *d* stems, illustrating the independent thinker who is not concerned with custom or convention. Indifferent to what other people think, independent thinkers prefer to make up their own minds according to self-prescribed standards. They want freedom from convention, which allows them to seek approval from within. They want to be autonomous and will therefore "do their own thing," sometimes out of defiance but usually as an adjustment to strong discipline or authority. They cannot be driven, but they can be led (note: independence is not stubbornness).

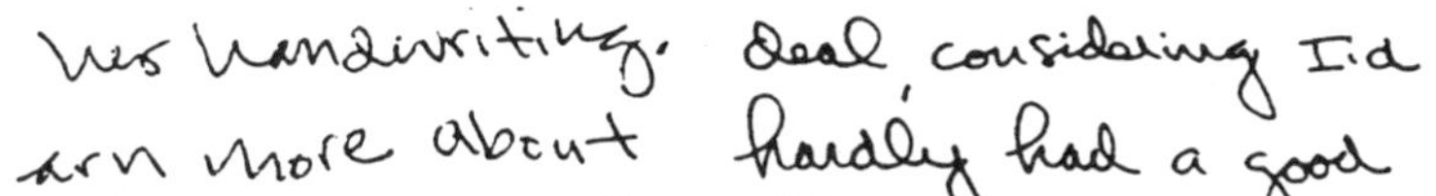

FIGURE 171
Short *t* and *d* stems: Independent thinking

Whether the *t* or *d* is made with a loop adds to what is revealed in the letter's height. A small or narrow loop in either letter exhibits mild sensitivity to criticism, which is, generally speaking, a positive trait in that it allows one to accept constructive criticism without becoming unduly upset. It also means (when supported by other indications) sensitivity to other people's feelings.

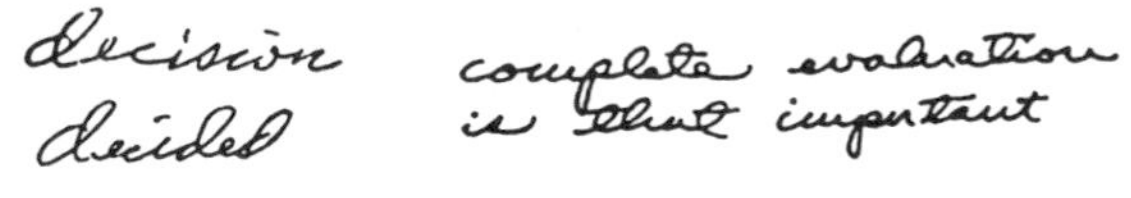

FIGURE 172
Small *t* and *d* loops: Mild sensitivity to criticism

An overly large loop in either the *t* or *d* labels the writer as one who is easily offended by real or imagined criticism. The larger the loop, the more imagination is involved and the more likely the criticism is unfounded. In fact, writers of large *t* or *d* loops put themselves into vulnerable positions where they may even expect to be criticized. Enlarged *t* stems indicate that the writer is sensitive about work, efforts, plans, intentions, and accomplishments. Enlarged *d* stems reveal sensitivity about one's personality, likes and dislikes, mannerisms and self-expression—who he or she is as opposed to what he or she does.

Figure 173
Enlarged *t* and *d* stems: Hypersensitivity to criticism

Very large loops that pull leftward (more frequently seen in the letter *d*) imply that the person is easily offended and withdraws to avoid further discomfort. Such writers are apt to sulk (Fig. 174).

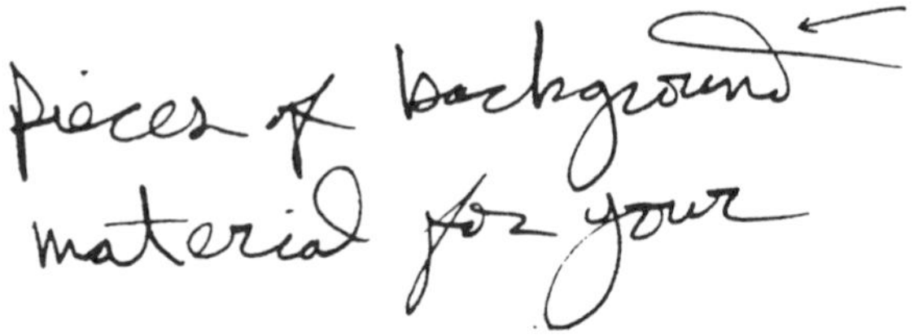

Figure 174
Sensitivity plus withdrawal

Enlarged loops, showing sensitivity to criticism, may demonstrate either pride, vanity, or independent thinking. Each combination produces a different reaction to criticism, ranging from hurt feelings that are eventually healed (pride), to a deeply wounded ego (vanity), to initial hurt that gives way to indifference (independence). For a true portrait of how sensitivity works in the personality, other traits must be considered.

T and *d* stems that are carefully retraced so that little or no paper shows through belong to writers who are careful to avoid criticism. These people are dignified and have a sense of decorum. Behind the dignity is a sense of self-worth based on conformity to a set of standards that the individual has adopted. The writer is able to accept criticism with composure. Dignity creates an impression of honor: the person tries to conform and thus gain approval. Custom and good taste are respected.

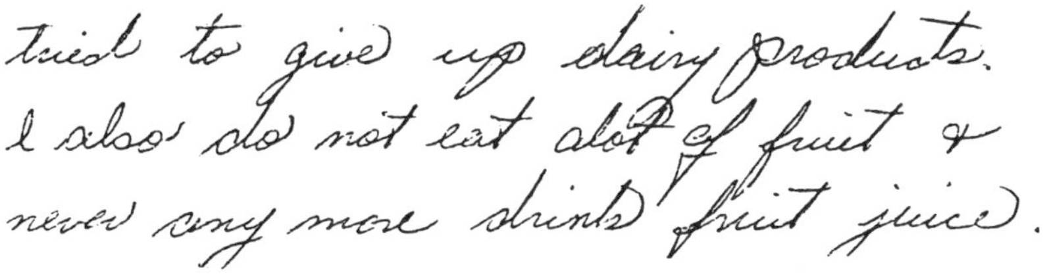

*Tried to give up dairy products.
I also do not eat alot of fruit &
never any more drinks fruit juice.*

FIGURE 175
Retraced *t*'s and *d*'s: Dignity

The height of the *t* or *d* modifies the indication of dignity. The retraced *t* or *d* that is also tall shows pride and increased dignity. The writer is likely to be a conformist and to be concerned with dress, usually wearing clothes that are proper for the occasion. Very tall *t*'s and *d*'s show that dignity increases the vanity by a feeling that the writer is better than others, a refusal to be influenced by criticism, and a resulting stuffed shirt attitude. Short *t*'s and *d*'s in combination with dignity reveal the person who makes an attempt to *appear* to conform while thinking and acting according to his or her own standards—such as jaywalking in an unconcerned manner.

Note that either pride or dignity may have a negative evaluation in the right setting. For example, some criminals have a high regard for their underhanded, antisocial activities and like to be seen as upstanding and above reproach. Evaluate these signs carefully with other characteristics.

Other implications of the letters *t* and *d* are as follows.

Braced stem, spread at the bottom to resemble a tent: stubbornness. The person is braced against influence and refuses to budge, especially if the letter is particularly stiff and if the stroke ending is blunt. If there is some give to the stem or if the ending fades out, the person has a resistant attitude but lacks the firm decisiveness necessary to remain stubborn and therefore eventually gives in.

End stroke comes down below the line: a strong need to be right. The writer is beyond stubborn and is unreasonably persistent in any decision or idea. The straighter and heavier the stroke, the more the resistance. The person may be underhandedly aggressive, especially when the final stroke juts straight out to the right. ( )

Arched top: deliberateness. The approach to work and goals (*t*) is very methodical and step by step; much forethought precedes action (see Georgia O'Keeffe, Fig. 145). The writer wants to impress with his or her personal tastes (*d*) and may be pretentious and calculating.

Lyrical d: one indication of interest in literature or the arts; a need for recognition of one's ideas and individual tastes, which are often expressed in poetry or music (see Percy Shelley, Fig. 81; Oscar Wilde, Fig. 112).

Simplified stem, formed without initial stroke: directness. The individual comes directly to the point, cutting out what is unnecessary and taking the shortest route to accomplish goals (*t*) (see Jacqueline Kennedy Onassis, Fig. 82). The writer is unpretentious, simple in taste, and direct in self-expression (*d*).

T bar placement indicates, among other things, how (or if) the writer plans for the future. The farther away from the baseline the *t* cross is placed, the more distant the person's intentions.

The normal placement for *t* crosses is about two-thirds up the letter stem (Fig. 176-C). This indicates an urge to reach out from the present and to work toward practical aims. The person is secure enough to stretch beyond the present, while still maintaining good common sense and reaching for achievable goals.

T crosses placed very low on their stems (near the tops of middle zone letters) reveal a desire to stay close to the here and now and a fear of stretching beyond the present. Fear of failure (or success) causes the person to underestimate his or her potential and to shun challenges. Anticipation of failure implies lack of self-worth or self-confidence.

A	**B**	**C**	**D**	**E**

FIGURE 176
T cross placement: Goal-orientation. (A) self-underestimation;
(B) low goals; (C) practical aims; (D) distant goals;
(E) far distant, visionary plans

Low goals are indicated by slightly higher *t* crosses (176-B). Such writers may not fear failure, but they do underestimate their full potential and hold themselves back by not taking on challenges. They are comfortable with the familiar and choose to deal with life on a day-to-day basis rather than to set plans for the future.

T crosses placed high on the letter, as in Fig. 176-D, are evidence that the writer reaches toward the future by setting distant goals. Such writers think of what is (or might be) ahead and are willing to take on challenges and the requisite a consistent program of action.

Far distant, visionary *t* crosses belong to the dreamer or the armchair planner. Such writers think far ahead and, with traits showing achievement potential, are able to envision the future and make their dreams come true. Often such high *t* bars, like other exaggerated traits, indicate overcompensation and perhaps a way of avoiding a poor sense of accomplishment by reaching far ahead and away from reality. Visionary writers want to do something important or be someone special; they feel there is room for them at the top.

However, great ideas need landing gear as well as wings if they are ever to materialize. High-flying *t* bars require a sense of purpose or willpower to give the writer a real sense of direction. Although willpower is not always a requisite, it lends a sense of direction or self-regulation where goals are concerned.

Strength of will is shown in heavy *t* crosses, a sign that the writer emphasizes whatever goal is set and exerts strong energy toward his or her aims. Exceptionally strong *t* bars reveal relentless willpower, which is negative in the sense that the person is unable to consider other methods but the chosen path, but positive in the sense that the person is likely to reach the goal (see signature of David Livingstone, Fig. 32).

Strong willpower is not to be considered a positive trait without evaluating other writing indications. For example, a strong-willed criminal uses strength of purpose in a negative way.

Figure 177
Heavy *t* crosses: Strong willpower

Light *t* crosses point toward lack of willpower or self-direction. Such writers sometimes need other people to help them envision possibilities. They may or may not have other characteristics that then help them achieve.

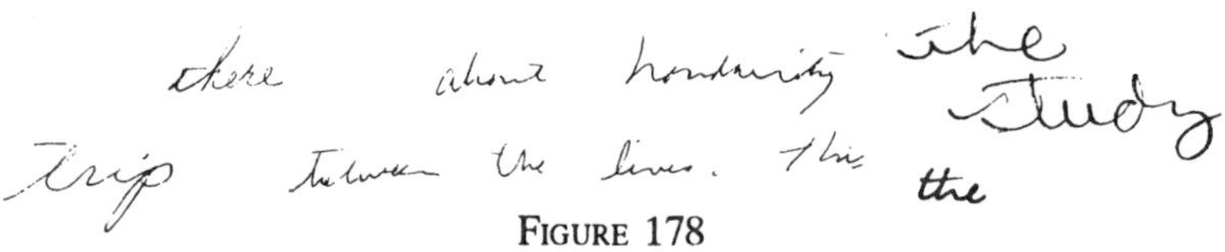

Figure 178
Light *t* crosses: Weak willpower

Consider again the person whose *t* bar is placed above the *t* stem. Without a sense of purpose the writer merely dreams of what might be without having the force necessary to achieve the dream. If the writer has firm willpower in addition to the vision, achievement is more likely. People who have demonstrated this combination of vision and personal willpower are Thomas Edison, George Bernard Shaw, Georgia O'Keeffe, and Albert Einstein.

Their chances for success are furthered by the added trait of enthsiasm, illustrated by very long *t* crosses. Lengthened *t* crosses illutrate willpower extended over a longer time. Enthusiastic people become excited about their goals and intentions as they proceed. Firmly convinced of their purpose, they often stir up excitement in others. Without strength of will, enthusiasm loses much of its effectiveness and sometimes becomes merely an outlet for emotion or impulsiveness (Fig. 179-A).

A   B

Figure 179
Extended *t* crosses: Enthusiasm. (A) Enthusiasm lacking in force;
(B) Enthusiasm plus strength of purpose

Short *t* crosses, on the other hand, imply conservation of energy and a lack of expended effort in working toward personal goals.

Other indications of *t*'s are as follows.

**T *cross well-placed, equal on both sides:* carefulness; attentiveness to detail; conservative efforts; perfectionism, if consistent.

**T *cross bowed downward:* self-control, bending the will in an effort to check any personal trait felt to be negative or undesirable.

**T *cross bent upward:* Superficiality, lack of conviction or overall purpose, easily swayed from objectives, may take the easiest route or leave the real work to someone else.

Flourished cross bar: flirtatiousness; wants recognition and attention (according to how flourished the bar is) and may achieve it through a sense of humor, mimicry, or antics.

**T *cross sharp at the end:* sarcasm, caustic thoughts or remarks that result from hidden hostilities.

**T *cross beginning with a hook:* acquisitiveness, desire to "hook oneself" to a goal or purpose.

**T *cross ending with a hook:* tenacity, clinging to one's objectives until the task or idea is completed, holding on to what one has achieved.

**T *cross ending with a barb:* frustrated tenacity, irritability or frustration regarding the outcome or possible outcome of a goal.

**T *cross does not follow through:* procrastination, putting off action where plans are concerned, indecisive regarding the future, avoids activity but may do well under pressure of a deadline, in managers or executives may indicate the person is putting off what he would really like to do in life.

**T *cross to the right:* impatience; wants to get on with things; dislikes delay; frustrated by time wasters and obstacles; if letter is heavy or clublike, indicates temper and possible explosiveness. (Note: Give the right-placed *t* cross less emphasis if the writer is British.)

Final stroke juts forward: initiative, sees opportunities and takes advantage of them, ready to move ahead when the time is right.

Final stroke retraces letter stem—variation of above: repressed initiative; contradictory, as the writer sees opportunities but puts off taking action.

Final stroke begins to jut forward, but droops—variation of above: before the initiative takes hold, the writer sees the negative possibilities and therefore does not act.

T *cross made from right to left, back to self (check with magnifying glass):* self-castigation; pushing or driving oneself to reach a goal; may feel obliged to work toward something but without much enjoyment; tendency to feel guilty, self-critical, or be willing to take blame. (Note: Give this sign less significance for left-handed writers.)

Final stroke of **t** *reaches up, then back to left:* same as above, except the person may want to be recognized for his or her self-driven attitude.

Final stroke of **t** *reaches up over the letter, then forward, not tied:* writer reaches to the past to consider what has been, then uses the experience to reach far into the future; visionary and imaginative; aware of possibilities; seeker of the abstract or the ideal.

Tied **t***:* persistence; ignores obstacles and temporary set-backs, returning to "try, try again"; "tied" to one's purpose or intentions; not easily defeated.

Star-shaped **t***:* the strategist; considers all angles and possibilities, evaluating both past and present in his approach to what lies ahead; if exceptionally angular, is relentless.

Downward **t** *cross:* domineering; needs to be in control; likes to have things his or her way; demanding; if light, frustrated because of inability to control others; if heavy, uses forcefulness to get what he or she wants.

Downward t cross to the right of letter: domineering tendencies added to impatience, temper, or both; wants what he or she wants when he or she wants it; pushy.

T *cross becomes part of next letter:* fluidity, mental agility, ability to quickly connect one thought or idea to another, comes up with quick alternatives to problems or situations.

No cross bar: forgetfulness, inattentiveness to detail, impulsiveness (if the cross bar is absent only once or twice, it may be due to hurried writing; check more than one sample).

Clublike t cross, heavy-ended: willfulness, dominating personality, must have own way, forcefulness, anger, may be brutal or explosive.

Upward slanted cross bar: optimism; hopefulness; no matter how difficult things are at the moment, they will be better tomorrow; looking toward the future; tends to like his or her work.

12
ARE YOU
INSECURE?

Everyone has occasional moments of insecurity or self-doubt. This is normal and can actually be beneficial if it leads to personal growth or if it serves as self-protection. When fears become habitual, however, the wholeness of the personality is at stake. Fearful people cope poorly with challenges. Their thinking, interpersonal relationships, and achievement potential or sense of purpose can be damaged.

Fear is often misunderstood and pushed from consciousness so that we don't have to deal with it. Graphology can point out habitual fears and how we cope with them. Handwriting reveals such traits as self-consciousness, repression, self-underestimation, sensitivity to criticism, and jealousy; it helps us to see objectively the areas we may improve.

Besides a closer look at your own shortcomings, graphology gives you a more objective view of the "sore spots" of people in your life. By recognizing their uncertainties you can better understand their reactions and encourage the more positive traits that show in their handwriting.

Do not worry when you discover that your writing reveals any of the traits covered in this chapter. Everyone has a smattering of one insecurity or another. If you happen to be a bit sensitive to criticism or somewhat shy in mixed company, don't despair. Recognize that your writing indicates the truth and that other people are sensitive and self-conscious, too.

Occasional or temporary insecurities are not revealed by handwriting so much as habitual ones. The fear elements discussed here usually result from unpleasant or inadequate situations in childhood. Parental teaching, environment, trauma, excessive criticism, abuse, or violence in the home can all leave emotional scars that may show up as chronic fears.

Reactions to fear are shown first in the gestalt of the handwriting (e.g., regularity, spacing, overall arrangement, and size). Handwriting of poor quality (irregular, disorganized, erratic, or inconsistent) shows less inner strength and self-discipline, whereas more regular, organized writing reflects a more solid personality and better coping mechanisms.

Tight or squeezed writing is more revelatory of inner fear than is more free-flowing, open script, although this is considered in relation to the overall quality of the writing. Very small writing can also indicate uncertainty and withdrawal because of fear, whereas large writing is more confident and self-expressive (again, depending on the gestalt of the script).

Emotional makeup is shown by slant, pressure, and baseline regularity. Forward, light writers are more reactive and less poised in the face of fear whereas heavy or vertical writers, or both, tend to be more self-disciplined. Consistent baselines also imply regulated feelings and a "feet on the ground" approach.

SELF-CONSCIOUSNESS

Ordinary self-consciousness is a social inhibitor that makes for uneasiness or embarrassment, especially when one is with strangers. Anyone can feel "on the spot" in a given situation, but the habitually self-conscious person may actually fear ridicule. Although they may not show it on the outside, self-conscious people believe that others are watching them or taking note of their inadequacies. Their perceived inadequacies may be physical (scar, physical handicap, torn clothing) or intangible (inadequate education, uncertainty). Truly self-conscious people are sometimes timid and shy, often blunder through life and social settings, and in extreme cases can be apologetic for being themselves.

Self-consciousness can sometimes have an adverse effect on goal orientation, making for uncertainty in day-to-day achievements and more distant plans, and therefore holding people back from getting what they want. Although this trait can be a deterrent to action, it need not be. Recognizing from your writing that you feel this uneasiness can give you the impetus needed to be yourself in spite of what people may think. In reality people are not likely to express ridicule or even think it. Ridicule is more often a perception than a reality.

Self-consciousness is shown in the letters *m* and *n* where the last section of the letter is taller than the preceding one. The intensity of the trait depends on the amount of times the stroke is found as well as the strength of the last segment of the letter (Fig. 180).

FIGURE 180
Self-consciousness

The self-conscious stroke can be found in either lower case or capital *m*'s and *n*'s: When it is found in capitals, the writer is not as likely to appear self-conscious. The implication of the enlarged capital is that the person wears a face of confidence while inwardly feeling insecure, and may be bold, confident, and forward-moving in daily activities, perhaps to compensate for the uncertainty within.

M's and *n*'s that are cramped as well indicate that the self-consciousness is closely tied to fear of expression. These people keep their true feelings concealed as a way of protecting themselves from possible ridicule; they tend to suffer in silence and need encouragement to express themselves (Fig. 181).

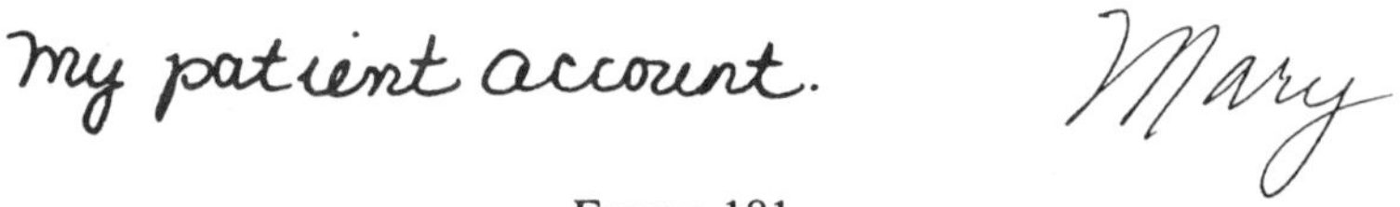

FIGURE 181
Self-consciousness and repression

Sharp-pointed *m*'s and *n*'s, which also reveal self-consciousness, imply that the person is so quick to perceive ridicule as to walk into a room full of people and "know" immediately who might evoke the inadequate feelings (Fig. 182).

FIGURE 182
Self-consciousness and quick perception

A very angular, self-conscious stroke suggests the writer who is willing to fight against self-consciousness (Fig. 183). A stubborn or aggressive attitude may cover the uncertain inner emotions.

FIGURE 183
Self-consciousness and combative approach

If the last stroke of the *m* or *n* is tucked in or turned back, the feelings of discomfort cause the person to withdraw (Fig. 184).

"JEANETTE"

FIGURE 184
Self-consciousness and withdrawal

This trait is intensified if the writing is also very small. The writer is then inclined to withdraw into a very small personal world of self-protection.

JEALOUSY

Webster's dictionary defines jealousy as "a suspicious fear or watchfulness, especially the fear of being replaced by a rival." It is a peculiar feeling of insecurity composed of fear and anger. Jealous people are afraid of losing their place of importance and angry at persons whom they perceive as rivals.

Entire books have been devoted to this trait, and psychologists say that it is common to many character disorders. Jealousy masquerades as forcefulness but is founded in weakness; it arises from a sense of inadequacy and emotional impotence (not importance).

In handwriting, jealousy is indicated by a proportionately small, reversed loop at the beginning of any letter. It is generally seen in the letters *m, n, I,* or *j.* The stroke reverts to the past, the self, then swings around to form the rest of the letter (Fig. 185). Jealous people reach to the past for security, but restrict themselves and their relationships out of frustration. Just as these small loops are closed off, so the jealous person squeezes people out.

FIGURE 185
Jealousy

In contrast, a larger initial loop indicates a desire for responsibility (Fig. 186). It is normal to wish to include many people and activities in one's life, as is implied by the larger loop size. Although jealous people want to feel responsible for their own lives, they have a fear of including others, so they exclude all but one or two intimate relationships or people to whom they cling tightly.

FIGURE 186
Desire for responsibility

In spite of its negative origins and the interpersonal difficulties it causes, jealousy can sometimes have positive results. In work or business affairs, for example, it can be translated into competition, which acts as a spur toward increased activity and greater accomplishments. This is likely when positive achievement forces are indicated and when the jealousy loops are not extremely small.

Often, however, jealousy is a demanding possessiveness that manifests in direct proportion to one's inner sense of powerlessness. It indicates an inner lack of self-worth. The jealous person craves attention, needs to be number one, wants to be favored, and is afraid of being unloved, unappreciated, or pushed aside.

In extreme cases, the trait shows ambivalence of feeling. The person may actually love and hate at the same time but be unaware of the contradiction. A jealous rage can be a way of externalizing a lack of faith in his or her relationship(s). In such a plight, the person half wishes to find the lover in the imagined disloyalty so that the situation, so plagued with inadequacy, can at last come to an end.

Both the past and future seem empty to jealous individuals because they relate only to immediate problems concerning the self. There is emotional distortion in the area of the jealousy. This may be intensified by emotional responsiveness, depth of feeling, sensitivity, resentment, or other fears.

When the personal pronoun *I* or the signature begins with a jealousy loop, the trait is deeply embedded in the writer's psyche and has a more pervasive influence on the personality.

REPRESSION

Another common insecurity is repression, which is an unconscious restraint of thoughts or emotions. A person develops repression as a way of withdrawing from thoughts or feelings that threaten the ego, and thereby pushes the perceived danger from consciousness. If the unpleasant feelings beneath the repression were to be recalled, the person would once again experience the feeling of danger.

In most cases repression begins as *suppression*, a more positive trait. Suppression is a conscious control mechanism whereby we temporarily put something out of mind to deal with it later; it is a healthy form of self-discipline.

Suppression is revealed by occasionally retraced letters, especially in the middle zone. Such retracing indicates that the writer periodically attempts to put thoughts or feelings temporarily out of mind (Fig. 187).

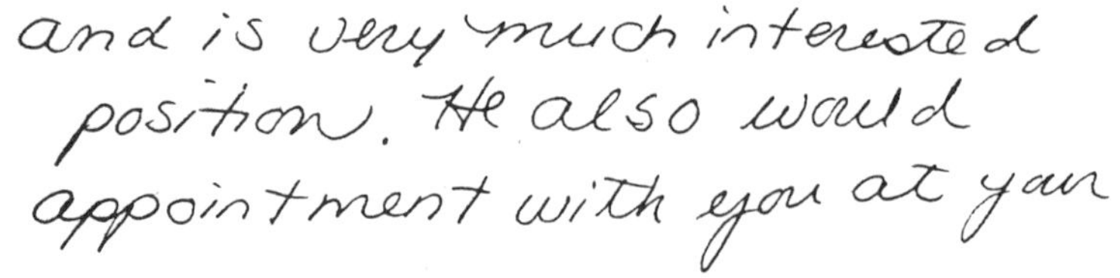

and is very much interested
position. He also would
appointment with you at your

FIGURE 187
Suppression

We previously saw a kind of suppression in dignity, shown by carefully retraced *t* and/or *d* stems and indicating that the writer is socially self-controlled (Fig. 175).

Repression is different from suppression in that the emotional control has become an unconscious habit so that the person no longer remembers the event or emotion that is being held in check.

Repression is indicated by *frequently* retraced strokes, which gives the writing a squeezed, tight look, especially when the trait is strong (Fig. 188). Note that downstrokes of letters on the baseline (especially *m*'s and *n*'s) are carefully retraced by the upstrokes that follow. Symbolically, the act of retracing keeps the writer from stretching forward and moving away from restrictions of the past, as if he or she were "marking time" and retracting from danger. It thereby detracts from achievement forces. The stroke, by its cramping, also replaces any relaxation. The more often these retracings appear, the more effect the trait will have on the writer's personality.

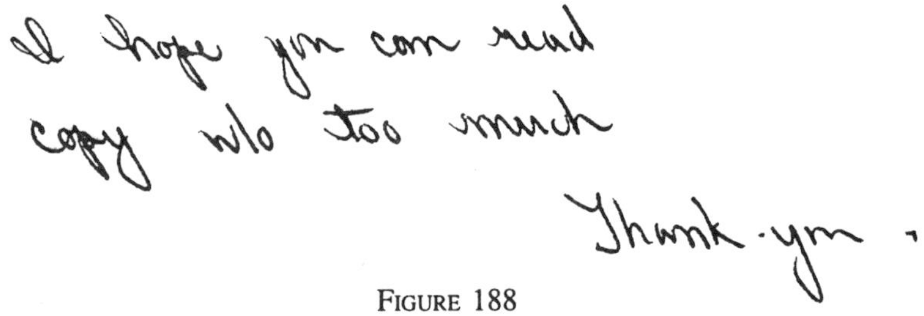

I hope you can read
copy w/o too much
Thank-you .

FIGURE 188
Repression

People who are repressed have strong tendencies toward timidity, stinginess, or selfishness, which other writing characteristics bear out. Generally speaking, handwriting that contains repression also shows other fear traits.

Repressed thoughts or feelings must periodically find expression, especially when the repression is strong. The release of pent-up feelings sometimes comes quite suddenly, much to the surprise of the repressed person and to other people around. When the writing is of strong pressure and also repressed, very intense feelings are beneath the surface waiting for the right moment to gush out.

Repression is frequently seen in writing that slants far to the right, suggesting an acquired control over strong emotional responses, but can, of course, appear in handwriting of any slant. This particular fear has a negative effect on thinking, as revealed by the way it closes up the angles that would otherwise show analytical ability. Repressed people tend not to know themselves in depth, since they repress any *self*-analysis as well. They seem to lack the ability to look at their feelings objectively.

Repression sometimes appears in the handwriting of people who had very strict or religious parents who taught the child that certain acts and thoughts were bad and punished the child for doing something the parents deemed unacceptable. At first the child is unaware that the behavior is not approved, but after being punished a few times the youngster consciously considers the consequences of performing the act again, and suppression develops. Eventually the suppression becomes habitual and turns into repression.

Determining exactly what is being repressed cannot be discerned from the handwriting and should be left to qualified therapists. However, handwriting can offer some clues in the area(s) where the repressed strokes occur. Tightly squeezed upper loops indicate repression of one's ethics and a tendency to accept beliefs on blind faith. Retraced baseline letters indicate repression of thought and feeling and difficulties in day-to-day social settings. Lower zone retraces reveal unfulfilled physical (sexual) needs and desires.

SELF-UNDERESTIMATION

A trait that detracts from achievement potential is self-doubt or self-underestimation. The main indicator of this characteristic is *t* crosses that are placed very low on their stems (Fig. 189). Very low *t* crosses graphically indicate people who are afraid to stretch toward the future.

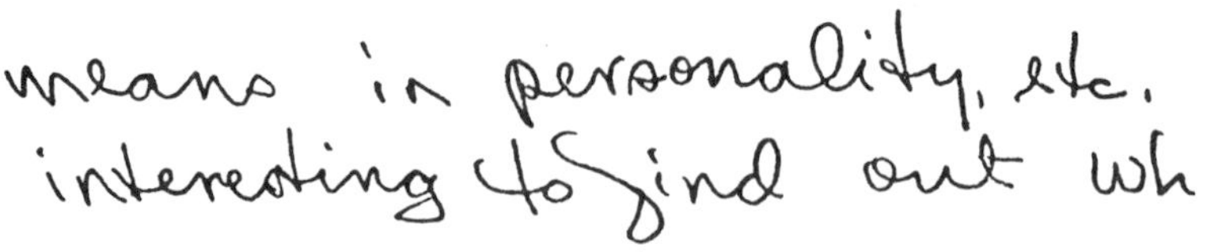

*means in personality, etc.
interesting to find out wh*

FIGURE 189
Self-underestimation

People who underestimate themselves are reacting out of an inner lack of faith and a fear of failure. Such people usually deal well with everyday affairs (as shown by regularity, clarity, and spacing) but they shun challenges and do not look to the future. They take care of today and let tomorrow take care of itself.

Although very low *t* bars have generally been associated with fear of failure, more recent observation suggests they may also indicate fear of success. This trait is suggested if the writing, in addition to having low *t* bars, is of high formlevel, if it is clear and well-organized, and if signs related to thinking and achievement are positive.

Writers with very low *t* crosses have a tendency to feel that they are beneath others and are unworthy of personal progress. They sell themselves short, anticipate failure, and stick with the familiar.

Writers of higher, more practical *t* crosses are more realistic in how they measure themselves. People who lack self-worth should be encouraged to develop a more realistic self-concept and to place their *t* crosses higher.

SENSITIVITY TO CRITICISM

Sensitivity to criticism is brought about by continued disapproval. People who are open to criticism actively seek to be recognized and respected for who they are, as their tall *t* and *d* stems illustrate. When these stems are also looped, imagination comes into play, allowing them to feel offense when unrecognized or disapproved of, or when they imagine disapproval. The larger the loop, the more the sensitivity is nurtured by frequent hurt and perceived rejection (Fig. 190).

Anyone's feelings can be hurt from time to time, but repeatedly injured feelings imply uncertainty regarding one's self-image. The overly sensitive person is readily affected by what people say, anticipates criticism and injuries, and may even imagine rejection or insult where none is intended. This can result in considerable unhappiness.

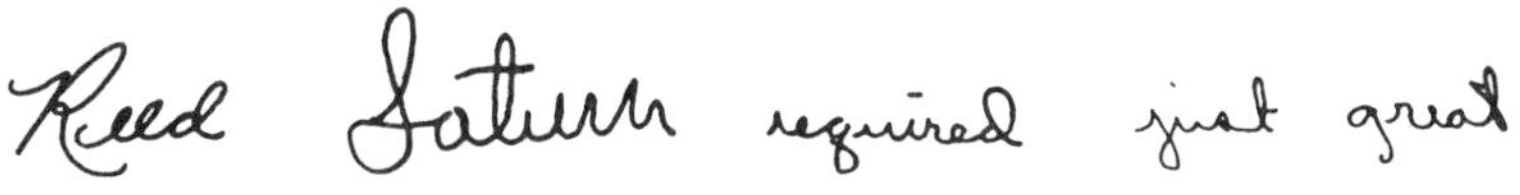

Reed Saturn required just great

FIGURE 190
Sensitivity to criticism

When looped *t*'s and *d*'s are proportionately very tall, indicating vanity, the writer is even more thin-skinned (Fig. 191). Here the self-esteem is distorted, causing the person to seek constant approval and recognition in order to feel whole. Such people have an imaginary view of what people think (or should think) about their actions, mannerisms, habits, and ideas. They tend to feel better than others and they are sometimes critical of others in order to avoid injury to themselves.

*one't do I've wanted it
I first found out*

FIGURE 191
Vanity and sensitivity to criticism

People who write short *t* and *d* stems can also be injured by criticism, but they set their own standards and seek approval from within. When they are also sensitive, as shown by an added loop, they can be initially offended but can easily cast sensitivity aside for a more independent attitude (Fig. 192).

good don't mistreatment bad

FIGURE 192
Independent thinking and sensitivity to criticism

Sensitivity to criticism, like other fear traits, need not be a burden. It can act as a driving force toward success, enabling the person to put forth a stronger effort and avoid censure. It may also help the person uphold personal values through pride and sincerity, and it allows for sensitivity to other people's needs and feelings.

13
HANDWRITING
REVEALS YOUR
SOCIAL LIFE

Do you like people? Are you expressive and outgoing, or quiet and reserved? How do you communicate? Are you pleasant or difficult to get along with? Do you like to share what is yours? Do you seek approval from others?

These questions can be answered from your handwriting. Your writing also shows other personality characteristics that influence your relationships with people and tells you how others are apt to relate to you.

A true picture of one's social attitudes is, of course, determined by evaluating many characteristics, including those covered in this chapter as well as others mentioned throughout this book. Especially noteworthy are the writer's insecurities, as discussed in Chapter 12. The person who feels exceptionally insecure does not feel at ease in social settings and may exhibit unpleasant characteristics born of an attempt to defend the ego. A more confident individual, however, has a healthy, pleasant disposition and an ease of expression.

DO YOU LEAN
TOWARD PEOPLE?

If you are fundamentally a "people person," your writing is likely to slant toward the right, an indication that you respond to other people's feelings because of your own emotional makeup. Rightward slant implies the ability to be sympathetic and is one indication of extroversion (Fig. 193). Whether or not you are outwardly expressive of your inner responses depends primarily on the size and spacing of your writing.

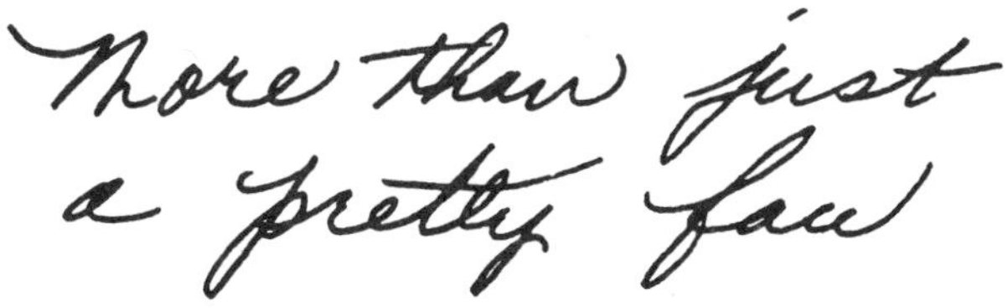

More than just a pretty face

FIGURE 193
Rightward slant: Responsiveness to people

Upright or leftward slant belongs to people who are likely to be emotionally reserved, self-contained, nonexpressive of inner feelings, and generally lacking in extroversion (Fig. 194). Such writers may *appear* to be extroverted, especially if the writing is large, expansive, heavy, or if it contains many strong, forward movements.

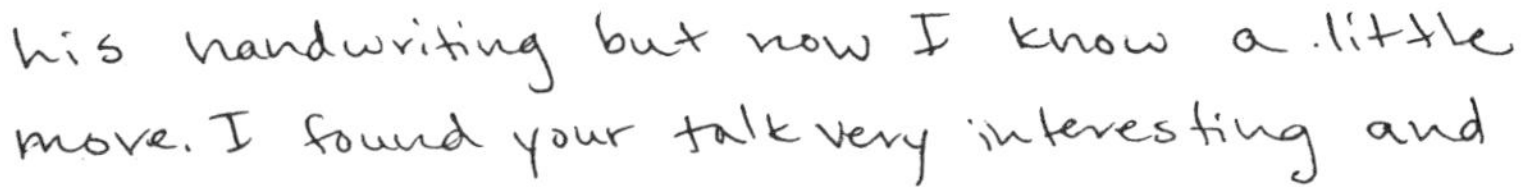

his handwriting but now I know a little more. I found your talk very interesting and

FIGURE 194
Upright handwriting: Emotional reserve

Emotional permanence, as shown by the heaviness of the script, is also an important component of social attitudes. Heavy writers tend to have more warm and lasting feelings toward people than do light writers, whether or not they express those feelings. Light writers can be quite responsive and expressive of feeling, but their emotions are generally not as lasting. Light-pressured strokes also imply lack of warmth, although you must look at other indications such as degree of roundness and spacing, length of finals, loop size, and the presence of any hostility indicators.

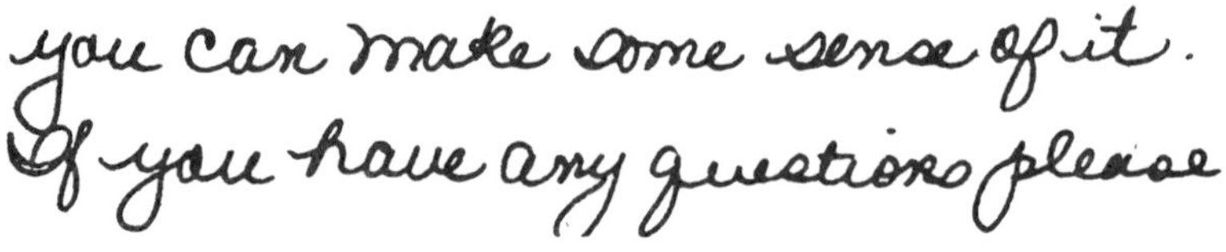

FIGURE 195
Heavy pressure: Lasting feelings

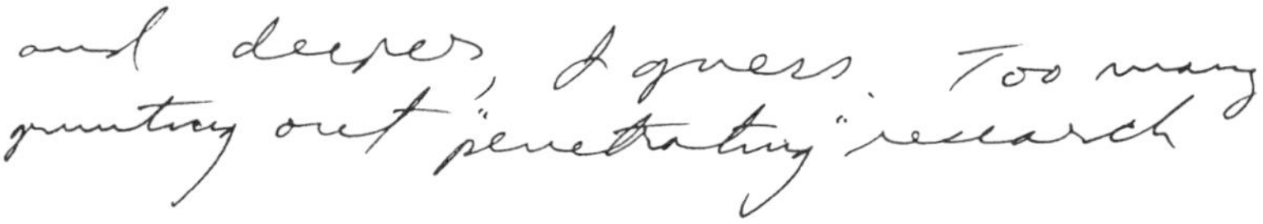

FIGURE 196
Light pressure: Short-lived feelings

DO YOU CONNECT
WITH PEOPLE?

Both letter spacing and word spacing indicate one's social attitudes, as suggested in Chapter 3. Narrow spacing between letters (Fig. 197) reveals the person who may not feel at ease with himself or herself. As a result, the person has a tendency to be reserved or unexpressive of inner needs and feelings. Sometimes the "tight" writer is repressed, finds it difficult to connect with others, and lacks self-acceptance or self-understanding. Sometimes (when there are no extended letter finals, for example) such writers are not able to share easily.

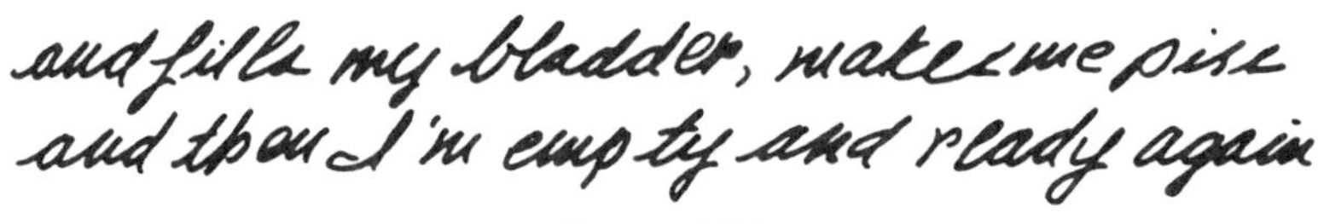

FIGURE 197
Narrow letter spacing: Uncomfortable with inner feelings

Wide spacing between individual letters shows more self-acceptance than narrow letter spacing, and a tendency to be more freely expressive. It shows that the person reaches toward others and readily shares his or her self and possessions (Fig. 198).

how much I enjoyed

FIGURE 198
Wide letter spacing: Comfortable with self

The degree of spacing between words shows how much distance the person wants between self and others. Narrow word spacing implies a willingness to be close, while wide spacing shows a need for elbow room. The writer of narrow word spaces can feel comfortable squeezed between two people on a bus, but the writer of wide word spaces may need an empty seat on either side.

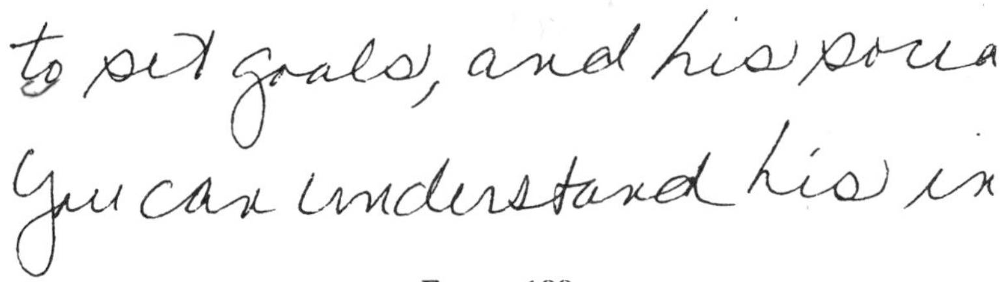

to set goals, and his sprea
You can understand his in

FIGURE 199
Narrow word spacing: Willingness to connect

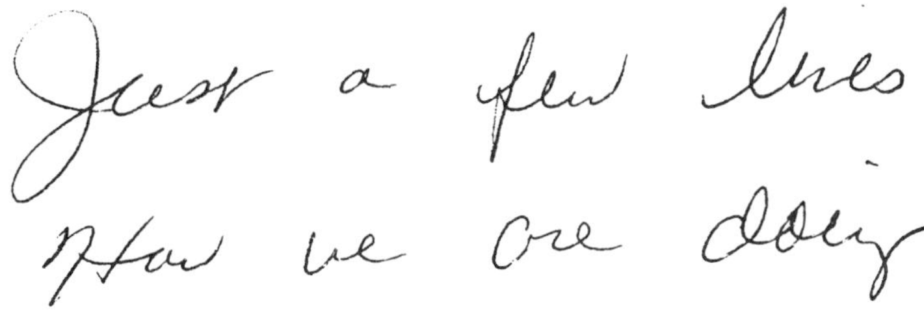

Just a few lines
How we are doing

FIGURE 200
Wide word spacing: Likes space between self and others

DO YOU SEEK OUT
SOCIAL ACTIVITY?

Writing size, especially the size of the middle zone, reveals the self-expressive qualities of the writer. The larger the writing, the more likely the person is to be outgoing, social-minded, and expressive. Those with large writing seek out a busy social life as a way of gratifying an inner need for recognition and a desire to be important. Their broad and expansive outlook on life usually allows them to mingle with a variety of people.

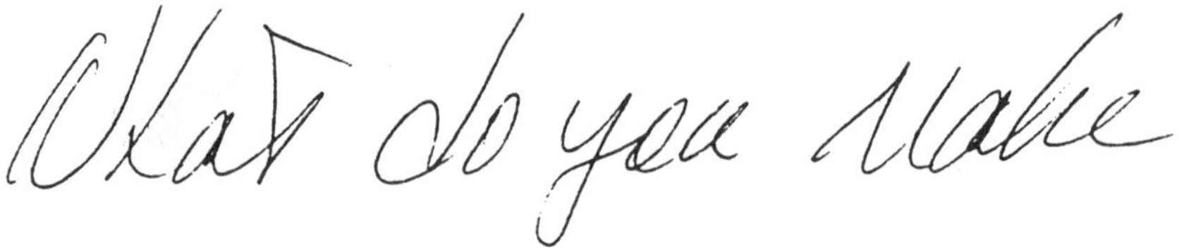

FIGURE 201
Large writing: Self-expressiveness

Those with very small writing are at the other end of the social spectrum: they are inclined to be modest, reserved, and quiet, sometimes because they are self-sufficient, and sometimes because of an inner fear of contact (check for indications of insecurity). They do not require a lot of attention and sometimes go without notice. Their narrow outlook on life causes them to be rather selective of their friends, interests, and activities.

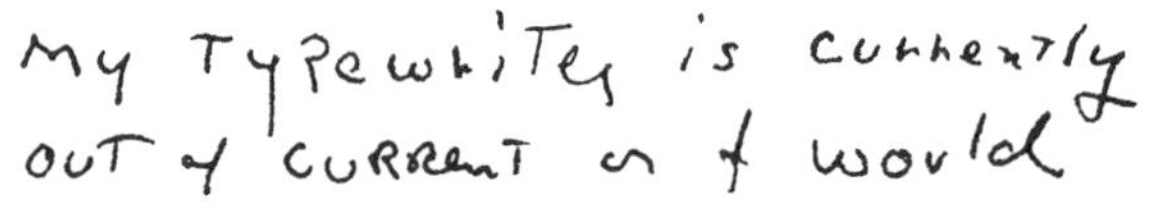

FIGURE 202
Small writing: Modesty and reserve

HOW DO YOU CHOOSE YOUR FRIENDS AND ACQUAINTANCES?

Loops, especially lower ones, further clarify the writer's approach to people: they indicate how we choose our friends and associates.* The larger these loops, the more likely the person is to have a variety of acquaintances and relationships. Wide or large loop writers seek a broad social scene, one in which they can be assured of frequent change and

---

*Further information regarding lower loops can be found in the next chapter.

interesting events. If the loops are exceptionally inflated, the writer may be a social butterfly, too restless to light for very long on any one flower.

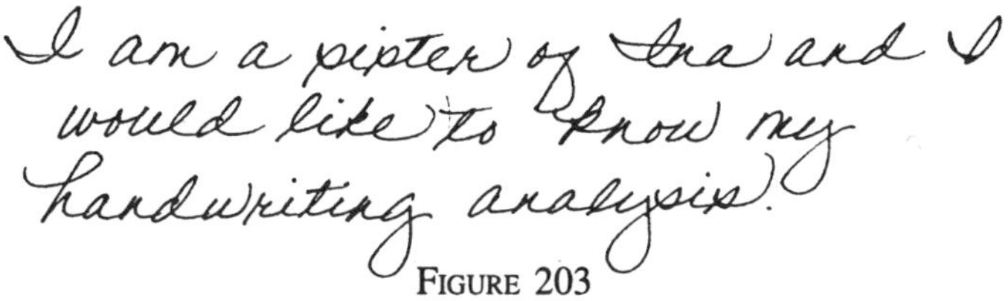

FIGURE 203
Large lower loops: Seeks social variety

At the other extreme are people who do not form loops at all (Fig. 204). Lack of loops, lower ones especially, implies that the person is able to spend time alone. He or she may not need many friends and activities, preferring instead to be more independent. Whether the need for solitude is a conscious choice or the result of inner uncertainty depends on other characteristics.

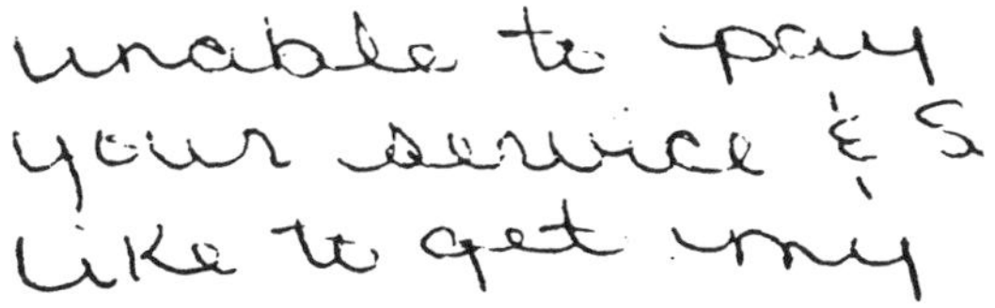

FIGURE 204
No lower loops: Prefers solitude

Narrow or retraced loops illustrate care in the selection of friends. These writers tend to choose friends who are like them in some way: who are in the same profession or have similar hobbies and interests. They sometimes prefer solitude and usually choose to be involved with small or close-knit groups. Although such writers can sometimes be gregarious, they are always a bit careful in choosing their close friends.

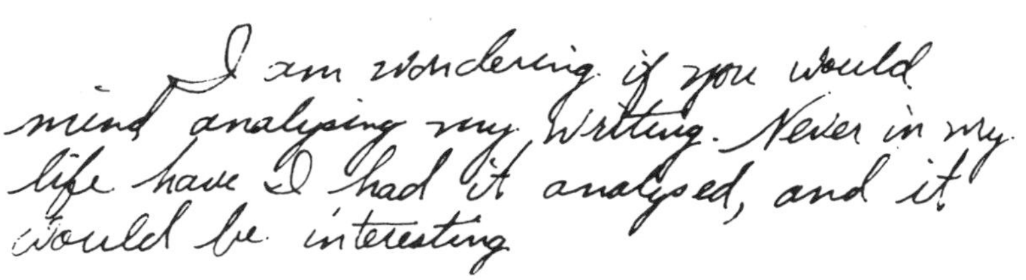

FIGURE 205
Narrow lower loops: Socially selective

Although writers of narrow loops are cautious about intimacy, writers of tiny lower loops are fearful of intimacy (Fig. 206). Their circle of intimate acquaintances is the proportionate size of their lower loops. Such writers are clannish and only open to those people who definitely have something in common with them; their real friends are a trusted few. They tend to shun outsiders but are likely to remain loyal to those within the remote, tight circle. Clannish writers may at times be good mixers, but only superficially.

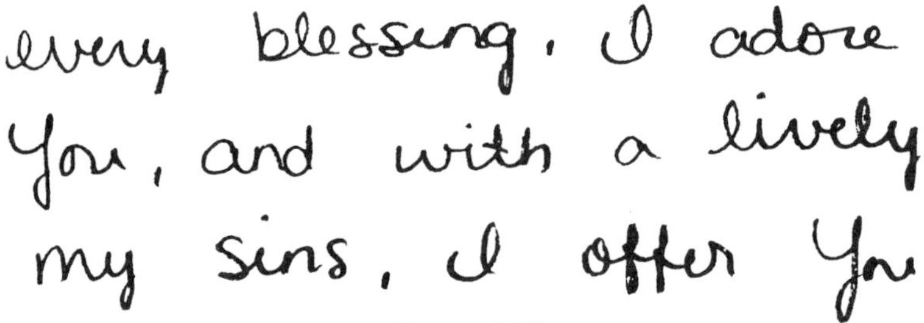

FIGURE 206
Tiny lower loops: Fears intimacy

ARE YOU GENEROUS?

A generally favorable social trait is generosity. Webster's dictionary tells us that the generous person has a "noble or forbearing spirit" and is "liberal, kindly, magnanimous, and openhanded." The truly generous person is able to give of self without reserve and without wishing for something in return. He or she is liberal, which implies a freedom from fear or self-restraint. The person is willing to share with other people whatever he or she values—money, material possessions, time, talents, ideas, or feelings. Generosity indicates that the writer is considerate of other people's needs and feelings. It adds positively to any relationship or social encounter.

In handwriting, generosity shows in outward-curved finals (Fig. 207). The terminal strokes move out toward people and upward, adding a philosophical bent. Like outstretched hands, generous finals seem to say, "Take it; I want nothing in return."

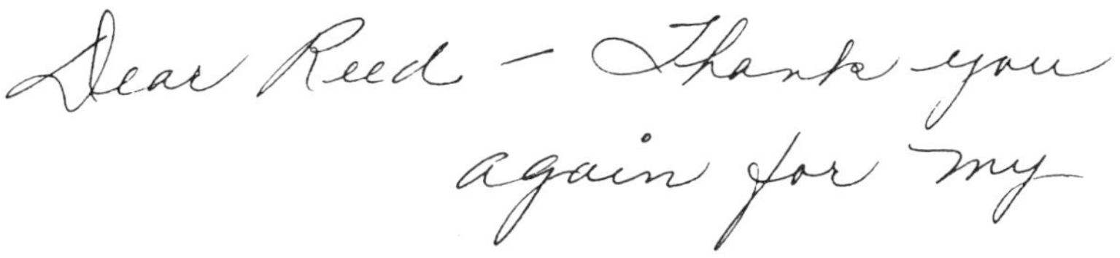

FIGURE 207
Outcurved finals: Generosity

Sometimes the writer *does* want something in return, in which case the generosity loses much of its sincerity. When the person wants to be recognized or appreciated for what has been given, or if he or she wants a gift in return, the outcurved finals will also reach back toward the left, lending a bit of self-concern: "I take care of you and give you nice things, and I want you to recognize me for it" (Fig. 208).

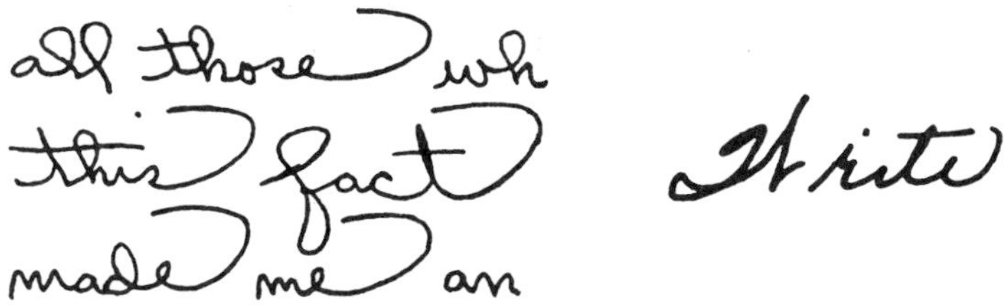

FIGURE 208
Finals curved outward and back: Seeks recognition for being generous

ARE YOU EASILY ANGERED?

Each of us at some time feels irritable, angry, or resentful. Usually we feel one of these shades of anger as a result of thwarted personal needs or desires and therefore, have good justification for feeling miffed. Some people are able to resolve situations that cause their anger to flare, whereas others remain peeved, ticked off, frustrated, resentful, quarrelsome, or sarcastic instead of dealing with their problems head-on.

People who have adopted anger as a way of life show strong anger indications in their handwriting. If the writing is exceptionally full of anger, the writer is carrying around feelings that are destructive to both self and others. Repressed anger can contribute to physical ailments such as headaches, stomach disorders, and high blood pressure, and it is guaranteed to spoil relationships if it is not handled constructively.

Irritability, resentment, and temper are all easily discerned in writing. A generally angry and critical approach to life is revealed in strongly angular script. Excessive angularity shows the writer to be rigid, unwilling to bend to the ideas or wishes of others, and ready to quarrel. This is especially true if the writing contains sharp, knifelike strokes, as in Fig. 209.

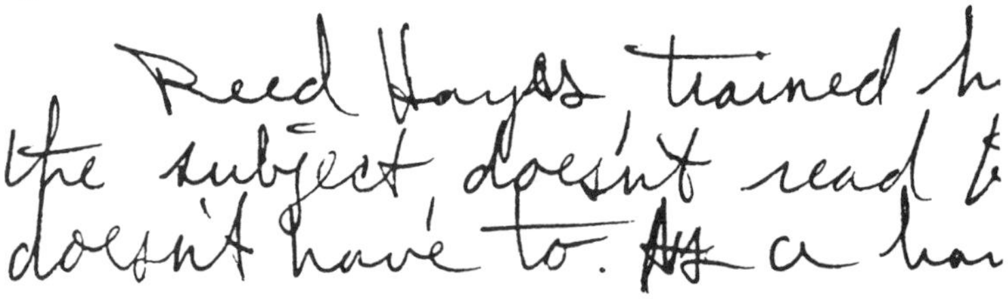

FIGURE 209
Excessive angularity: An angry, critical approach

IRRITABILITY

Irritability is a sign that the writer is easily annoyed by everyday situations, frustrated, tense, and ready to become irked by insignificant matters. It implies temporary or habitual dissatisfaction, according to how frequently it appears, and it reveals the person who may become snappy when faced with problems. The irritable person can alienate people by a peevish attitude, perhaps more so than the person who explodes in a fit of temper and releases the negative feelings.

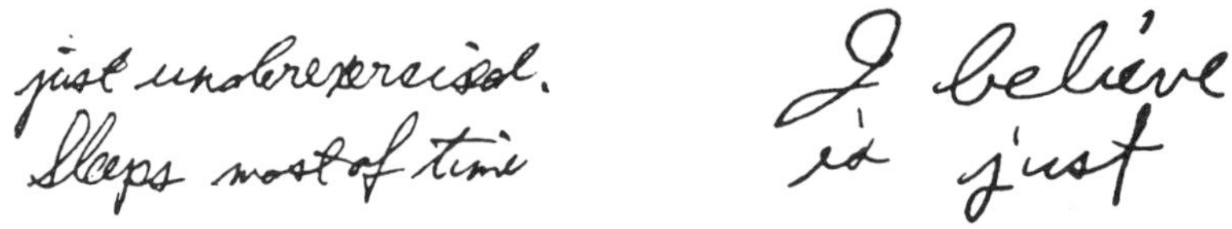

FIGURE 210
Jabbed dots: Irritability

Irritability is shown by jabbed *i* dots (Fig. 210). The heavier and more intense these jabs, the more torrid the irritability. If very heavy, real temper is shown and the person may be explosive. Light, slightly jabbed dots are much less effective than heavier, stronger jabs; short jabs are less irritable than longer ones. Strong jabs can be explosive, whereas weak jabs reveal more of an inner, unexpressed frustration. Dots that are more curved than jabbed suggest mild frustration, which can turn to wittiness if combined with a sense of humor.

RESENTMENT

The sign of resentment (unresolved anger) can be seen at the beginning of words and letters. Resentment strokes are straight, inflexible initial strokes that come up from the baseline or below (Fig. 211).

FIGURE 211
Straight initial brace strokes: Resentment

These strokes reveal that the writer is guarded, alert to intrusion, resistant to influence, and wary of being taken advantage of. The writer has experienced interpersonal difficulties in the past and anticipates more problems that might restrict freedom and self-expression. Such writers carry anger from the past and are suspicious of any situation likely to reactivate the anger. Their "once burned, twice shy" outlook indicates they are alert to the possibility of being used or abused. For this reason, they tend to keep people at arm's length.

Resentful people are concerned with their individual rights and can become very emotional about such issues. They can become indignant if someone appearing less qualified succeeds where they have failed.

Resentment strokes feature the past, especially if they come from far to the left or from well below the baseline. If exceptionally long, and especially when heavy, the resentful feelings surge from the past and are apt to be released in retaliatory action at an opportune moment. Truly resentful writers carry grudges that may explode when least expected. See the writing of Winnie Ruth Judd, Fig. 212-A, convicted of murdering two women and sending their bodies in trunks to California. The handwriting of serial killer Ted Bundy, Fig. 212-B, also shows extreme resentment stemming from deep-rooted feelings of injustice.

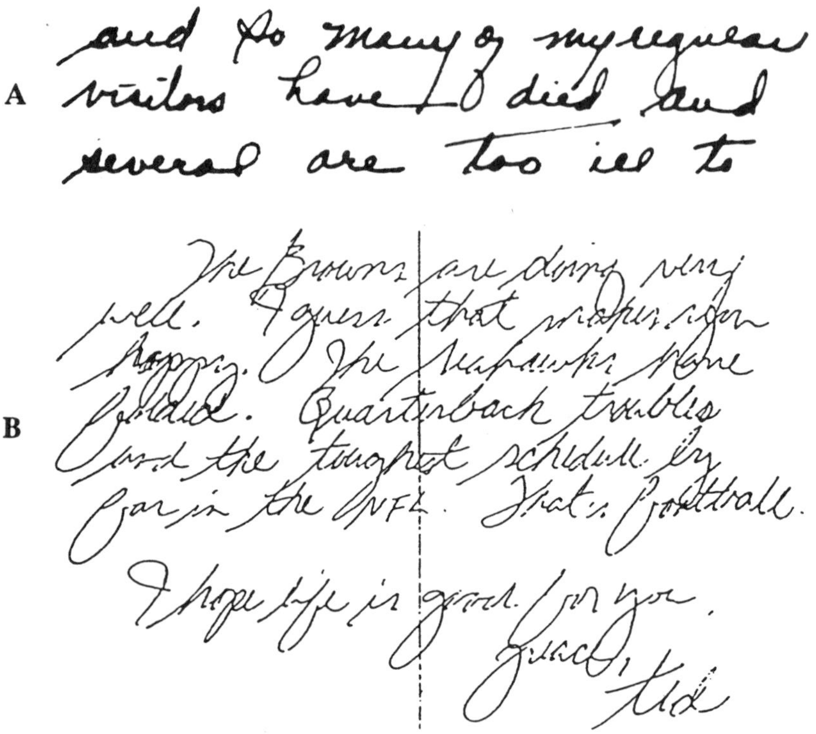

FIGURE 212
(A) Unresolved resentment: Winnie Ruth Judd, "Trunk Murderess"
(B) Deep-rooted feelings of injustice: Ted Bundy, serial killer

When the resentment stroke is somewhat curved, the person will put up with a certain amount of imposition before finally reacting. The trait is softened according to the degree to which the stroke curves.

TEMPER

Temper is a predisposition to react with feelings of hostility. By feeling or expressing anger, the writer keeps problems (and the people who cause them) at bay. Temper is an active resistance that serves to protect the ego through attack.

Temper can of course be controlled, and it may remain unexpressed until conditions are just right for its release. The presence of pride, dignity, suppression, repression, or a conventional approach indicate that the temper is held in check. When provoked, however, the person with temper may flare up.

A shortened version of the resentment stroke implies a shorter fuse, so that the anger is more immediate. These short initial strokes (called tics) indicate a proclivity to an angry reaction (Fig. 213). Such reactions are sometimes concealed and may never actually be expressed outwardly, but the feeling of anger is immediate. The writer is ticked off.

FIGURE 213
Temper tics

The heavier and more angular the temper tic, the more intense the anger. The frequency with which the stroke appears is also significant. Very short, light tics reflect an irritable or frustrated nature, showing that the writer can become irked but that the anger is short-lived. Heavy or pronounced initial tics reflect a more pervasive anger that lasts longer and has a strong influence on the person's life.

Temper may also be seen in *t* crosses to the right of their stems and illustrates "flying off the handle." Such writers are impatient; they want to get on with things and are frustrated by delays, especially about their plans and intentions. When such writers' plans are thwarted, they become annoyed (Fig. 214).

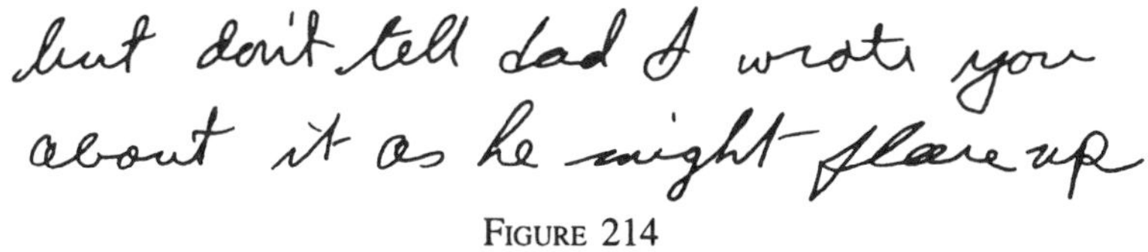

FIGURE 214
Temper *t*'s

If the temper *t* bar is light or short, the reaction is immediate but not lasting. On the other hand, a straight and heavy *t* bar to the right reveals temper of a more lasting nature because of the depth of feeling shown in the pressure of the stroke. If the stroke is also long, the temper is enduring and it feeds on itself. When the temper *t* cross is also bowed downward at either end (⌐⌐) the writer may be making a conscious attempt to control the anger.

SARCASM

Another unpleasant trait is sarcasm. The sarcastic person wards off difficulties and keeps people at a distance with cutting remarks. The sarcasm may be thought but not expressed or in extreme cases it can be released as vicious, cruel insults. However it is expressed, sarcasm always suggests inner frustration, often unconscious. It is frequently the result of injured feelings, jealousy, or other feelings of inadequacy.

Sarcasm is illustrated by sharp-pointed *t* crosses. The trait is strong when the *t* cross starts heavily and comes to a very sharp, knifelike ending. It is especially devastating when it also points downward and to the right, indicating a relentlessly bossy attitude, as in the case of Carry Nation, American temperance movement agitator (Fig. 215-B). Sarcasm is intensified by rigid or angular writing and heavy pressure, and is further emphasized when accompanied by other negatives such as temper, irritability, argumentativeness, or resentment.

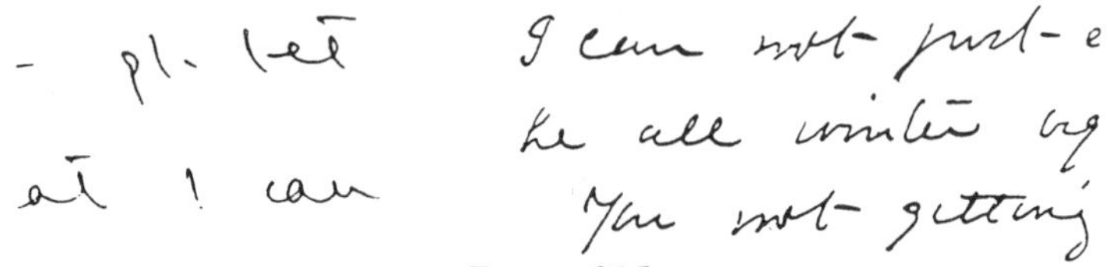

FIGURE 215
Sharp *t* bars: Sarcasm

Although negative feelings are always hidden behind sarcastic comments, the expression of sarcasm can have positive results. This is especially true when it is found in combination with a sense of humor, which serves to soften the sting and allows a comment to be made pointedly but with less severity. With humor, sarcasm turns to wit (see page 161). Sarcasm can be beneficial to the public speaker and is frequently found in the handwriting of literary greats.

ARGUMENTATIVENESS

Closely related to anger is argumentativeness, a readiness to be defensive and to protect one's opinions at all costs. Although a good debate may be healthy, in an argument no one really wins. The argumentative person is seldom willing to back down, as that would mean losing face.

Argumentativeness is shown in the letter *p* where the initial stroke comes up higher than the circle part of the letter (Fig. 216). The more pronounced this stroke, the more unreasonable the person is likely to be. If the letter starts with a resentment stroke (*ℓ*) the person will be defensive as a result of an I've-been-burned-before attitude. When the stroke forms a figure eight (*ℓ*), imagination will come into play so that the writer enlarges on the subject and expresses his or her position skillfully.

FIGURE 216
Tall initial *p* stroke: Argumentativeness

Someone once said that to win an argument is to lose a friend. If you write argumentative *p*'s, consider why you need to defend yourself so vehemently.

ARE YOU OPEN-MINDED?

If you are open-minded, the circle letters of your writing, especially the *e*'s but also the *a*'s and *o*'s, will be well-rounded (Fig. 217). Rounded circle letters show you to be open to new ideas and approaches and willing to listen to advice before coming to final conclusions. A broad-minded attitude allows for possibilities outside of your own thinking. It suggests consideration for others and aids in cooperation. Broad-mindedness is enhanced by nonangular "soft" writing, wide spacing, flexible baselines, and a lack of hostility traits.

FIGURE 217
Rounded circle letters: Open-mindedness

A narrow-minded attitude is reflected in tightly closed circle letters, indicating that the writer is closed to ideas or approaches other than his or her own (Fig. 218). The narrow-minded person's mind is already made up. Although the writer may be open to persuasion, the person will initially reject anything that does not fit with his or her preconceived notions. A narrow-minded approach can also be positive, as it serves as a screen against irrelevant information. However, if the trait is strong, it implies defensiveness and may contribute to inner tensions and limited understanding of other people and their ideas. It can also reduce one's thinking capacities if very pronounced. The person is further closed-minded if the writing is also rigid or shows strong emotional bias, stubbornness, ultraconservatism, argumentativeness, or hostility traits.

FIGURE 218
Narrow circle letters: Narrow-mindedness

If your writing shows you to be narrow-minded, consider the possibility of opening up your circle letters and taking a look at approaches outside of your own.

HOW DO YOU COMMUNICATE?

Communication plays a vital role in your interpersonal relationships. If you or your associates are frank, open, and honest, your relationships will be enhanced. Positive relationships do not have room for secrecy, deceit, or manipulation.

How we communicate is shown primarily in the formation of our circle letters, especially *a*'s and *o*'s.

FRANKNESS

Clear, open, rounded *a*'s and *o*'s without extraneous loops or marks (as in Fig. 219) illustrate frankness, the willingness to be honest with yourself and to communicate clearly what is on your mind. Clear circles indicate a lack of secretiveness, concealment, or deceit and are a major component of integrity and dependability. (If the formlevel of the writing is good and the letters are clear and legible, the writer's integrity and clarity of communication are enhanced.)

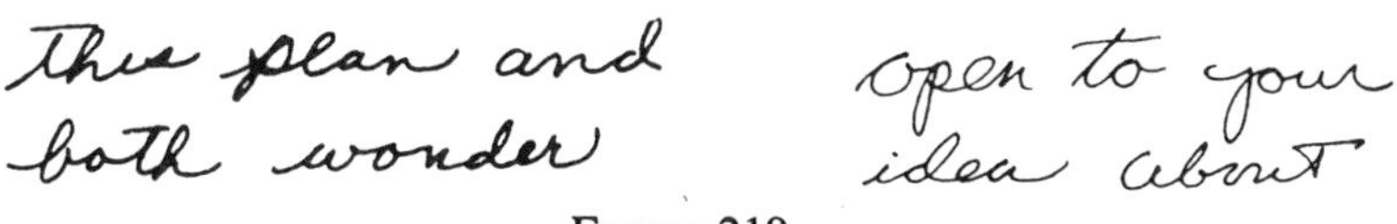

[handwriting sample]

FIGURE 219
Clear circle letters: Frankness

TALKATIVENESS

When circle letters are open at the top, a willingness to communicate is indicated (Fig. 220). Think of these letters as open mouths that are ready to reveal what is inside. (If the writing is also very small the writer may not actually be talkative, but you can be certain that he or she is open under the right circumstances and voices an honest opinion when asked for it.)

[handwriting sample]

FIGURE 220
Open-topped circle letters: Talkativeness

Circle letters closed at the top suggest closed mouths. Such writers do not always reveal what is on their minds. If the circle letters are free of loops, hooks, or additional marks, the writer is quiet, not from an urge to cover or deceive but from a simple need for privacy. These people usually tend to their own business and are likely to be honest, if all other signs indicate so (Fig. 221).

[handwriting sample]

FIGURE 221
Closed circle letters: Quiet about personal matters

SECRETIVENESS

When *a*'s and *o*'s are looped on the right, the writer is secretive in proportion to the size of the loops (Fig. 222). Secretiveness implies that the person deliberately withholds personal information as a means of self-protection, perhaps as a result of deception but always from a strong need for privacy. Secretive writers sometimes need to be drawn out and they usually make good confidants.

FIGURE 222
Circle letters looped on the right: Secretiveness

SELF-DECEIT

Circle letters looped on the left reveal the writer who withholds information from the self (Fig. 223). Such writers are self-deceptive; they tend to believe only what they want to believe, and they habitually withdraw from the truth, especially if it is painful. Denial and rationalization are common with these people, and therefore they often see the world through half-closed eyes or rose-colored glasses. They dislike owning up to their own problems.

FIGURE 223
Circle letters looped on the left: Self-deceit

If your own writing contains many of these leftward looped circles, you may want to take a good hard look at how you deal with reality. Self-deception is often so habitual that the person is no longer aware of concealing the truth. When this is the case, the trait works as an unconscious mechanism, tainting the writer's integrity and relationships to self and others. A professional therapist is perhaps the best person to help you discover what you have been hiding from yourself for so long.

DELIBERATE DECEIT

Circle letters that are looped on both the left and the right give evidence of deliberate deceit (Fig. 224). The deceptive person cannot be honest with self (left-hand loops) and at the same time is unwilling to be honest with others (right-hand loops). The result is a lack of truthfulness and an inclination to purposely mislead or manipulate through one's speech or actions. Deceptive people lack forthrightness and frankness, purposely mislead as a self-protective measure, and often show many faces.

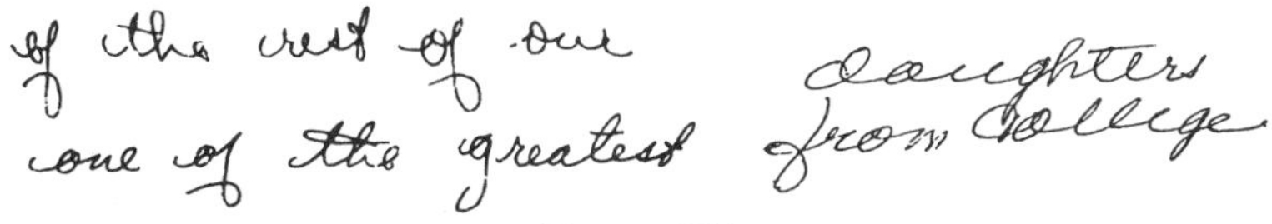

FIGURE 224
Circle letters looped both left and right: Intentional deceit

Deceit is usually born of emotional difficulties; it is a way of dealing with deep-rooted guilt complexes or emotional problems. If you or someone you know is deceitful, therapy is suggested to get to the bottom of unresolved emotional conflicts. Learning to look at the truth about yourself will greatly improve your relationship to yourself and those people around you. (Dishonesty will be further discussed in a later chapter.)

DO YOU HAVE A SENSE OF HUMOR?

The person with a sense of humor is able to see the pleasant side of unpleasant situations. If you have a well-developed sense of humor, you are able to see and appreciate the absurdities in life. You are likely to be optimistic and adaptable when confronted with problems, and you can probably make light of your own mistakes. A sense of humor always creates a cheerful atmosphere and adds positively to any interpersonal contact.

Humor is shown by wavy lead-ins, especially on the letters *m* and *n*. It is also indicated by "flirtatious" *t* crosses (Fig. 225).

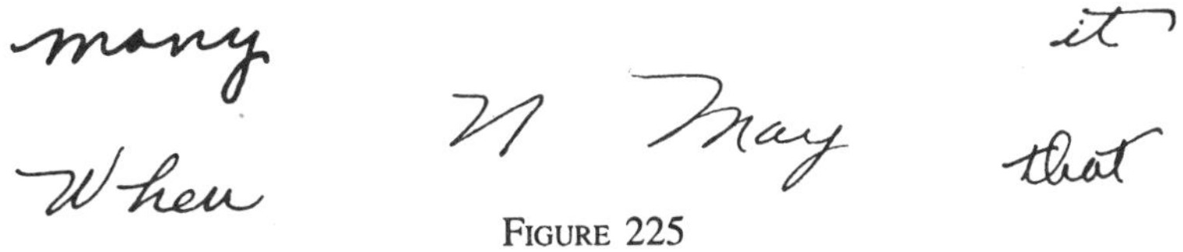

FIGURE 225
Sense of humor

The handwriting of actress Meryl Streep shows a fine sense of humor and other personality traits that enhance her social life (Fig. 226).

The humor strokes appear in the first word of the specimen, in the word "But" (line 3), in "Wishes" (line 5) and in the signature. This jovial approach adds to her warmth and responsiveness (moderately heavy pressure, forward slant) and her spontaneity (fluctuating letter formations and bouncy baseline). Streep has a hot temper (as shown in the tic on the personal pronoun *I* of line one and the rightward flung *t* bar of line 2), and she is argumentative (tall initial *p* strokes), but the sense of humor allows her to be generally pleasant. She also seeks a variety of social encounters (moderate-to-large lower loops) and is relatively generous (occasional outcurved finals).

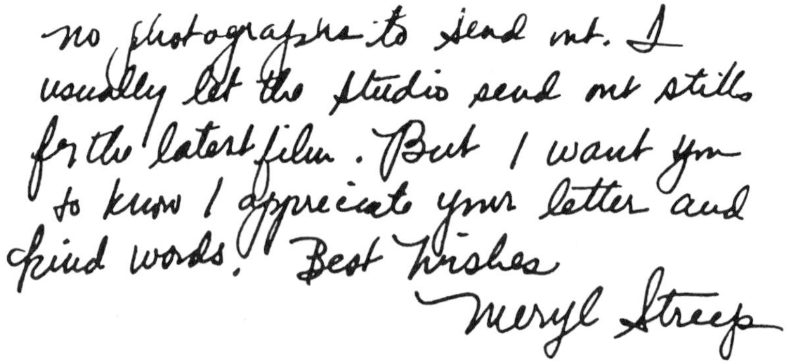
no photographs to send out. I
usually let the studio send out stills
for the latest film. But I want you
to know I appreciate your letter and
kind words! Best Wishes
Meryl Streep

Figure 226
Meryl Streep, actress

14
YOUR
LOWER LOOPS
ARE SHOWING

This chapter presents some basic considerations about attitudes toward sex and the expression of sexual urges. Graphology can tell you a lot about your sexual needs and how they relate to the other aspects of your personality. It can aid you in understanding the inner motivations of lovers, partners, or partners-to-be.

Sex is only one small piece in the entire personality puzzle; all other traits in the writing must be evaluated as well. Emotional makeup, mental development, social attitudes, and insecurities must all be considered for an accurate picture of how sex operates in a given personality. The writer's upbringing is also important, as are peer influence (especially in children and young adults), religious background, health, age, environment, and attitudes of parents and partner(s).

It must also be cautioned that although truth about the sexual needs of your acquaintances will help you know them on a different level, you must use discretion in how such information is used. Anything disclosed by a person's writing is very personal. It should not be used to fuel the fires of gossip or as a way of gaining the upper hand over those close to you. Instead, it should enhance your life by allowing you to look at yourself and others more objectively.

ENERGY, THE UNDERLYING FORCE

Sex is energy. To have healthy sex drives and good physical stamina, a person must have energy. Mental and physical energy are determined primarily by the amount of pressure applied to the writing instrument. Firm, clean pressure denotes strong energy, lasting emotions, warmth and sensuousness—an appreciation for color, taste, smell and touch, and an enjoyment of "the good life" (Fig. 227).

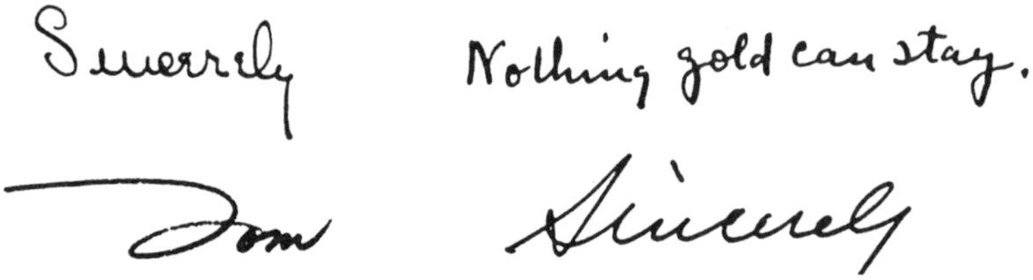

FIGURE 227
Clean, heavy pressure: Sensuousness

Writing that is ink-filled (when not the fault of the writing instrument) or exceptionally heavy denotes sensuality—very strong physical urges and a propensity for hearty interest in food, drink, sex, or any activity that will bring physical pleasure. Muddy or pasty script sometimes shows the person's appetites to be excessive, whereas clean, heavy-pressured writing relates to less intense pleasure seeking.

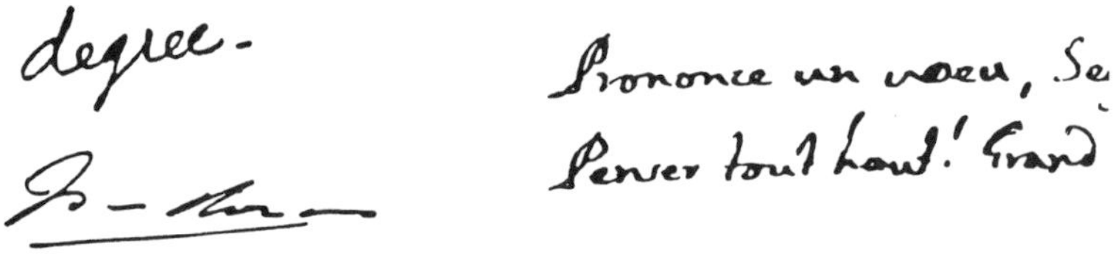

FIGURE 228
Muddy writing: Sensuality

SECRETS
OF THE LOWER ZONE

The mental or imaginative aspects of sex are revealed in lower zone structures. This area deals with subconscious drives and the degree of emotional involvement. (Because these structures represent unconscious motivations, they can sometimes be quite revealing about inner drives of which a person may be unaware.) Attitudes about security are determined here also, as are general feelings about food, money, and material possessions. One's social life is strongly influenced by this area, too, as discussed in the preceding chapter.

In general, the more pronounced the lower zone, the more emphasis is placed on physical acitivity, including sex. Conversely, the less pronounced or smaller this area, the less energy is directed into the physical.

FIGURE 229
Pronounced lower zone: Emphasis on the physical

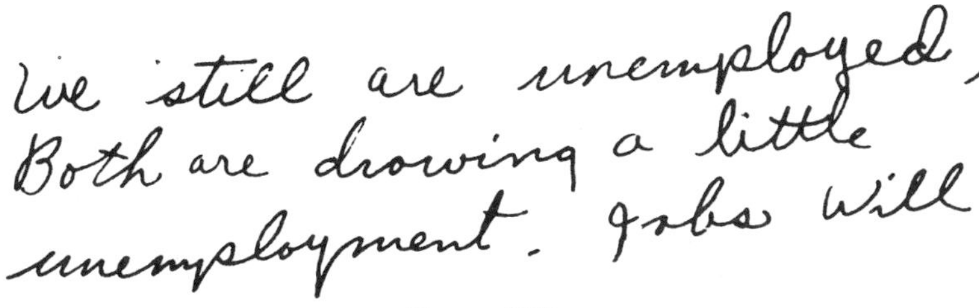

FIGURE 230
De-emphasized lower zone: Lack of interest in the physical

Ideally, the upper zone should balance the lower zone, showing a code of ethics surrounding one's everyday activities, including sex. When these two areas are balanced, the writer's mental and physical aspects are in harmony (check other indications, too).

SO WHAT'S NORMAL?

Some people need frequent sex, while others seem to live comfortably without expressing it. What is normal for one person or group may be quite abnormal to another person or group. In handwriting it is the writer's own attitudes about normality that show up. If the person *feels* sexually normal, the writing reflects that attitude, and if the person feels abnormally adjusted, the writing reflects abnormal adjustment. (In light of these statements, the words "normal" and "abnormal," as used in this book, refer to whether the lower zone strokes are written proportionately correctly compared with other writing strokes.)

A normal lower loop, which implies that the writer feels he or she is normal sexually, is a loop that is rounded, but not exaggerated. It is smooth, lacks angularity, is neither disproportionately heavy nor light, and is not squelched or otherwise distorted. The final stroke of a normal loop makes a smooth return to the baseline. To be classified as normal the loop should not exceed two to two and one-half times the height of the middle zone letters.

A   B   C

FIGURE 231
Proportionate loop sizes

People who write well-developed lower loops (Fig. 231-B) are able to gain satisfaction from sexual activity. They view sexual experiences of the past and the present as being enjoyable. Sex is neither a threat nor an obsession but a normal part of everyday life.

Very small lower loops (Fig. 231-A) indicate a lack of emphasis on sex and sometimes a retreat from both social and sexual acitivity. Large lower loops (Fig. 231-C) show strong sexual urges and a need for close human contact. Although such large loops are not "normal," the strong sexual needs may be adequately integrated into the person's life, if the loops are in no way distorted and if other indications in the writing are positive. (If the writer is not strongly sexual, he or she may choose sports or other activities that will satisfy the urge for physical movement.)

Abnormal lower zone structures are any formations that deviate strongly from our definition of normal. They may be proportionately too large, too small, or otherwise exaggerated; angular, twisted, or distorted; forceful or weapon-shaped; tightly closed, retraced, or finished with tiny circles.

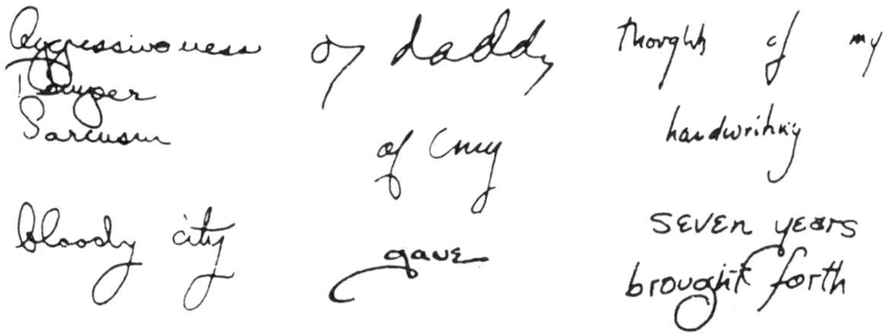

FIGURE 232
"Abnormal" loops

Poorly formed lower zone strokes suggest that sexual attitudes and encounters pose a problem in the manner(s) indicated by each specific structure. A few examples of distorted loops appear in Fig. 232. Because there are so many possible ways to write lower zone strokes, only some basic ones will be discussed here.* Common sense will guide you in your study of this interesting area of life.

Desire may fluctuate according to mood, health, and other reasons, and because our handwriting changes as we do, it is important to look at more than one sample of writing before accurately deciphering sexual urges.

There may be several types or sizes of lower zone formations in one handwriting that alert you to the writer's varibaility or instability (according to other indications) in the sexual sphere. Consider which structures are the most prevalent in the writing and which are likely to have less effect. Too much variability in the lower zone suggests that the writer is unsettled or uncertain regarding sex and emotional

---

*For a more complete discussion of sexuality as related to handwriting analysis, see *Handwriting: Its Socio-Sexual Implications,* by Reed C. Hayes.

involvement. Too much consistency implies a lack of emotional and sexual spontaneity and a tendency to want things "just so" where intimacy is concerned.

Exaggerated lower loops, such as those in Fig. 233, reveal the person who has exaggerated ideas about sex, has an excessively sexual imagination, and so seeks out a great deal of variety in sexual expression. (The expression may or may not happen, depending on other traits.) Exaggeration also spills over into the person's emotional expressions and social life: He or she is likely to overemphasize emotional issues, may have many acquaintances and, where morals and circumstances permit, a variety of sexual partners, techniques, or positions.

FIGURE 233
Exaggerated loops: Excessive physical drive

When lower strokes are incomplete and do not reach back to the reality of the baseline (Fig. 234), the writer is apt to feel unconsciously uncomfortable or unfulfilled about the expression of sexual needs. This may or may not be a handicap, and the reason the person chooses not to be sexual is important in deciding this.

FIGURE 234
Incomplete loops: Unfulfilled urges

Retraced lower loops (Fig. 235) show repression of sexual drives, whether the writer's physical needs are strong (long loops) or weak (short loops). In repressed lower zone structures there is little room for the inclusion of anyone else; the writer squeezes people out. The degree of sexual repression is dependent on how often the retraced loops appear and to what degree they are retraced.

great you from you. pay alleyway

FIGURE 235
Retraced loops: Sexual repression

Lower loops that are quite narrow but not entirely closed (Fig. 236) show careful selection of close friends and partners, denoting a healthy caution about relationships as long as the writing does not contain strong signs of inadequacy and if the lower loops are not distorted in addition to being narrow.

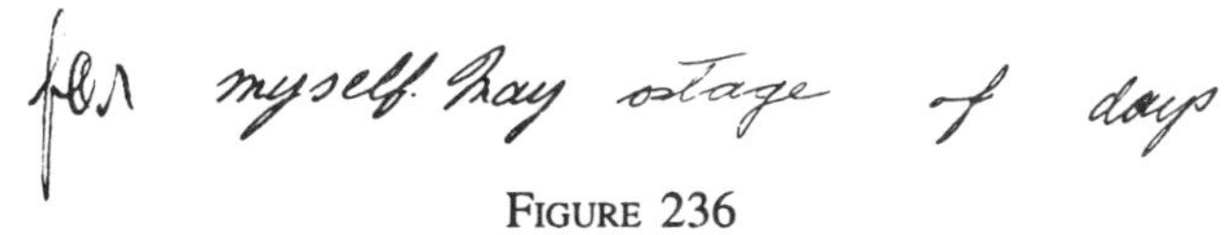

for myself. May ostage of days

FIGURE 236
Narrow loops: Selectivity

Tiny, remote lower circles show the writer to be exceptionally careful in admitting people to his or her intimate world. Tiny lower circles leave room for only one or two people and limited experiences; they are the result of a restrictive, exclusive sexual attitude (Fig. 237).

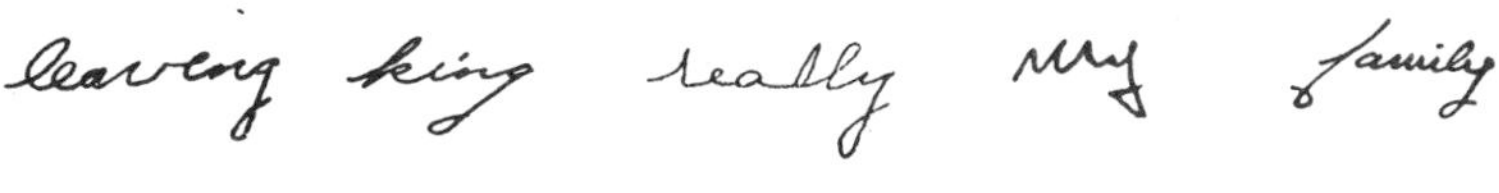

leaving king really my family

FIGURE 237
Tiny loops: Sexually exclusive

Angular lower zone structures imply tension in the sexual area and an overall nonacceptance of oneself sexually. Somewhere along the line (perhaps in childhood) the person learned that sex was bad, dirty, or in some other way unpleasant. The guilty or inadequate feelings remained in the person's unconscious so that now they seep into everyday life.

The person who writes angular lower loops is usually a strategist, often ambitious and aggressive. Sometimes these people find general frustration at every turn owing to the tension that lies under the surface of consciousness, all the while not understanding where the tension originates.

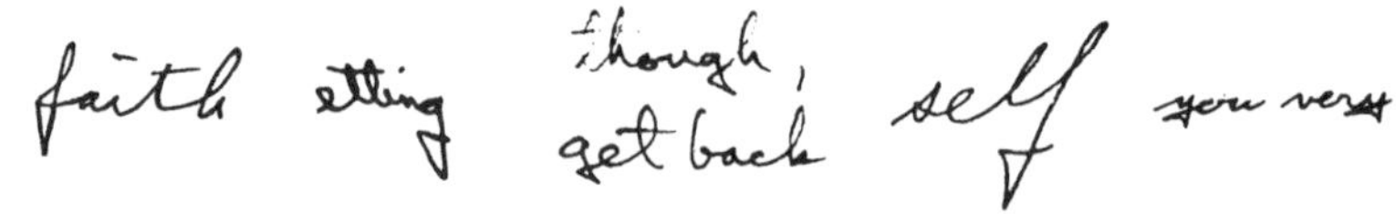

FIGURE 238
Angular loops: Sexual tension

When angular lower structures are exceptionally sharp or weaponlike, as in Fig. 239 and in the handwriting of Adolf Hitler (Fig. 240) there is tremendous anger wrapped up in the person's attitudes regarding sex. Such nasty formations are frequently found in the writings of criminals in general and sex offenders in particular. Whether or not such people actually act out sexual aggressiveness, they are bound to be cruel on one level or another. Sexual difficulties are further indicated by muddy writing. If you are involved with someone who writes these tics and barbs, *watch out!* If you are wondering whether you should become involved with such a writer, *don't!*

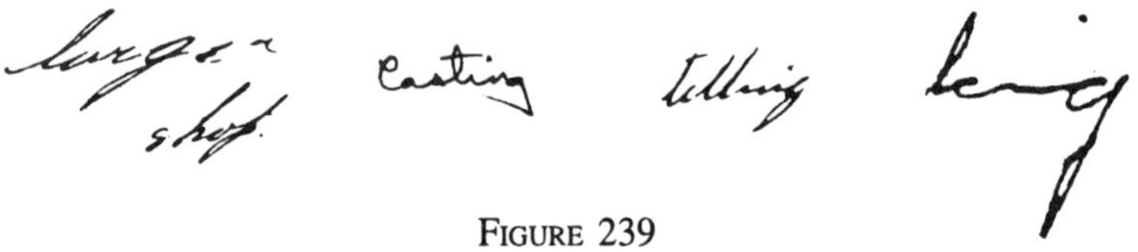

FIGURE 239
Sharp, weaponlike lower zone: *Watch out!*

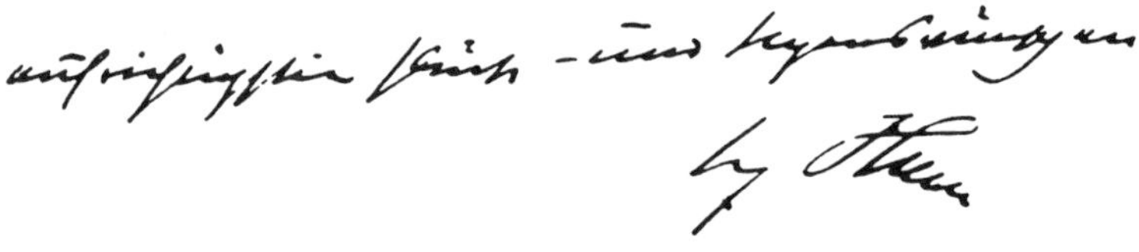

FIGURE 240
Adolf Hitler: Angry and aggressive

In addition to aggressive lower zone strokes, Hitler's writing shows other negatives that add to the unpleasant picture. Muddy strokes reveal strong, uncontrolled passion. There is such intense irritability in the jabbed dots that it can be considered explosive. Further indications of Hitler's deep-seated anger are the initial tic on the *H* of "Hitler" and the angular, "glassy" strokes pointing toward cool emotions and criticism. An extremely narrow outlook (squeezed circle letters) adds to the negative, pessimistic attitude illustrated by the drooping signature. When sexual aggression combines with this many negative traits, the outcome can only be disruptive and cruel.

Somewhat less negative are the "breakaway" strokes of Fig. 241. Although these formations imply some sexual unpleasantness (in the angle), they do not have the sting of those previously discussed. Writers of breakaway strokes are forward moving, energetic, and willing to get into new and different activities. When combined with positive traits, such initiative can be used positively (e.g., in business affairs). As we saw with Hitler, when such energy combines with negative traits the result is negative.

Yours very truly

FIGURE 241
"Breakaway" strokes: Strong initiative

The meaning of particular lower zone formations may be more easily determined by referring to the following.

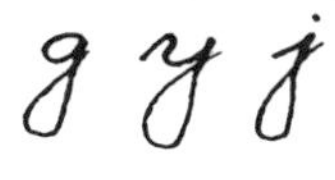

"Normal" loops, well rounded and well proportioned: normal sexual urges, comfortable feelings surrounding sex and intimacy.

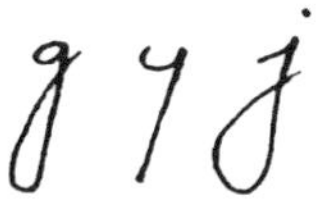

Proportionately very long, whether looped or not: strong sexual appetites.

Proportionately very short, whether looped or not: lack of interest in sex or material comforts, may be uncomfortable with intimacy.

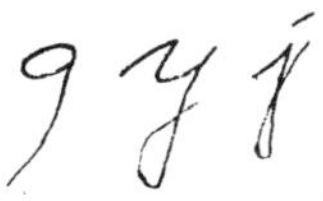

Weak, poor pressure: lack of physical stamina, follow-through, or "staying power."

Inflated: exaggerated sexual and emotional needs, seeks material comforts relative to the proportionate loop size, may be physically vain (preoccupied with appearance), tends to exaggerate intimate involvements and emotional issues, personal issues are blown out of proportion.

No loop: sexual self-denial, prefers solitude over intimacy, may have a general lack of interest in sex.

Unfinished, resembling a large cup: is emotionally and sexually unfulfilled; the cup never seems to be full enough and, therefore, the person is on a constant quest for something new, better, and more fulfilling.

Pulled leftward, no loop: sexual guilt, especially if the end is sharp; sexually unfulfilled; a tendency to pull toward mother or what mother represents, especially in a man's writing.

Bent leftward: sexual withdrawal and preoccupation with the past; guilt related to past activities, especially if loops are squeezed or twisted; emotional dependency; a tendency to pull toward mother or what mother represents, especially in a man's writing.

Pushing rightward: pushes forward, often against the norm; preoccupation with future security of a sexual or material nature; reaching toward father or what father represents, especially in a woman's writing.

Narrow: sexual self-control; caution in the selection of friends, acquaintances, and partners; conservative interests and activities.

Tiny loop at bottom: sexual mistrust, closes people off, very selective of intimate acquaintances, escapes reality out of guilt.

Retraced: sexually repressed, unconsciously controls expression of desire and intimacy, narrow scope of interests and involvements.

Angular: under-the-surface tension related to emotions, relationships, and sexual urges; hardened, rigid approach; angry, frustrated

(check the degree of angularity), or both; sexual strategy.

Tic at bottom of stroke: irritable or frustrated regarding unfulfilled needs and/or nonsatisfying relationships.

Very sharp, weaponlike formations: intense anger related to sex, can be mean and cruel either sexually or emotionally, unpleasant aggression.

Angle to the right and up toward baseline: aggressive; forward-moving; dislikes delays in activities, relationships, or sexual expression; if combined with negatives, can be sexually forceful; may use the aggressiveness in a positive manner, when combined with positive indications.

Drooping final: feels dejected or pessimistic about personal life, relationships feel unfulfilling or burdensome: "Poor little me; I'm so sad."

Final curves up and leftward: craves recognition for feelings and sexual needs, dissatisfied with relationships: "Poor little me; give me more love and attention."

Reversed loop: rejection; feels unwanted and sometimes pushes people away: "Do unto others before they can do unto you"; "I reject you before you get a chance to reject me."

Distorted, twisted, bizarre: strange sexual attitudes; may feel "twisted" or sexually misunderstood; sexually neurotic, especially if exaggerated.

Upstroke runs close to downstroke, compressed but not retraced: impotence or frigidity; sexual anxiety, especially if loop is weak and/or incomplete; may be physically weak or ill.

15
IS THE WRITER
HONEST?

Graphology can act as an insurance policy. Before forming a business or personal relationship you would be wise to check out the person's handwriting to determine ahead of time whether he or she is likely to be dishonest, untrustworthy, or unreliable.

Before looking at indications of dishonesty we must first establish how to recognize honesty. Honest people are clear and direct in their thinking, motivations, and communication. The honest person has integrity. His or her overall personality is characterized by balance and wholeness, character traits are in harmony with one another, and there are no exaggerated traits that dominate the others. Personality integration implies that the individual is able to hold consistently to a code of ethics or principles, thereby lending stability to actions and motivations. Honest people are sincere, conscientious, responsible, reliable, and socially mature, and they are able to blend with society without altering their personal ideals or losing their identity.

The writing of an honest person is usually of high formlevel, as described in the earlier pages of this book: It is likely to be balanced, well-organized, and consistent. (However, look carefully at the writer whose script is too regular or perfectionistic, which may indicate that he or she is carefully covering the truth.)

The strong traits of the personality—those which exert a dominant influence—are to be looked at with care. If these traits are primarily negative, the chances for honesty are proportionally diminished.

Clarity is also important. If you cannot read the writing, how can the writer be clear? Check the legibility of the signature, too: Can you decipher who the person is? Simplicity and uncomplicated structures point to a willingness to be direct.

Communication is also an important component of honesty. The circle letters, as previously mentioned, tell much about whether the person is willing to reveal what is going on inside. Uncontaminated *a*'s and *o*'s are an especially positive sign, showing that the writer feels no conscious need to alter, cover, or otherwise distort the facts.

The person's upper zone should also be examined: Balanced and moderate upper loops imply adherence to a set of standards (provided this sign is backed by other indications), whereas squelched, twisted, or exaggerated upper zone formations are unfavorable.

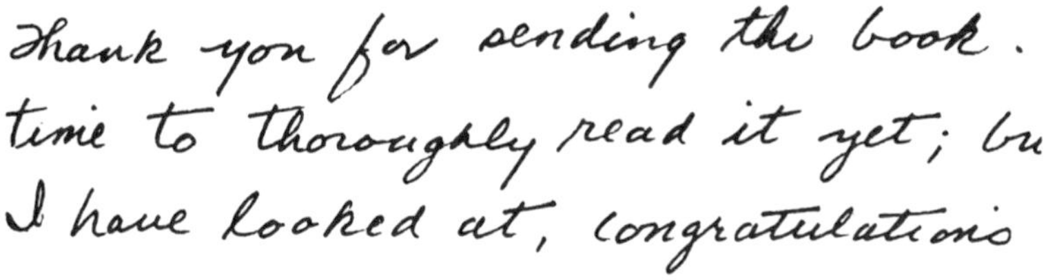

FIGURE 242
Handwriting showing honesty

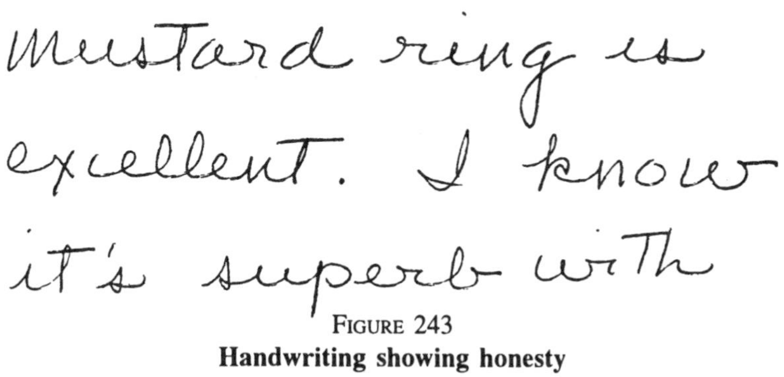

FIGURE 243
Handwriting showing honesty

The two handwriting samples on page 175 are each indicative of well-integrated personalities. On the basis of these criteria, you will find them to be honest, upstanding individuals.

DISHONESTY
HAS MANY FACES

Except in clear-cut cases, determining dishonesty from writing is tricky. Dishonesty comes in many varieties and is influenced by many factors. To evaluate it requires a thorough knowledge of many handwriting factors and experience in putting that knowledge into practical use (not to mention a solid understanding of people and their various and complicated motivations). Needless to say, these important considerations cannot be reduced to a few simple rules. However, there are some guidelines that allow you to make a more informed decision about a person's trustworthiness.

Dishonesty is not a single trait but any number of trait combinations added to the right circumstances. Graphologist Paul de Sainte Colombe writes that dishonesty results "when certain moral and/or intellectual qualities are lacking in the presence of such corruptive characteristics as a craving for luxury or power, love of risk and gambling, self-indulgence, overpowering sensuality, intemperance, excessive materialism or ambition, inconstancy, hypocrisy, envy, aimlessness, selfishness, laziness, indecisiveness, prodigality, instability, weak will, willfulness, rebelliousness, anti-social feelings, etc."* Emotional distress can be as much a cause for dishonesty as a conscious desire to mislead.

I learned the hard way that it is not always possible to detect dishonesty from writing. I was once asked by a hospital to analyze the writings of several applicants in order to help them choose a new staff member. After completing and delivering the analyses I called the hospital administrator to further discuss my reports. He agreed with my findings with one small exception—an exception that tainted my

---

*Colombe, Paul de Sainte. *Grapho-Therapeutics*. (Hollywood, Calif.: Laurida Books, 1971), 174.

professional image and taught me an important lesson. I had reported that one of the applicants was "honest and direct" when he had in fact falsified the information on his resume. My response to this was that the applicant *was* honest and direct in his everyday affairs and that neither the administrator nor I could possibly know why he altered the facts under the circumstances. Perhaps the applicant was under temporary personal pressure and felt it necessary to make himself look good in order to obtain the position.

Unethical behavior, such as that of the applicant who falsified his resume, is only one method of lying, cheating, and stealing. We all know at least one person who fudges on taxes or "innocently" takes company supplies or a few extra minutes of company time for lunch breaks. Blatant dishonesty can be observed in government and business, and in both business and personal affairs dishonesty can include manipulative deception, infidelity, unkept promises, broken agreements, forgery, theft, embezzlement, and so on.

TWENTY-FIVE SIGNS
OF DISHONESTY

Following is a list of 25 possible components of dishonesty. No one sign is indicative of dishonesty but must be found in combination with other signs from the list. To qualify for dishonesty, the writing must consistently show at least seven indicators. (Note: These signs are not necessarily in order of importance. Items not accompanied by handwriting illustrations have been discussed elsewhere in this book.)

1. *Unclear, illegible writing:* unwillingness or inability to be clear.
2. *Tangled, twisted lines:* confusion of ideas and interests, indecision.
3. *Excessive regularity or artificial writing:* pretense, desire to impress or to cover what is really going on.
4. *Overly complicated or overly simplified writing:* adds too much to the story or does not include enough.
5. *Exceptionally thready writing:* opportunistic, eases into a number of situations and settings, may have poor thinking habits.

6. *Sudden changes in slant, pressure, size, or other components:* moody, changeable self-image, fluctuating responses and attitudes, unreliable.

7. *Complicated or double looped circle letters:* poor communication skills, deliberate deception, emotional manipulation.

8. *Initial hooks inside circle letters or "shark's teeth" (especially in letter m or n):* emotional hunger, gets what he or she can.

9. *Fragmented letters, especially circle letters open at the bottom, or numbers separated into two or more segments (not breaks between letters):* anxiety, breaks in one's thought processes, has trouble connecting ideas, one hand may not know what the other is doing.

10. *"Trick letters" (letters which, when taken out of context, cannot be deciphered):* the trickster, wants you to see things different than they are.

11. *Initial or terminal strokes that are scrolled and complicated:* hypocrisy, pretense, vanity, secrecy.

12. *Frequently corrected, retouched, patched, or repaired letters:* goes back to cover, fix, or alter what has been done before; covering one's tracks.

13. *"Felon's claw" formation (lower zone stroke reaching leftward and ending in a definite hook):* underhanded behavior, sneaky, devious.

14. **Smeary or spotty writing:** "dirty," uncontrolled sensuality.

find to the bad gestation Annie

15. **Signature and text very different:** the writer's inner life and outer life are very different.

16. **Omitted letters:** part of the story is being left out.

institution (INSTITUTION)   *cruel* (CRUEL)   *monotous* (MONOTONOUS)

17. **Curled under arches:** secrecy, concealment, afraid of being found out.

hound   dummy   home   them

18. **Angles and arches in the same writing:** hypocrisy, mental disturbance, lack of sensitivity to others.

'Imply'   consuming   met one
REMEDY.   hound and

19. **Ambiguous numbers (unless written in a hurry):** may be untrustworthy with money.

10/3/85.   7-5   87

20. **Two or more distinct handwriting styles, especially if in the same sample:** strongly varied responses and attitudes, unreliability.

21. **Combination of initial hooks and double looped circle letters, especially if also with exaggerated lower zone:** acquisitiveness, wants things and may stoop to taking them.

22. **Distorted lower loops:** unconscious frustrations, may become involved in criminal activities out of inner dissatisfaction.

23. **Blotched upper loops:** muddied thinking and morals.

school bubbles.   each night   that her

24. *Distorted, twisted, or stunted upper loops:* distorted, twisted, or undeveloped sense of morals.

spoken. this is how I last a hound.

25. *Capital letters out of place:* strongly resists authority, has own ideas of right and wrong.

I Was a thing Self and I am my very best but

HANDWRITING SAMPLES
SHOWING DISHONESTY

The handwritings of some known criminals are included to illustrate dishonesty. By use of the list presented above you can determine for yourself some of the indications of dishonesty.

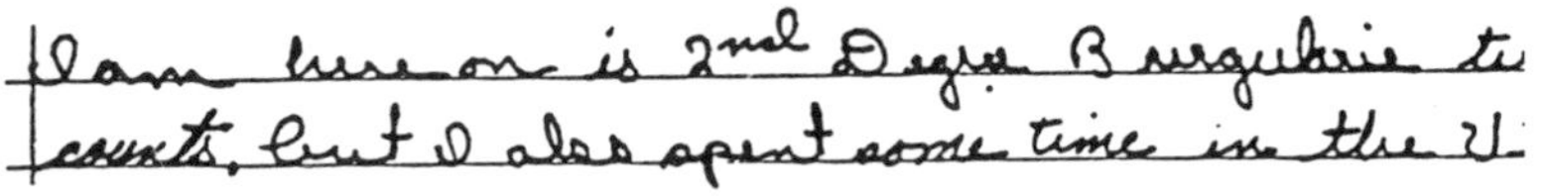

FIGURE 244
Auto thief and burglar

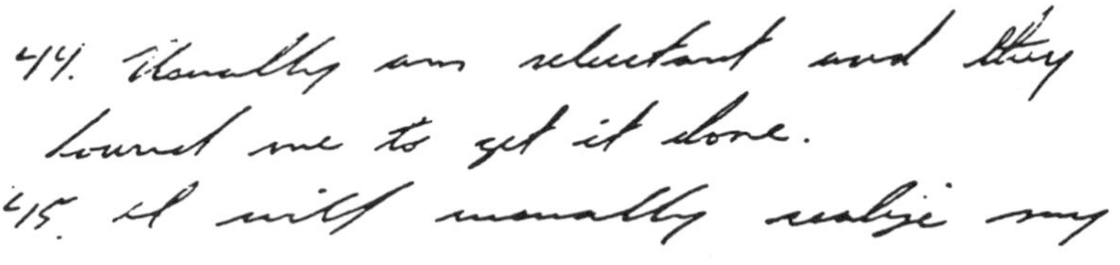

FIGURE 245
In prison for robbery and assault

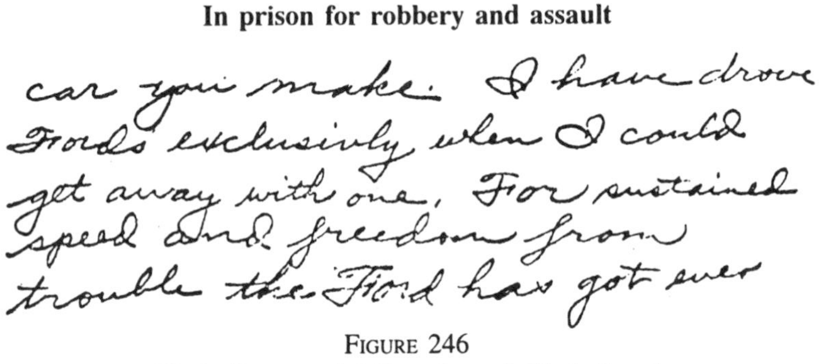

FIGURE 246
Clyde Barrow (of *Bonnie and Clyde* fame)

Clyde Barrow (of *Bonnie and Clyde* fame) writes to Henry Ford, telling him "I have drove Fords exclusively when I could get away with one" (Fig. 246).

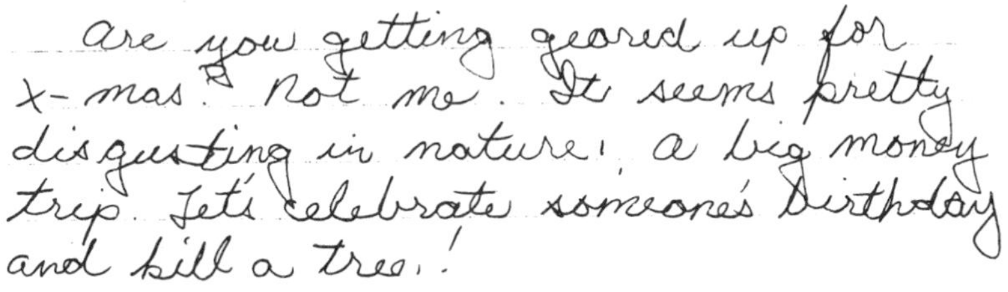
are you getting geared up for x-mas? Not me. It seems pretty disgusting in nature, a big money trip. Let's celebrate someone's Birthday and kill a tree!

FIGURE 247
Drug trafficking and child molestation: Note angular lower loops and retraced upper zone

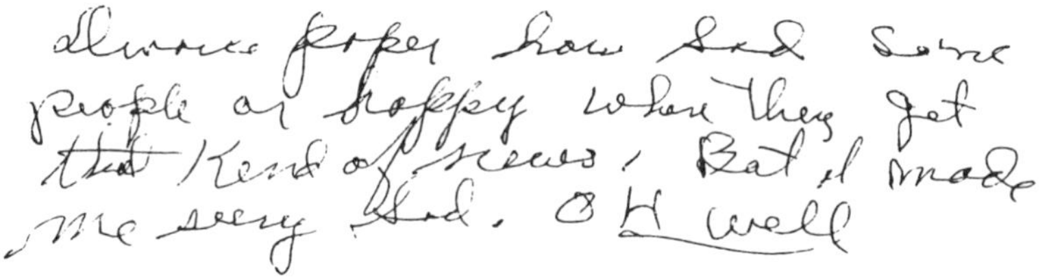
Always proper how sad some people are happy when they get ~~that~~ kind of news, But it made me very sad. OH well

FIGURE 248
70-year-old pathological liar who repeatedly molested his granddaughters

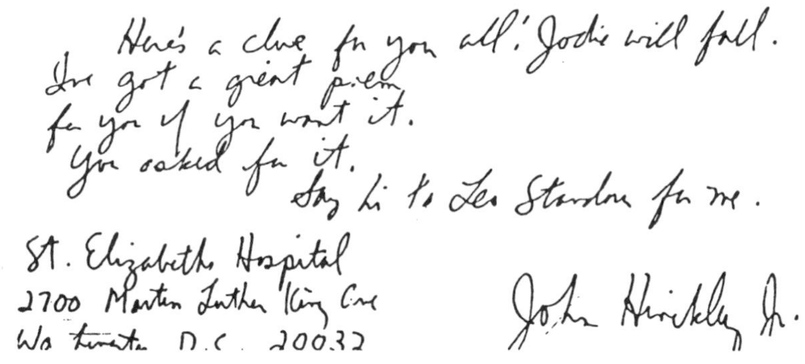
Here's a clue for you all: Jodie will fall.
I've got a great poem
for you if you want it.
You asked for it.
Say hi to Leo Stanton for me.

St. Elizabeths Hospital
2700 Martin Luther King Ave
Washington D.C. 20032

John Hinckley Jr.

FIGURE 249
John Hinckley, Jr: Attempted to assassinate President Ronald Reagan

16
HANDWRITING
REVEALS YOUR SPECIAL
APTITUDES

Your handwriting shows a variety of aptitudes. It can confirm whether you are imaginative or creative, cultural, business oriented, mechanically inclined, or scientific.

Handwriting analysis is beneficial when it uncovers talents of which you were perhaps unaware, allowing you to seek out fulfilling hobbies or avocations that you may not have believed possible. It is especially advantageous when parents are able to unlock potential talent in their children or employers can take full advantage of their workers' natural aptitudes rather than trying to fit them into positions for which they have no real skill.

For practical purposes we can divide aptitudes into four categories: cultural, mechanical, business, and scientific.

In their global effect, some character traits, like imagination and a sense of rhythm, influence more than one of these categories. To understand fully which of the four areas you fit into best, score yourself on each trait, then determine which group receives the highest percent

182

of the tallies. Remember that aptitudes are expressed according to the overall personality structure.

SENSE OF RHYTHM

Rhythm has an influence on the overall personality and is especially beneficial to creativity. It suggests that the individual's "inner machine" is well-tuned, stable, and self-disciplined, and that he or she has an integrated personality and inner harmony.

Rhythm is illustrated by letters in which the strokes regularly return to the baseline; there is a smooth up–down, up–down motion throughout the writing. Tracing over the writing with a dry pen gives you a feel for the individual's inner timing. Rhythm is further indicated by consistency of letter size, spacing, slant, and pressure and is given added emphasis when writing movements are smooth and fluid.

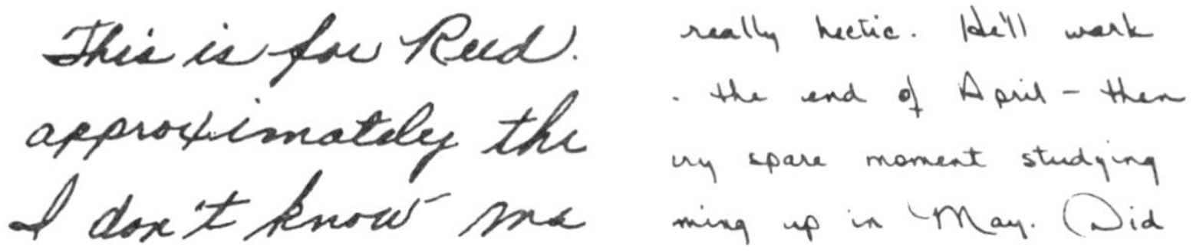

FIGURE 250
Sense of rhythm

People with rhythmic writing are able to think and act in a smooth, orderly fashion as rhythm implies that the person is at one with the self. Generally speaking, the person with this trait is able to deal with day-to-day situations with consistency and dependability.

The trait of rhythm can be viewed as a continuum, with mechanical, monotonous, and artificial writing on one end, and loose, disorganized, changeable writing on the other. Neither extreme is positive. Monotonous rhythm results in an overly controlled and stereotyped personality that is unable to experience spontaneous reaction or creative expression; extreme lack of rhythm, on the other hand, belongs to the person who has little self-discipline and is apt to be scattered, disorganized, unpredictable, or unstable.

People whose handwritings show a sense of rhythm are responsive to music, poetry, or dance. They are often very much aware of proportion, balance, and symmetry, which are all characteristics that can be used in the arts and in most creative endeavors. Rhythm can also be a positive trait for people who are mechanically inclined.

IMAGINATION

Imagination allows us to enlarge on concepts and to envision the outcome of projects: It expands on anything that is perceived through the five senses. It can enable you to appreciate the creative ideas and efforts of others and it encourages you to seek new experiences through reading, travel, entertainment, social encounters, and activity in general. Imagination also indicates that you are likely to be resourceful.

Imagination can produce negative results when it is channeled in the wrong direction or is combined with negative characteristics. For example, it can blow emotions out of proportion, making a person exceedingly sensitive to benign remarks or feeling exceptionally thwarted by jealousy. It can cause the argumentative or stubborn person to be relentlessly argumentative or stubborn. It can add even more sting to already unpleasant anger or sarcasm. In *A Midsummer Night's Dream,* Shakespeare summed it up by saying, "The lunatic, the lover and the poet are of imagination all compact" (5.1.7).

Imagination is practically indispensable in creative endeavors and is, as Albert Einstein said, "more important than knowledge." Imagination can allow the familiar to take on new form or to be seen in a new light and helps us envision that which is not present. It gives the artist the capacity to "see" a painting before it is finished, adds new dimensions to literary characters, and helps the actress or actor to portray roles more dramatically. Imagination can help the businessperson to see more possibilities in his or her work and give the scientist the ability to envision what might be.

Two types of imagination are illustrated by handwriting. One, shown by unique, unusual formations and letter connections, belongs to the person with an unusual way of looking at life and a special way of connecting ideas. Truly creative people are willing to deviate from the structures they were taught in grade school penmanship classes and to create those that suit their own purpose. They may, therefore, be "different" from their peers in thought or action.

How the person is different depends on the shape, size, direction, and pressure of the unique structure. It is important to keep in mind that unique structures can belong to both creative people and very unbalanced people, and you must consider the formlevel and the influence of other personality traits before drawing a final conclusion.

FIGURE 251
Unique formations: Imagination

The other indication of imagination is enlarged loops, especially lower ones. The larger the loops, the more imagination influences the person's thinking and expressions. Enlarged loops can have positive implications if used wisely, but exceptionally large loops are often problematic in that much of the writer's life becomes exaggerated or dramatic.

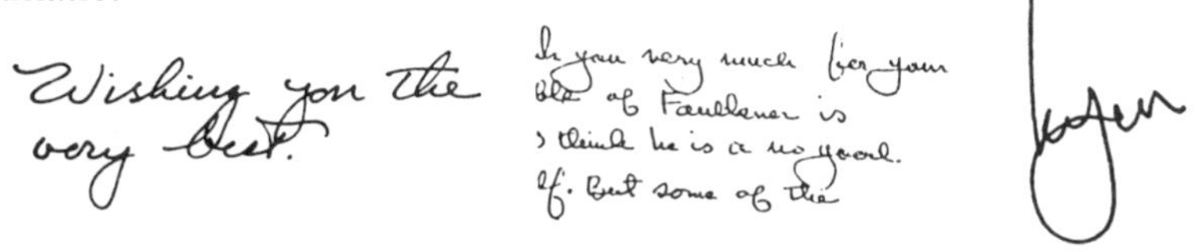

FIGURE 252
Enlarged loops: Imagination

CULTURAL APTITUDES

LITERARY INTEREST

Literary interest (or talent for literature when accompanied by other cultural indications) is shown by Greek *e* formations, as those of

Fig. 253. Greek *e*'s may be seen in uppercase or lowercase *e*'s, or they may be found in the letter *r*.

Literary indications suggest that the writer has a way with words, either written or spoken, and that cultural matters draw his or her attention. If the writer has well-developed thinking habits and if the handwriting scores high in other cultural signs, there is apt to be actual talent for writing. The writer of Greek *e*'s who does not have other cultural signs may simply enjoy the theater or the ballet or may be fond of reading. Culturally inclined people like harmonious surroundings and intellectual environments.

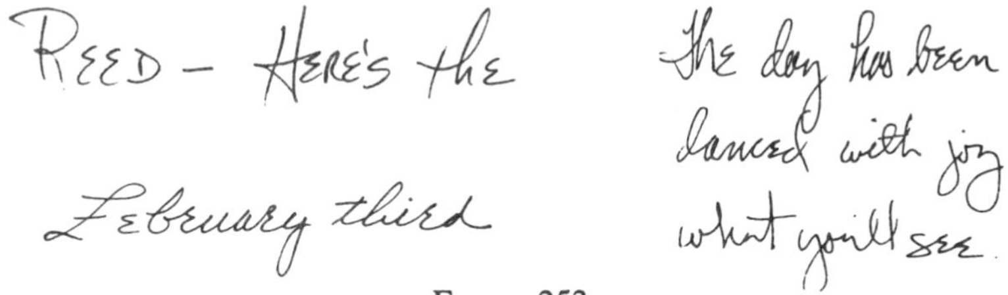

FIGURE 253
Greek *e* formations

Delta *d*'s (Fig. 254) are also indicative of cultural interests and are often found in the handwriting of literary greats. Delta *d*'s are similar in formation to desire-for-attention strokes in that they reach leftward and thus feature the self. Since these *d*'s reach into the philosophical area, the implication is that the person wishes to be noticed for his or her ideals. Recognition can be achieved by publishing how one thinks and feels.

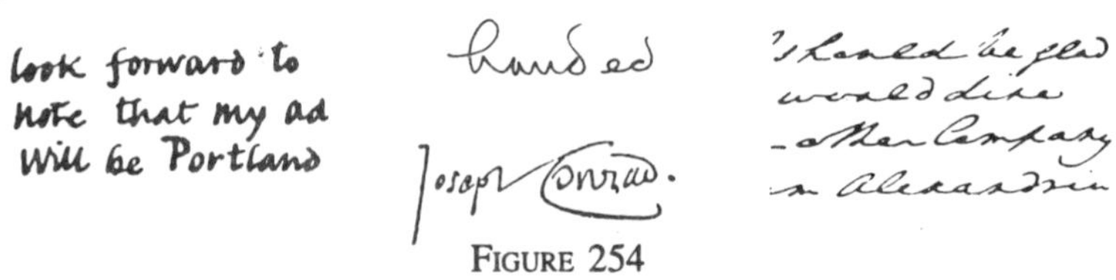

FIGURE 254
Delta *d*'s

Further suggestions of literary inclinations are figure-eight forma-tions, found primarily in the letters *g* or *f* but also elsewhere, as in the lowercase *s* or in other unusual structures (Fig. 255).

Figure-eights show fluidity and ability to think and communicate smoothly. Fluid thinkers move easily from one subject or idea to another, express themselves with ease, and can quickly come up with alternatives. This is especially helpful to anyone involved in the art world, as it helps to envision and express new approaches. Fluidity is often accompanied by rhythm, an appreciation for line value and imagination, and is certainly enhanced by fast writing and indications of clear and well-developed thinking (see Chapter 6).

FIGURE 255
Figure eight formations: Fluidity

COLOR SENSE

An appreciation for color is advantageous for creative people, especially those involved in visual art.

The person who writes broad or colorful pen strokes is one whose sense of color is well developed. He or she has a feel for color, likes deep and rich hues, and is able to sense which colors go well together and which have good contrast. A sense of color also implies, as previously suggested, the writer has deep and lasting feelings, likes and dislikes with intensity, and has a feel for anything related to the senses. Heavy writers are often "grounded" and like to work with objects that can be touched, tasted, or smelled.

When heavy pen strokes are accompanied by round-topped or flat-topped letters (especially *m*, *n*, or *r*) there is further emphasis on visual impressions as well as an ability to work with the hands, so that the writer wants to do something physical with the color sense, perhaps paint or sculpt (see Fig. 267).

A feeling for color is illustrated in the heavy pen strokes of Pablo Picasso (Fig. 256), Marc Chagall (Fig. 257), Henri de Toulouse-Lautrec (Fig. 258), Richard Diebenkorn (Fig. 259), and Georgia O'Keeffe (Fig. 260). A strong color sense is not a necessity to artistic expression, provided there are other cultural indications. Frederic Remington (Fig. 261), noted for his paintings of the American West, did not possess a strong color sense, but his writing does show good rhythm (evenness of writing tempo), a sense of line value (carefully arranged writing), simplicity of expression (lack of superfluous strokes), and a smattering of interpretive skill (breaks between letters).

FIGURE 256
Pablo Picasso: Spanish painter and sculptor in France

FIGURE 257
Marc Chagall: Russian painter in France

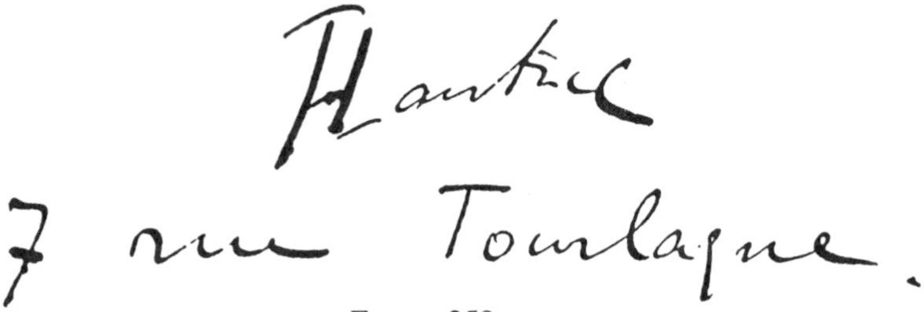

FIGURE 258
Henri de Toulouse-Lautrec: French painter

FIGURE 259
Richard Diebenkorn: U.S. artist

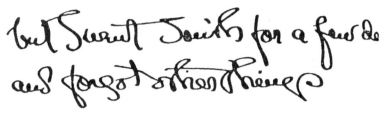

FIGURE 260
Georgia O'Keeffe: U.S. artist

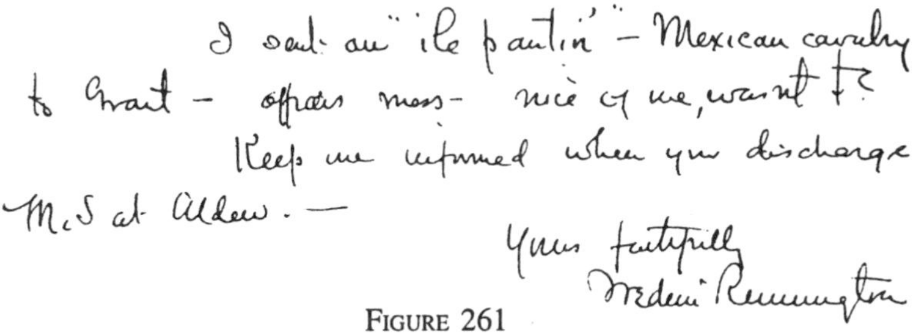

FIGURE 261
Frederic Remington: U.S. artist

TALENT FOR MUSIC

In addition to a good sense of rhythm and timing, musical interest is shown by breaks between letters (Fig. 262). This implies a feel for music—an intuition or sixth sense that can be a boon to any artist. Such breaks indicate an interpretive ability or spiritual attunement that allows the person to know what the artist or composer is trying to convey. The intuitive person often gets a deeper meaning from a painting, a sculpture, or a piece of music than do those without this skill.

Musicians sometimes do not have these breaks between letters yet have developed an ability to read music, to play by ear, or to handle an instrument with ease. In such cases, the musician may be very competent in his or her renditions but does not have the innate ability that takes music from wonderful to the sublime. (Check also the person's imagination, sense of balance and line value, and so forth.)

(Note: When breaks between letters occur at a syllable or after a capital letter, the indication is somewhat discounted as these are natural breaking points.)

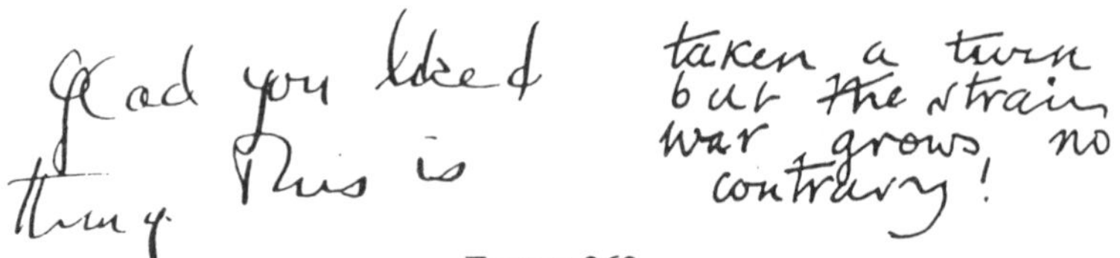

FIGURE 262
Breaks between letters: Intuition and a feel for music

SIMPLICITY OF EXPRESSION

Simple, direct, efficient handwriting formations are a plus in any creative endeavor. When capital letters are printed or written without superfluous movements, the writer likes simplicity and can be said to have an understanding of the essence of things. He or she prefers not to deal with extraneous matters or unimportant details and often finds efficient ways of getting from point A to point B. The useful and practical is preferred, and if there are also artistic indications, the artistic expression is streamlined.

FIGURE 263
Simplified capitals: Simplicity of expression

LINE VALUE

A person who has a feel for shapes, forms, proportion, and balance produces writing with gracefully formed letters. Lower loops and capital letters are especially likely to show line value in their graceful, fluid movements. People who have a sense of line value have a feel for the decorative. This aptitude may be expressed through fashion design, interior decoration, floral design, window display, or landscaping.

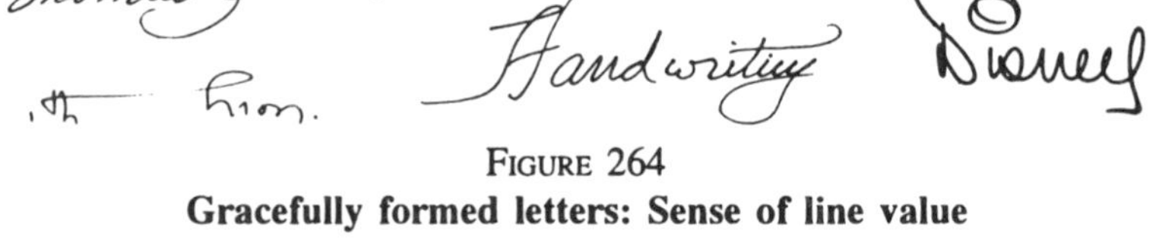

FIGURE 264
Gracefully formed letters: Sense of line value

When such balanced, well-proportioned writing is more angular or composed of squared structures, the writer's sense of line value may lean toward architecture, structures, buildings, bridges, or machinery. (See Thomas Edison's graceful *T* cross, flattened *m*'s and *n*'s , and simplified formations; and Frank Lloyd Wright's rooflike *F* and "*L-l*" combination that resembles a foundation in Figs. 265 and 266.)

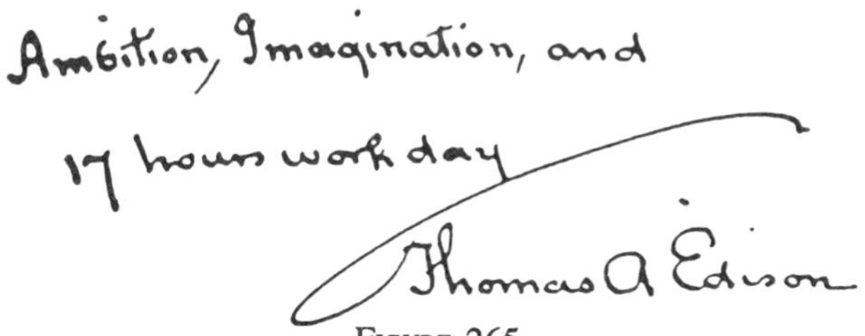

FIGURE 265
Thomas Edison: Inventor

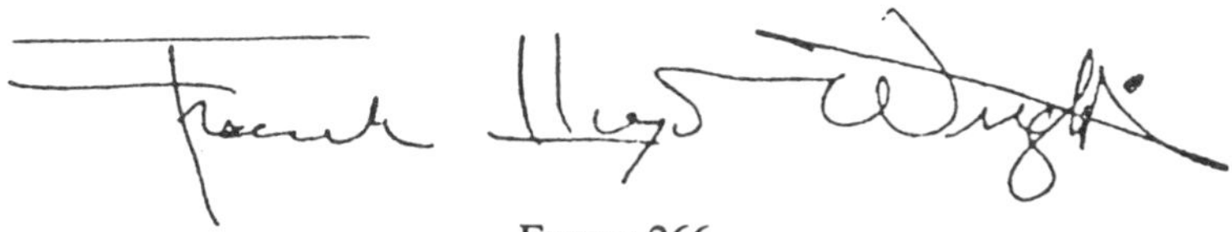

FIGURE 266
Frank Lloyd Wright: Architect

MECHANICAL APTITUDES

MANUAL DEXTERITY

Skill for mechanics requires that the person have good manual dexterity—a natural ability to work with the hands—shown by flat-topped *r*'s and well-rounded *m*'s and *n*'s (Fig. 267). Such flat-topped letters imply an urge to do something practical and workable; the writer may want to "get his or her hands on" something.

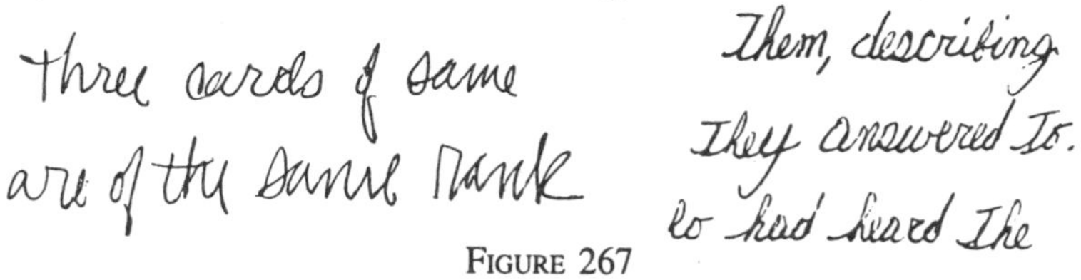

FIGURE 267
Flat-topped *r*'s: Manual dexterity

In combination with a sense of rhythm, manual dexterity points toward an ability to work with machinery or computers, or perhaps play an instrument if there is also other evidence of talent. Skill in these areas is supported by attentiveness to detail, good thinking habits, and fluidity, as well as precise letter formations and spacing. (See Fig. 265.) When manual dexterity is added to imagination, the result is a sense of form or structure and a good visual memory. Attentiveness to details is also helpful in the mechanical realm, as shown by carefully placed dots and punctuation and consistent letter formations.

BUSINESS SKILLS

Several character trait combinations are useful in business, depending on the nature of the business as well as whether the person is a top executive or a subordinate.

Confidence and thinking habits are important considerations, especially for executives. Their willingness to take chances shows in large capital letters, strong, bold handwriting, or both. The executive's thinking must be quick and perceptive (fast writing, needlepoint formations) as well as direct (lack of lead-ins). Intuition (breaks between letters) is also advantageous. Executives generally have great ideas (unusual letter structures, enlarged loops, and breaks between letters) but they usually cannot be bothered by petty details, so they are not likely to be careful about evenness of letter size or placement of dots and punctuation. Sometimes their writing is lacking in organizational ability.

ORGANIZATIONAL SKILLS

The person chosen by the executive to carry out ideas needs the ability to put ideas into some sort of workable order. This requires a sense of organization, which is the ability to assemble the elements needed for productivity and to coordinate them into a working whole. The person with this ability can coordinate time, plans, people, or projects.

The organized person is careful about making upper and lower loops of relatively equal size (Fig. 268). The letter f is a good place to look for the writer's sense of order. If the f loops are balanced, indications are that ideas (upper loop) are brought down to a practical level (lower loop). Organization is enhanced by good formlevel, evenness of spacing and formations, consistency of slant, even baselines, and careful punctuation.

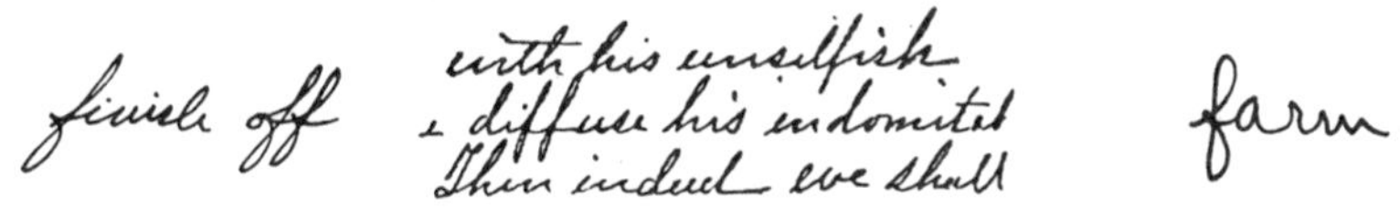

FIGURE 268
Balanced loops: Organizational ability

DECISIVENESS

The ability to make firm decisions is essential in the business world. An uncertain person is likely to vacillate between one possibility and another, wasting time, effort and energy in the process. But when one makes a firm decision and sticks with it, everyone involved is more likely to follow through. You can't get anywhere until you take the first step, and you can't take the first step until you know where to put your foot.

Decisiveness shows in letters that come to a firm stop (Fig. 269). There is no fading of pressure, no "feathering" of the stroke—just a strong finish, a resolute stop of the pen: "Here is where I stop and this is where I stay." (Too much decisiveness, however, results in stubbornness or bluff, both negative qualities.)

FIGURE 269
Firm endings: Decisiveness

DETERMINATION

Once a decision has been reached, determination is necessary to act on it. Determination is a willingness to work steadfastly toward a goal or project, ignoring defeat and persisting even when things do not look good. The determined writer makes long, firm downstrokes in the lower zone, indicating firm control and good follow-through (Fig. 270). Determination is increased proportionally to the amount of pressure and the length of the stroke and is enhanced by good overall pressure, even spacing between lines, tied structures (see Chapter 11 on the letter *t*), balanced *f*'s, and rhythmic writing.

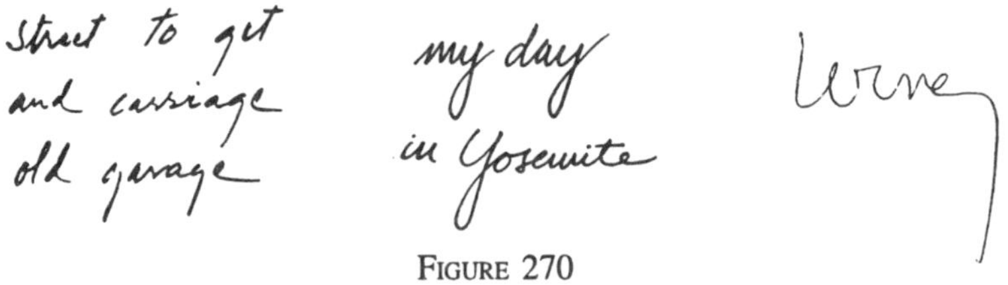

FIGURE 270
Strong downstrokes: Determination

DIPLOMACY

A tactful, diplomatic approach is helpful in business. The diplomatic person eases into situations, especially those involving people. Usually the diplomatic person understands others' needs and motives and is effectively persuasive, especially when confidence is also shown. Diplomacy suggests that the person can state his or her wishes without inviting friction.

Diplomacy is illustrated in individual letters (*m*, for example) or entire words that gradually diminish in size (Fig. 271). When the letter or word maintains legibility, the tactful approach is further emphasized. Diplomacy is augmented by fluid thinking, quickness of perception, and positive social traits.

FIGURE 271
Tapered letters: Diplomacy

INITIATIVE

Victor Hugo said, "Machines move mountains, but initiative moves men." People with initiative are good at getting things off the ground. They are able to see and take advantage of opportunities and are ready to take the next step forward. They can see what needs to be done and are usually eager to act, depending on how strong the trait is and what other traits support it.

A readiness to take advantage of opportunity is illustrated in "breakaway" strokes, which may be located in either the middle or lower zone (Fig. 272). In the middle zone they are sometimes seen in the final letter *t*, which ends with a final forward stroke in place of a crossbar. Initiative can also be seen in the letter *h* or *p* where the second part of the letter juts forward.

FIGURE 272
Breakaway strokes: Initiative

In the lower zone, breakaway strokes usually carry more impact because this is the action area (see Fig. 241). When such strokes are curved or move forward softly, the initiative has less force than when the stroke is firm and angular and has a strong forward thrust. In the latter case, aggressiveness is evident; the person pushes forward into new territory. (In business, this is generally a positive characteristic, whereas in one's personal life it can be offensive; check other traits as well.)

SCIENTIFIC APTITUDE

An aptitude for science requires, first of all, good thinking skills. In addition, it calls for both material and abstract imagination as well as the ability to organize.

The person with a scientific mind often has very small handwriting, showing the ability to focus on details. If the person is also careful about the placement of punctuation, the ability to concentrate on small matters is increased. Such writers are good candidates for research because they are able to spend long hours digging into one specific topic. This skill may be enhanced by a general lack of loops (especially lower ones), implying that the person is able to spend much time alone.

Besides being able to concentrate, the scientific mind needs to be interested in the unknown and to be able to analyze carefully what is discovered there. Exploratory thinking is shown in upward-pointed wedges in the abstract area but also in the middle zone if the angles are pronounced. The ability to separate and evaluate the facts is indicated by downward-pointed wedges between letters, as between the sections of *m*'s and *n*'s (see also Chapter 6).

The scientist must be able to consider many possibilities, so the baseline may be a bit bouncy and the writing should be lacking in stiffness. Breaks between letters will be of help here, showing that the person senses what the next approach might be. Imagination increases the ability to see what lies ahead. If the scientist is to work with instruments or machinery, manual dexterity is a plus, as is a good sense of rhythm.

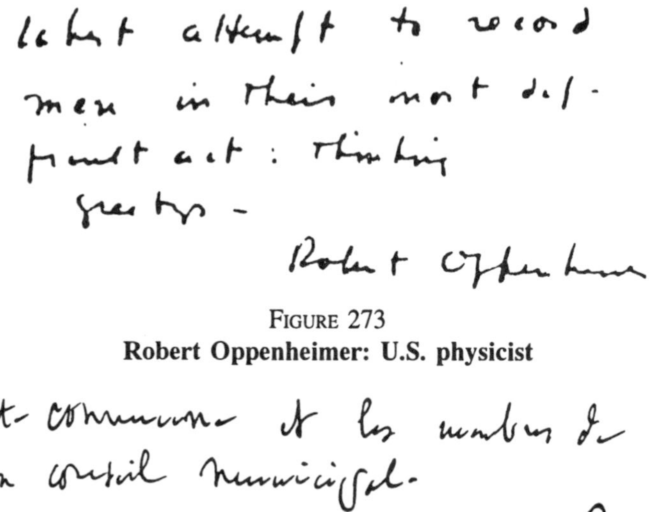

FIGURE 273
Robert Oppenheimer: U.S. physicist

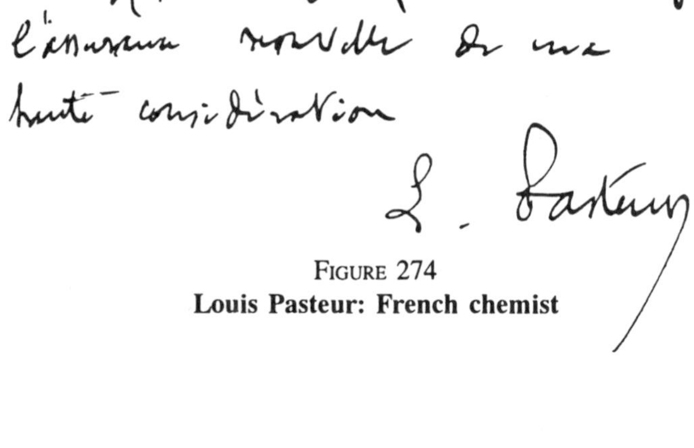

FIGURE 274
Louis Pasteur: French chemist

DICTIONARY
OF PERSONALITY
TRAITS

The personality indications given here must be carefully evaluated. Various possibilities are indicated for each trait, the most important indications appearing first. Italicized descriptions are primary indications of the trait in question. Descriptions not italicized must be found in combination to reveal the trait. When several indications for any trait are discovered in the writing, the trait will score high; if there are only one or two, the trait will have a lower rating.

Abbreviations: esp, especially; hw, handwriting; LZ, lower zone; MZ, middle zone; PPI, personal pronoun *I*; sig, signature; UZ, upper zone.

Absent-minded	Missing letters; missing *i* dots and *t* crosses; disorganized writing; poor spacing.
Accurate	Carefully formed letters; accurately placed *i* dots and *t* crosses; careful spacing; organized writing.
Acquisitive	*Initial hooks*; enlarged LZ structures; "felon's claw" formations.

Adaptable	*Figure-eight formations*; garlands; soft baseline; rounded circle letters, esp *e;* connected letters; lack of angularity.
Affectionate	Rightward slant; enlarged lower loops; moderate-to-heavy pressure; middle-to-large size; rounded hw.
Agreeable	Soft hw; forward, light hw; broad circle letters, esp *e*; moderate-to-wide spacing.
Aggressive	*Angular LZ strokes jut forward;* finals jut into LZ; strong angularity; clublike formations; large size; large capitals; heavy pressure; strong downstrokes; firm *t* crosses.
Ambitious	High and heavy *t* crosses; heavy downstrokes; small reversed initial loops; tall capitals; upward slanted *t* crosses; heavy pressure; angularity.
Analytical	*Downward-directed* v *formations, esp at baseline;* vertical writing; middle-to-small size; carefully placed *i* dots.
Angry	Excessive angularity; intense pressure; initial tics or barbs; initial brace strokes; club formations.
Argumentative	*Tall initial stroke of* p; angularity; initial brace strokes; glassy writing; downward *t* crosses; sharp *t* crosses; strong capitals; heavy pressure.
Arrogant	Extra tall *t*'s and *d*'s; very large capitals; excessive ornamentation; inflated UZ; heavy pressure; rigid writing; argumentativeness; sarcasm.
Artificial	Excessively careful writing; embellished capitals; left slant; sig different from text.
Artistic	Tasteful ornamentation; simplification; rounded letters; flat-topped *r*'s; good shading; heavy pressure; good layout.
Athletic	*Enlarged* p *loops;* LZ emphasis; firm pressure, esp in LZ; large hw.
Attention, desire for	*Final stroke swings up and leftward*; artificial writing; large or embellished capitals; exaggerated loops; wavy *t* crosses and initial strokes; large sig or PPI.
Bossy	See Demanding.
Broad-minded	*Rounded circle letters, esp* e; enlarged upper loops; rounded writing; garlands; soft baseline; nonjabbed dots.
Brutal	Clubbed *t* crosses and final strokes; strong angularity; slow speed; coarse hw; very heavy or muddy hw.
Business sense	Good layout; sharp, penetrating, and angular *m*'s and

n's; moderate-to-small size; firm endings; strong downstrokes; figure-eight formations; initials or first name joined with surname of sig.

Calm

Consistent baseline; consistent spacing, size, formations; vertical hw; small hw; carefully placed dots; rounded hw.

Careful

Consistent formations; carefully placed dots and *t* crosses; moderate-to-slow speed; initial lead-ins; legibility; closed *a* and *o*.

Cautious

Finals extend straight out; left slant; *t* bars remain left of stem; precise hw; retraced letters.

Change, desire for

Long lower loops, esp if enlarged; tangled lines; flying *i* dots; expansive writing.

Clumsy

Inconsistent formations; irregular baseline; poorly formed LZ; slow hw; tangled lines.

Communicative

Open-topped a*'s and* o*'s;* large hw; broad formations; figure-eight formations; large capitals; rightward slant.

Conceited

Very tall *t*'s and *d*'s; extra large or embellished capitals; exaggerated loops; flourished hw; large PPI or sig.

Concentration

Very small hw; carefully placed punctuation and *t* crosses; legible letters; simplified hw.

Confident

Large MZ; moderate-to-large capitals; underlined sig; moderately strong sig or PPI; firm pressure; ascending lines; *t* crosses at upper third of stems.

Conservative

Schoolbook hw; retraced letters; curtailed finals; moderate-to-small UZ and LZ; simplification; regularity; arcades.

Creative

Original formations; figure-eight structures; disconnections between letters; large loops; some size fluctuation; moderate-to-strong pressure.

Critical

Angular hw and sharp *t* crosses; jabbed *i* dots; sharp or angular LZ strokes; curtailed finals.

Cruel

Clublike *t* crosses and finals; downward-slanted *t* bars; very heavy pressure; muddiness; abrupt finals; finals descend sharply below line and to the right; coarse hw; triangular loops; whiplike formations in combination with preceding signs.

Cultured

Greek *e*'s; figure-eight formations; delta *d*'s; graceful loops and capitals; breaks between letters; balanced spacing; consistent formations; colorful hw.

Daydreamer	T *crosses placed above stems; floating* i *dots;* light, uncertain hw.
Deceitful	Double-looped circle letters; artificial hw; backward or tricky letters; illegible sig; frequent patching; broken letters; felon's claws; muddiness; inconsistencies.
Decisive	*Firm letter endings; strong downstrokes;* consistent formations; even spacing; carefully placed dots; firm *t* crosses; vertical writing.
Defiant	*Lowercase letters (esp* k*) jut out;* angular hw; very firm pressure; backward letters, esp PPI.
Demanding	*Downward-slanted* t *crosses;* very heavy *t* crosses; finals come straight down below line; angular hw; braced formations, esp *t* and *d.*
Dependable	*Even, consistent hw; straight baseline;* well-formed MZ; firm endings; carefully placed dots and cross bars; balanced zones.
Dependent, emotionally	*Downstrokes of LZ structures pull leftward;* strong forward slant; basin *t* bars; very soft writing; poorly formed PPI.
Depressed	*Descending baselines; end of lines droop;* drooping finals, esp on lower loops; drooping garlands; line cancels out sig.
Detail-mindedness	*Carefully dotted* i*'s;* very small hw; careful spacing, regularity, letter formations; even baseline.
Determined	*Strong downstrokes, esp below baseline;* angular hw; firm *t* crosses; regularity; heavy pressure.
Dignified	*Retraced* t *and* d *stems, esp if tall;* vertical hw; graceful formations; lack of coarseness.
Diplomatic	*Tapering words or letters, esp if maintaining legibility;* closed circle letters; few direct strokes (without lead-ins).
Direct	*No lead-ins;* simplified letters; legible hw; clear circles; LZ downstrokes without loops.
Disciplined	See Self-disciplined.
Dishonest	See Deceitful.
Disorganized	Irregular hw; poor layout; tangled lines; changeable slant or formations; differences in size of upper and lower loops, esp letter *f.*
Domineering	*Downward-slanted* t *bars, esp if sharp;* sharp final strokes

that jut forward and downward; strong angularity; tall initial stroke of *p;* clublike formations.

Dreamer — T *cross above the stem, esp if light;* full upper or lower loops; very light *t* crosses; basin *t* bars; light pressure; feathered end strokes.

Earthy — Heavy or pasty pressure; LZ emphasis; lack of UZ emphasis.

Easily influenced — *Rounded formations; indefinite* m*'s and* n*'s;* rounded *s;* broad circle letters; light pressure; thready connections; indefinite finals.

Economical — *Curtailed or short finals;* narrow letter, word, or line spacing; no exaggerated movements; simplified hw; small size.

Efficient — *Simplified formations;* lack of lead-ins; no exaggerated movements; balanced *f* loops; consistent letter size; small hw.

Emotional depth — *Heavy pressure;* consistent formations; even baseline.

Emotionally expressive — *Rightward slant;* large hw; expansive movements; enlarged loops, esp lower; lack of retracing; open-topped circle letters; moderate-to-light pressure.

Emotionally responsive — *Far rightward slant;* fluctuating baseline; large loops, esp lower; expanded writing.

Energetic — Heavy pressure; angular hw; large size; large capitals; strong LZ downstrokes; long *t* crosses; fast hw.

Enthusiastic — *Long, heavy* t *crosses;* expansive movements; enlarged loops; large hw; rightward slant; ascending baseline.

Envious — *Small, initial loop and initial and final hooks;* tight spacing; curtailed finals; glassy hw; double-looped circle letters.

Evasive — *Initial loops cutting into body of circle letters;* basin *t* bars; poor legibility; thready hw; double-looped circle letters; changeable size; inconsistencies.

Exaggerates — Very large loops, esp lower; large writing with flourishes; very tall *t* or *d* stems; any grossly exaggerated forms.

Extravagant — *Very wide spacing; long, curved finals;* large hw; rightward slant.

Extroverted — Large hw; large capitals; enlarged lower loops; right-

	ward slant; open-topped circle letters; broad hw; rightward movements in general.
Fair	Rounded circle letters; moderate and rounded upper loops; vertical or slightly rightward hw; light-to-moderate pressure; lack of hostilities.
Faithful	See Loyal.
Fastidious	Carefully placed *i* dots and *t* bars; precise letter forms; consistency; amended letters.
Flamboyant	*Embellishments;* very large hw; enlarged loops, esp lower; showy signature; extravagant movements.
Flexible	See Adaptable.
Flirtatious	*Wavy initial strokes; wavy* t *crosses;* light, rounded hw with showy loops and forward slant; final strokes go upward and back to self.
Forgetful	*Undotted* i*'s and uncrossed* t*'s; omitted letters or parts of letters;* jerky style; disorganized hw.
Frank	*Clear, legible hw; uncontaminated circle letters;* open-topped *a*'s and *o*'s; simplification; broad letters; signature same as text.
Friendly	Garland formations; rightward slant; medium-to-large size; wide lower loops; open-topped *a*'s and *o*'s; finals reaching out and upward; moderate spacing between words.
Generous	*Finals reach out and upward*; open letter formations (no tight letters); wide spacing (letter, word, line); large size.
Gentle	Garland formations; soft hw; round-topped letters; light pressure.
Gossipy	Open-topped *a*'s and *o*'s and sharp-pointed *t* crosses and large LZ; tall initial *p* stroke.
Graceful	*Smooth, full, rounded LZ formations, esp* p; rhythmic hw; good organization, line spacing, etc.
Hesitant	Long, curved lead-ins, esp if from below baseline; left-placed *t* crosses; left-placed *i* dots; initial blobs of ink; jerky hw.
Honest	Clear, legible hw; uncontaminated circle structures; open-topped circle letters; simplified formations; lack of lead-ins; quick speed; sig matches text.
Humorous	*Wavy initial strokes;* wavy *t* crosses; moderate-to-large size; broad letters; light-to-moderate pressure.

Hypersensitive	Wavering baseline; very light pressure; poorly formed letters; light *t* crosses; incomplete finals; leftward trend.
Hypersensitive to criticism	*Enlarged* t *or* d *loop;* very tall *t* and *d* stem; angularity and forward slant and enlarged lower loops, esp with light pressure.
Imaginative (easily affected)	*Enlarged loops, esp upper;* unique formations; very high *t* crosses and *i* dots; broadness; full letters; enriched capitals.
Immature	*Rounded, very slow hw;* copybook style; irregularities; presence of many fear traits and few adjustment traits.
Impatient	T *cross to right of stem;* rightward slant and jabbed dots, esp with light pressure; lack of consistency; fast hw; incomplete finals; light pressure.
Impulsive	Rightward slant and irregularity; rightward slant, neglected letter formations, and incomplete finals; fast speed; rising lines; extended *t* crosses.
Inconsistent	Changeable slant, size, formations; poor layout; thready formations; variable *t* crosses; same letter made different ways; light *t* crosses and light pressure.
Indecisive	*Indefinite finals (feathered endings);* inconsistent slant, size, formations; thready formations; irregular baseline.
Independent	*Very short* t *and* d *stems;* vertical hw; simplified PPI; consistent size, slant, formations; firm finals.
Inefficient	Poor organization; slow hw; changeable formations; imbalanced *f*; ornate or extravagant movements; poorly dotted *i*'s.
Inflexible	See Rigid.
Intelligent	Quick-to-fast speed; simplified formations; unique structures; clearly written letters, esp *m*'s and *n*'s; clear spacing; well-developed UZ.
Introverted	Tiny hw; leftward slant; tightly closed circle letters; tiny circle letters; perfectionistic hw; last hump of *m* or *n* taller; narrow letter and word spacing.
Intuitive	*Breaks between letters;* sharp *m*'s and *n*'s; sharp UZ formations; light pressure.
Irresponsible	Dish-shaped or weak *t* crosses; irregularities; poor MZ formations; weak downstrokes.
Irritable	*Jabbed* i *dots; initial or final tics;* variable size, pressure and spacing; sharp-pointed *t* crosses; angular connections; very light pressure.

Jealous	*Small, reversed initial loops;* initial brace strokes plus forward slant plus angularity.
Law-abiding	*Schoolbook writing;* moderate-sized and consistent UZ structures; lack of unusual formations; consistent baseline, size, and slant.
Leadership skills	Firm, moderately large capitals; strong signature; strong, slightly downward pointed *t* crosses; firm downstrokes; clear, legible hw; good over-all balance and regularity.
Lecherous	*Smeary, blotched writing; distorted LZ structures;* excessive pressure and poor UZ development; erratic pressure and changeable size, slant, structures, etc.
Literary	*Greek e's; delta d's; figure-eight formations;* rhythmic hw; disconnected hw; graceful loops; simplified structures.
Logical	Connected hw; vertical hw; well-formed *m*'s and *n*'s; legibility; clear, balanced MZ; rounded circle letters.
Loyal	*Rounded* i *dots (not circle dots);* rounded, non-contaminated circle letters; consistent UZ; vertical-to-slightly rightward slant; consistent baseline.
Manic	Excessively large and/or expansive hw; strongly upward slanting baseline; exaggerated movements; very long *t* crosses; very large loops.
Manipulative	*Contaminated circle letters (double loops, hooks, distortions);* thready hw; "shark's tooth" or "felon's claw" formations; flattened arcades.
Mechanical aptitudes	*Flat-topped* r*'s; very round, broad letters, esp* m *and* n; supported by rhythmic hw, consistency, and moderate speed.
Memory	Carefully placed dots and punctuation; consistent and carefully written *m*'s and *n*'s; well-formed letters; consistent formations, spacing, size, etc.
Methodical	*Rounded* m*'s and* n*'s and consistent formations;* connected hw; good overall layout; lacking in exaggerations.
Modest	*Small hw;* moderate-to-small capitals, esp PPI; non-embellished signature; short *t*'s and *d*'s; simplified formations (lack of ornate letters).
Moody	*Erratic slant and/or baseline, or both;* changeable size; inconsistent formations; variable pressure; far forward slant.

Nagging	Downward-slanted, sharp *t* crosses; tall initial stroke of *p*; angular LZ formations; initial tics.
Narrow-minded	*Narrow (squeezed) circle letters, esp* e; tight spacing; rigid or angular hw; squeezed loops, esp upper; braced final strokes.
Nervous	*Shaky, trembling, erratic hw;* light pressure with lack of consistency; corrected or amended letters.
Objective	*Vertical hw;* connected hw; clearly formed *m*'s and *n*'s; legible hw; rounded circle letters; simplified formations; regularity.
Observant	Carefully placed dots and punctuation; small hw; consistent and carefully written *m*'s and *n*'s; angular formations; vertical hw.
Obstinate	See Stubborn.
Open-minded	*Rounded circle letters, esp* e; moderate-to-wide spacing; rounded hw; rounded, open loops.
Opinionated	Very tall upper loops, esp *t* and *d;* inflated UZ; strong endings and downstrokes; heavy pressure; exaggerated capitals (see also Narrow-minded).
Optimist	*Ascending baselines,* t *crosses, or both;* rising endstrokes; high *i* dots and *t* crosses.
Original	Original letter formations; unusual connections; nonschoolbook hw; enlarged loops.
Ostentatious	*Overly embellished hw;* enlarged or exaggerated sig; very tall, enlarged *t*'s and *d*'s, or both; exaggerated size; enlarged capitals; excessive underlining.
Patient	Regularity; rhythm; carefully placed dots and punctuation; rounded dots (not jabbed); slow hw; close spacing; no exaggerated movements.
Perceptive	*Needlepoint formations, esp at baseline ("sharp" hw)*; disconnected hw; fast hw; wide spacing.
Perfectionist	*Excessively accurate and regular hw;* precisely placed dots, punctuation, and *t* crosses; frequent corrections or amendments; clear letter formations; small size.
Persistent	*Tie strokes, esp letter* t; regular hw; consistent formations; straight baseline; firm downstrokes; final hooks; blunt endings.
Pessimistic	*Descending baseline; baseline falters at end of line;*

	drooping final strokes of y *or* g; weak, low *t* crosses.
Poised	Vertical hw; straight baseline; consistent formations; close, careful spacing; retraced *t*'s and *d*'s.
Prejudiced	*Very heavy hw, esp. with rightward slant;* tight hw; narrow upper loops; narrow circle letters; very strong downstrokes; final strokes descend vertically below line.
Pretentious	*Artificial hw; ornate hw;* embellished, enlarged capitals, or both, esp sig; embellished PPI; very large hw; dominant UZ.
Procrastinator	*T bars and* i *dots to the left;* long, curved initial strokes; slow hw; overly rounded hw.
Reliable	*Clear, consistent formations;* straight baseline; consistent size (esp MZ), slant and spacing; sig same as text; firm downstrokes; lack of excessive movements.
Repressed	*Excessively retraced structures, esp MZ;* tight hw; narrow circle letters and loops; tiny hw; very low *t* crosses.
Resentful	*Straight, inflexible initial strokes from at or below baseline, esp with pressure;* very angular hw; tight hw; dagger formations.
Reserved	Small hw; small capitals; closed *a*'s and *o*'s; tight letter spacing; wide word spacing; vertical or leftward slant.
Resourceful	*Enlarged lower loops, clear letter formations, and rounded circle letters;* original formations; simplified hw.
Responsible	Regular, consistent hw; even baselines; consistent, moderate slant; well-placed *t* crosses; firm downstrokes; clear letter formations.
Restless	*Tangled hw;* large hw; inconsistent formations; changeable slant, pressure, size; uneven spacing.
Rigid	*Very angular, "stiff" hw;* narrow or retraced UZ structures; narrow circle letters; initial or final braced strokes; final clublike formations.
Sadistic	Dagger formations; strongly jabbed *i* dots; very sharp LZ formations; sharp strokes that invade circle letters; supported by blotchy hw, inconsistent pressure, curtailed finals, angularity.
Sarcastic	*Sharp* t *crosses;* glassy hw; angular formations; sup-

ported by open-topped circle letters and very tall initial *p* stroke.

Secretive — *Loops on right-hand side of circle letters;* consistently closed circle letters; narrow circle letters; narrow hw generally; illegible sig or sig very different from text.

Self-blaming — *Sharp, backward-moving strokes, esp at end of words or letters; leftward-directed* t *crosses.*

Self-confident — *Large or bold capitals, or both; large MZ; underlined sig;* large PPI or sig; heavy pressure; angularity.

Self-conscious — *Last hump of* m *or* n *taller than preceding strokes; very small hw with small capitals, esp with light pressure;* leftward slant; slow hw; emended PPI.

Self-controlled — See Self-disciplined.

Self-disciplined — *Regular hw, esp size; consistent baseline; firm* t *crosses;* t *crosses bowed downward;* no exaggerated formations; vertical hw; simplified structures; lack of enlarged loops.

Self-underestimating — *Very low* t *crosses; very small capitals;* very small hw; leftward slant; *t* crosses left of stems.

Selfish — *Curtailed finals, narrowness, or close spacing, or or all three;* narrow circle letters; very tall *t*'s and *d*'s; leftward slant; exaggerated PPI.

Sensitive (easily affected) — Light pressure; variable baseline; changeable slant; changeable structures; wide or changeable spacing.

Sensitive to criticism — *Enlarged* t *or* d *stems; angularity, forward slant, and initial brace strokes, esp with light pressure.*

Sensual — *Extra heavy pressure resulting in unclean edges and muddy spots;* exaggerated loops, esp lower.

Sensuous — *Very heavy-pressured hw with clean edges;* enlarged loops, esp lower.

Shallow (lacks purpose) — *Basin* t *crosses;* light *t* crosses; light or uncertain downstrokes, esp in LZ; wandering baseline; changeable formations; irregular hw.

Simple tastes — *Simplified hw; lack of lead-ins; printed capitals;* no exaggerated movements; clear, legible hw.

Sociable — *Forward slant with enlarged LZ and broad circle letters;* open-topped circle letters; garland connections; moderate-to-wide spacing; legible hw.

Spontaneous	*Nonrigid, freeflowing hw;* changeable baseline and size; variable formations; large hw; wide spacing; wide formations; lack of retraced structures.
Stressful	See Tense.
Stubborn	*Final braced strokes, esp if blunt;* rigid formations; angularity and heavy pressure; narrow circle letters; very tall *t*'s and *d*'s.
Suspicious	*Initial brace strokes; narrowness and rigid formations;* reversed initial loops; very large *t* or *d* loops.
Sympathetic	*Forward slant and light pressure, garlands, and open formations;* supported by enlarged loops (esp lower) and wide circle letters.
Tactful	*Letters or words decreasing in size;* closed circle letters; retraced *t* or *d* stems; thready formations.
Talkative	*Open-topped circle letters, esp in large hw;* large MZ; broad letters; open spacing; supported by ascending baselines.
Tenacious	*Final hooks;* tied structures; regularity; consistent formations; firm downstrokes; consistent pressure, esp if firm.
Tense	Narrow, angular movements; rigid hw; very heavy pressure; isolated letters; frequently distorted loops; incomplete or light downstrokes; changeable size and formations; small MZ.
Thrifty	*Close, careful spacing;* curtailed finals; moderate-to-small size; no exaggerated movements; well-placed *t* crosses.
Truthful	See Honest.
Unconventional	*Nonschoolbook hw; unusual formations;* exaggerated movements, esp capitals; circle *i* dots.
Unpredictable	Changeable hw (size, slant, baseline); variable formations; changing pressure; tangled lines.
Vain	*Very tall* t*'s and* d*'s;* overly embellished letters, esp capitals; very large capitals; very tall or inflated upper loops, or both; exaggerated sig or PPI.
Variety, desire for	See Change, desire for.
Versatile	Somewhat variable hw, esp baseline; variable (not erratic) size, spacing and formations; soft hw; wide spacing; enlarged loops.

Violent tendencies	Clublike or daggerlike formations; heavily jabbed *i* dots; childish script when combined with previous indications; hw that digs into paper; muddy hw; spotty pressure; erratic hw; distorted letters, esp PPI, *e* and *d;* felon's claw or shark's tooth formations; supported by distorted LZ and restricted UZ; expression of violence diminished by regularity.
Weak-willed	*Weak* t *crosses;* changeable baseline; weak downstrokes; variable formations and hw size; very soft hw, esp if light.
Will power	*Strong* t *crosses;* consistently straight baseline; firm downstrokes; consistent formations and hw size; firm, angular, or rigid hw.
Withdrawn	Strong leftward slant; tiny hw; LZ formations pull leftward; closed circle letters; retraced letters, esp in MZ; very small or retraced LZ structures.
Worrier	*Loops between humps of* m *and* n; wavering or hesitant structures; indefinite downstrokes, esp at baseline; corrected letters.
Yielding	*Rounded formations, esp* s; light pressure; indefinite formations; garland connections; light *t* crosses; uncertain downstrokes; forward slant and outreaching finals.

SUGGESTED
READING LIST

Allport, Gordan, and Philip Vernon. *Studies in Expressive Movement.* New York: Macmillan, 1933.

Amend, Karen, and Mary Ruiz. *Handwriting Analysis: The Complete Basic Book.* North Hollywood, Calif.: Newcastle Publishing Co., 1980.

Bernard, Marie. *The Art of Graphology.* Troy, N.Y.: Whitston Publishing Co., 1985.

Bunker, Milton N. *Handwriting Analysis.* Chicago: Nelson-Hall, 1971.

Colombe, Paul de Sainte. *Grapho-Therapeutics.* Hollywood, Calif.: Laurida Books, 1971.

Green, Jane Nugent. *You and Your Private I.* St. Paul: Llewellyn Publishers, 1975.

Gullen-Whur, Margaret. *What Your Handwriting Reveals.* New York: Avanel Books, 1984.

Hayes, Reed C. *Handwriting: Its Socio-Sexual Implications,* rev. ed. Van Nuys, Calif.: Astro-Analytics Publishers, 1986.

Hayes, Reed C. *Handwriting, an Expression of Energy.* Honolulu, Hawaii: Private publication, 1987.

Hayes, Reed C. *The Handwriting of Problem Children.* Honolulu, Hawaii: Private publication, 1987.

210

Hayes, Reed C., and Mary H. DeLapp. *Guide to Children's Handwriting.* Minneapolis: Private publication, 1987.

Hayes, Reed C., and Kimon Iannetta. *Danger Between the Lines.* Honolulu, Hawaii: Private publication, 1993.

Kurtz, Sheila, and Marilyn Lester. *Graphotypes.* New York: Dell, 1983.

Lazewnik, Baruch. *Handwriting Analysis.* West Chester, Pa: Whitford Books, 1991.

Mahony, Ann. *Handwriting and Personality.* New York: Ivy Books, 1989.

Marne, Patricia. *Crime and Sex in Handwriting.* London: Constable, 1981.

Marne, Patricia. *Practical Graphology: How to Analyze Handwriting.* London: Kogan Page Publishers, 1990.

Mendel, Alfred O. *Personality in Handwriting,* reprint of 1947 ed. North Hollywood, Calif.: Newcastle Publishing Co., 1990.

Nezos, Renna. *Graphology.* London: Rider Books, 1986.

Solomon, Shirl. *How to Really Know Yourself Through Your Handwriting.* New York: Taplinger, 1973.

Solomon, Shirl. *Knowing Your Child Through His Handwriting and Drawings.* New York: Crown, 1978.

HANDWRITING ANALYSIS
WORKSHEET

1=low score; 3=moderate score; 5=high score.

Feature/Trait	1	2	3	4	5	Comments
Regularity						
Size						
Large						
Medium						
Small						
Spacing						
Wide line spacing						
Medium line spacing						
Narrow line spacing						
Consistent line spacing						
Wide word spacing						
Medium word spacing						
Narrow word spacing						
Consistent word spacing						
Wide letter spacing						
Medium letter spacing						
Narrow letter spacing						
Consistent letter spacing						
Baselines						
Consistent baselines						
Straight across page						
Uphill baselines						
Downhill baselines						
Handwriting Form						
Arcades						
Angles						
Garland						
Threads						

FEATURE/TRAIT	1	2	3	4	5	COMMENTS
Zones						
Predominant UZ						
Predominant MZ						
Predominant LZ						
Moderate Size MZ						
Large MZ						
Small MZ						
Moderate (balanced) UZ						
Narrow UZ						
Retraced UZ						
Neglected UZ						
Stick-like UZ						
Wide UZ						
Exaggerated UZ						
Moderate (balanced) LZ						
Narrow LZ						
Retraced LZ						
Neglected LZ						
Stick-like LZ						
Wide LZ						
Exaggerated LZ						
Rightward trend						
Leftward trend						
Emotions						
Vertical HW						
Slightly inclined HW						
Rightward slant						
Far forward slant						
Leftward slant						
Far leftward slant						
Consistent slant						
Moderate pressure						
Light pressure						
Heavy pressure						
Muddy HW						

Feature/Trait	1	2	3	4	5	Comments
Thinking Style						
Moderate speed						
Fast speed						
Slow Speed						
Arcades (methodical)						
Angles (investigative/analytical)						
Needlepoints (perceptive)						
Threads (adaptable)						
Connected HW						
Disconnected HW						
Simplified HW						
Embellished H						
Careful dots and punctuation						
Small size						
Signature						
Legible						
Illegible						
Simplified						
Embellished						
Signature larger than text						
Signature smaller than text						
Slant of signature and text differ						
First name emphasized						
Surname emphasized						
Underscored						
Encircled						
Crossed out						
Patched/repaired						
Beginning/Ending Strokes						
Simplified capitals						
Embellished capitals						
Omitted lead-ins						
Long lead-ins						
First letter attached						

FEATURE/TRAIT	1	2	3	4	5	COMMENTS
First letter separated						
Initial hooks						
Wavy lead-ins						
Initial spirals/curlicues						
Large, reversed initial loops						
Small, reversed initial loops						
Initial "tics"/barbs						
Initial brace strokes						
Firm endings						
Clublike or blobbed endings						
Finals fade out						
Finals do not reach baseline						
Thready endings						
Gradually tapered endings						
Endings increase in size						
Final letter suddenly larger						
Finals extend below baseline						
Curtailed finals						
Finals reach outward and upward						
Finals reach upward and leftward						
Finals reach straight upward						
Finals reach straight out						
Final hooks						
Drooping finals						
LZ downstrokes fade						
Firm LZ downstrokes						
Letters T and D						
Tall stems						
Very tall stems						
Short stems						
Looped stems						
Retraced stems						
Braced stems						
Arched stems						
"Lyric" (delta) *d*						

FEATURE/TRAIT	1	2	3	4	5	COMMENTS
No initial stroke						
Low *t* crosses						
Medium-high *t* crosses						
High *t* crosses						
Heavy *t* crosses						
Light *t* crosses						
Long *t* crosses						
T crosses bowed downward						
T crosses bent upward						
Sharp *t* crosses						
Barbed *t* crosses						
Hooked *t* crosses						
T crosses left of stems						
T crosses right of stems						
T crosses written right to left						
Tied *t* crosses						
Downward directed *t* crosses						
Upward directed *t* crosses						
Clublike *t* crosses						
Other *t* formations:						
Insecurities						
Self-conscious (last hump of *m* higher)						
Jealous (small, reversed initial loop)						
Repressed (tight, retraced letters)						
Underestimates self (low *t* crosses)						
Sensitive to criticism (looped *t* or *d*)						
Social Traits						
Responsiveness (slant)						
Letter spacing						
Word spacing						
Writing size						

FEATURE/TRAIT	1	2	3	4	5	COMMENTS
Large lower loops						
No lower loops						
Narrow lower loops						
Tiny lower loops						
Outcurved finals						
Finals curve out and back						
Excessive angularity						
Jabbed dots						
Straight initial brace strokes						
Temper tics						
T bar to right						
Sharp *t* crosses						
Tall initial *p* stroke						
Rounded circle letters						
Narrow circle letters						
Clear circle letters						
Open-topped circle letter						
Closed circle letters						
Circle letters looped on right						
Circle letters looped on left						
Circle letters looped on left and right						
Wavy lead-ins						
Sexuality						
Pressure						
Muddy writing						
Pronounced lower zone						
De-emphasized lower zone						
"Abnormal" lower loops						
Exaggerated lower loops						
Incomplete lower loops						
Retraced lower loops						
Narrow lower loops						
Tiny lower loops						
Angular lower loops						
Weaponlike lower loops						

FEATURE/TRAIT	1	2	3	4	5	COMMENTS
Unfinished, cuplike lower loops						
Bent leftward lower loops						
Pushed rightward lower loops						
Lower loops with drooping finals						
Reversed lower loops						
Other lower loop formations:						

Dishonesty

FEATURE/TRAIT	1	2	3	4	5	COMMENTS
Unclear, illegible writing						
Tangled lines						
Excessive regularity or artificiality						
Overly complicated or simple						
Exceptionally thready						
Sudden changes (slant, pressure, etc.)						
Complicated circle letters						
Hooks inside circle letters						
Fragmented letters						
Trick letters						
Scrolled initial or terminal strokes						
Corrections, retouches, patches						
"Felon's claws"						
Smeary writing						
Signature and text differ						
Omitted letters						
Curled under arches						
Angles and arches in same writing						
Ambiguous numbers						
Two or more distinct styles						
Initial hooks plus double looped circles						
Distorted lower zone						
Blotched upper zone						

Feature/Trait	1	2	3	4	5	Comments
Distorted, twisted upper zone						
Capitals out of place						
Aptitudes						
Sense of rhythm						
Imagination (unique structures)						
Imagination (enlarged loops)						
Literary interest						
Fluidity						
Sense of color						
Interpretive skill (intuition)						
Simplicity						
Line value						
Manual dexterity						
Organizational skills						
Decisiveness						
Determination						
Diplomacy						
Initiative						
Scientific aptitude						

Additional Comments:

INDEX

Abstract concepts, 43, 46
Acquisitiveness, 118
Adaptability, 35, 76. *See also* Flexibility
Age, indications of, 13, 69
Aggressiveness, 54, 75, 113, 120, 128, 195
  sexual, 170–71
Alcott, Louisa May, 27
Allport, Gordon, 17
Ambiguous letters/numbers, 178, 179
Amiability, 40
Analytical thinking, 73–75
  repression of, 140
Analyze handwriting, how to, 97–101
Anger, 151–55. *See also* Temper
Angular formations, 40, 73–75, 137, 173
  and arcades in same writing, 179
Anthony, Daniel, 18
Anxiety, 94, 109
Aptitudes, 182–96

Arcade formations, 39, 71–73
  and angles in same writing, 179
  curled under, 179
Argumentativeness, 156–57
Aristotle, 14
Armstrong, Herbert W., 94
Arrogance, 87
Artistic talents, 116, 185–89
Asimov, Isaac, 79
Astor, John Jacob, 92
Attention, desire for, 23, 49, 116–21, 15
Authority, resistance against, 180

"Back-to-self" strokes, 132
Backhand writing, 60–61
Baez, Joan, 72
Bailey, Pearl, 23
Baldi, Camillo, 15
Ballpoint writing, 66

Barbs, 131
Barger, Ralph "Sonny," 107–9
Barrow, Clyde, 180–81
Baselines, 33–39
  arched, 39
  ascending, 36
  concave, 39
  consistent, 34
  descending, 34
  direction of, 36–39
  flexible, 35
  rigid, 35
  straight, 38
  wandering, 36
Bell, Alexander Graham, 80
Bias, 65
Binet, Alfred, 16
Black, Shirley Temple, 86
Blass, Bill, 86
Boldness, 22
Braced strokes, 118, 153
Bradley, Tom, 64
Brainwriting, 16
Breakaway strokes, 171, 195
Breaks between letters, 189–90
British handwriting, 132
Broad-mindedness, 157
Broken letters, 178
Brutality, 133
Bryant, Anita, 38
Bundy, Ted, 153–54
Bunker, Milton, 17
Burnett, Carol, 81
Business, aptitude for, 192–95

Calligraphy, 99
Camp, William B., 93
Capital letters, 114–16
  flourished, 115–16
  large, 115–16
  out of place, 180
  overly embellished, 115

simplified, 115
small, 115
Carefully formed letters, 8
Carefulness, 131
Carter, Jimmy, 52
Casanova, Giovanni, 65
Castro, Fidel, 92
Caution, 27, 30, 117, 121
Chagall, Marc, 188
Chaplin, Charlie, 92
Childhood, tied to, 117
Children's handwriting, 8
Circle letters, 157–61, 175
  clear, 175
  closed, 159
  initial hooks in, 178
  looped, 159–60, 179
  narrow, 157–58
  open, 159
  open on bottom, 178
  rounded, 157
  wide, 157
Clannishness, 150
Clarity, 8, 175
Closed-mindedness, 158
Clublike strokes, 51, 92, 119, 120, 133
Colbert, Claudette, 27
Color, sense of, 187–89
Collins, Joan, 49
Communication, 24, 44, 86, 117, 158–61
Concentration, 45, 83–84
Confidence, 6, 44, 87, 192
  lack of, 45
Conflicting personality traits, 100
Confusion, 26
Connected letters, 80
Connected words, 80–81
Conservatism, 120, 131
Control, desire for, 132, 133
  lack of, 35
Conventionality, 7
Corrected letters, 94, 178

Cousteau, Jacques, 74
Crépieux-Jamin, Jean, 15–16
Criminals, 12, 170, 180–81
Crippen, Hawley H., 92, 93
Critical, 75
Criticism, sensitivity to, 125–26
Cruelty, 170. *See also* Brutality
Cultural indications, 185–91

D (letter), 123–27, 128
de Sahagún, Fra Bernardino, 95
Dean, James, 78
Deceit, 160. *See also* Dishonesty
Decisiveness, 73, 119, 193
Defiance, 180
Deliberateness, 68, 128
Delta *d*'s, 186. *See also* Lyrical *d*
Demanding, 132, 133
Dependency, emotional, 55
Detail, attentiveness to, 23, 83, 131
Detail, inattentiveness to, 133
Determination, 51, 122, 193–94
Dickinson, Emily, 30
Diebenkorn, Richard, 188
Dignity, 126–27, 140
Diller, Phyllis, 35
Diplomacy, 41, 77, 120, 194
Directional trends, 53–55
Directness, 82, 116, 128
Disconnections, 80, 81
Discouragement, 37–38
Dishonesty, 176–81
Disney, Walt, 96
Disraeli, Benjamin, 6
Doctors, 77
Domineering tendencies, 29, 133
Downey, June, 17
Downstrokes
    fading, 122
    firm, 122, 193
Duncan, Isadora, 45, 60

E's, Greek, 185–86

Eastwood, Clint, 59
Edison, Thomas A., 72, 130, 191
Edward VIII, 92
Egotism, 115–16
Einstein, Albert, 23, 67, 68, 84, 130
Embellished handwriting, 82
Emotional conflicts, 161
Emotional control, 58
    lack of, 34–35
Emotional permanence, 62–66
Emotional responsiveness, 56–62, 135,
    145–46
Energy, 36, 64, 111–13
    lack of, 112
    related to sex drive, 164
Enthusiasm, 130
Ethics
    conservative, 47
    lack of, 46
    narrow, 47
    tolerant, 48
Evaluation, importance of, 8–9
Excesses, tendency toward, 65, 113
Executives, 77, 192
Exploratory thinking, 73–74
Expressiveness, 22, 147–48
Extravagance, 7
Extroversion, 32, 54

Factual, 47
Failure, fear of, 128. *See also* Self-
    underestimation
Fast handwriting, 67–68, 70
"Felon's claw," 178
Figure eight formations, 186–87
Final strokes
    curtailed, 120
    drooping, 122
    outstretched, 121, 150
First name emphasized, 90
Fixed Signs, School of, 15
Flandrin, Abbé Louis J. H., 15
Flexibility, 24

Flirtatiousness, 131, 161
Fluidity, 80, 133, 186–87
Footwriting, 16
Forcefulness, 133
Ford, Gerald, 47
Ford, Henry, 181
Forgetfulness, 133
Formlevel, 16, 174
Fragmented letters, 178
Frankness, 86, 158–59
Freud, Sigmund, 6, 42, 91
Frost, Robert, 47
Frustration, 169. See also Tension

Gabor, Zsa Zsa, 29
Gandhi, Mahatma, 23, 84
Garland formations, 40–41, 75–76
Garland, Judy, 93
Gender, indications of, 12
Generosity, 33, 40, 121, 150–51
Gershwin, George, 48
"Glassy" strokes, 75, 170
Goals, 128–29
Gould, Chester, 95
Grable, Betty, 90
Graceful formations, 190
Graphoanalysis, 17
Graphology, history of, 14–18
Griffith, D. W., 28
Guarded attitude, 153

Hamilton, Alexander, 21, 25, 101–4
Hancock, John, 86
Handwriting, description of, 5
Handwriting, practical applications of, 3, 10–12
Handwriting specimens, how to collect, 97
Handwriting styles, variable, 98
Hauptmann, Bruno, 46, 69
Hess, Rudolph, 39
Hinckley, John Jr., 181
Hitler, Adolph, 60, 170–71
Honesty, 174–80

Hooks
    final, 121
    initial, 118
Hubbard, L. Ron, 49
Hugo, Victor, 194
Humor, 131, 161–62

I, personal pronoun, 139. See Personal
    pronoun I
Idealism, 49
Illness, diagnosis of, 12
Image, 44, 142. See also Signatures
Imagination, 43, 48, 184–85
Immaturity, 45, 69
Impatience, 7, 131, 133
Impulsiveness, 59, 62, 67, 133
Inadequacy, feelings of, 87
Inconsistent personality, 20
Indecisiveness, 24, 41, 62, 67, 119
Independence, 45, 51, 149
    fear of, 29
Independent thinking, 125, 143
Indirectness, 82, 117
Ingenuity, lack of, 50
Initiative, 132, 194–95
Insecurities, 134–43
Integrity. See Honesty
Intellectual inferiority, feeling of, 49
Intimacy, fear of, 150
Introversion, 32, 55
Intuition, 80–81, 189
Investigative, 73
Irregularity of handwriting, 19–20
Irresponsibility, 26, 41
Irritability, 152–53
Isolation, 30, 32

Jabs, 152. See also Ticks, Barbs
Jackson, Michael, 37
Jacoby, Hans, 17
Jealousy, 118, 137–39
Johnson, Don, 93
Johnson, Lady Bird, 79

Johnson, Lyndon B., 51
Jones, John Paul, 89
Judd, Winnie Ruth, 153–54

Kennedy, John F., 67, 68, 76, 77
Kindness, 40
Kissinger, Henry, 77
Klages, Ludwig, 16
Klein, Felix, 18

Large handwriting, 20, 22–23, 135, 147
Lavater, Johann Kasper, 15
Lead-in strokes, 116–17
    omitted, 116
    wavy, 118, 161
Left-handedness, 61, 132
Leftward slant, 60–61
Leftward-directed strokes, 55, 132
Legal field, use of handwriting in, 3, 11
Letter spacing, 31–33
    narrow, 32, 135, 146
    wide, 33, 146
Lewinson, Thea Stein, 18
Lewis, Jerry, 76
Liberace, 94, 95
Lincoln, Abraham, 25, 32
Lindbergh, Charles, 69
Line spacing, 24–28
    exaggerated, 27
    narrow, 27
    variable, 28
Line value, 190–91
Lined paper, 34
Literature, interest in, 128, 185–87
Livingstone, David, 29, 74, 129
Logic, 80
Longfellow, Henry Wadsworth, 25
Loops, lower, 49–53, 148–50, 163–73,
    185. See also Zones of handwriting
    abnormal, 166–71, 179
    angular, 169–71, 172
    incomplete, 168

lack of, 148
large, 52–53, 148, 166, 168
narrow, 149, 169, 172
neglected, 50
normal, 166
proportionate size of, 166
retraced, 169
tiny, 150, 166
weaponlike, 173
Loops, upper, 46–49, 175. See also
    Zones of handwriting
    blotched, 179
    distorted, 180
Lower zone, 49–53
    de-emphasized, 166
    exaggerated, 53, 166
Lyrical d, 128. See also Delta d

Maltz, Maxwell, 37
Manual dexterity, 191–92
Marcuse, Irene, 18
Materialism, 49, 51
Mechanical aptitudes, 191–92
Memory, 83
Mendel, Alfred O., 18
Mesmer, Friedrich Anton, 96
Methodical approach, 40, 71–73
Michon, Abbé Jean Hippolyte, 15
Middle zone, 43, 44–45
Mimicry, 131
Modesty, 23, 148
Monotonous handwriting, 21, 34, 183
Monroe, Marilyn, 53
Mood, indications of, 35, 36–38
Muddy handwriting, 65, 92, 113, 164, 170
Music, feel for, 184, 189–90

Narrow-mindedness, 157–58
Nation, Carry, 156
Negative outlook, 37
Newton, Wayne, 32, 76
Nightingale, Florence, 86

Nixon, Pat, 30
Nixon, Richard M., 30, 88
Numbers, ambiguous, 179

Objectivity, 58
O'Keeffe, Georgia, 104–77, 128, 130, 189
Olyanova, Nadya, 18
Omitted letters, 179
Onassis, Jacqueline Kennedy, 60, 128
Open-mindedness, 157
Oppenheimer, Robert, 196
Optimism, 36–37, 121, 133
Organization, 7
Organizational skills, 25, 192–93
Originality, 7, 184
Ostentation, 87
Oswald, Lee Harvey, 62
Outgoing, 7

P (letter), 157
Paranoia, 31
Parrish, Maxfield, 96
Pasteur, Louis, 196
Patched letters, 94, 178
Patience, 7
Peevish attitude, 152
Perceptive thinking, 67, 75–76
Perfectionism, 83
Persistence, 132
Personal pronoun I, 139
Personnel selection, 11
Pessimism, 37–38, 173
Physical activity, 54, 65
Picasso, Pablo, 188
Pickford, Mary, 46
Pissarro, Camille, 27
Poe, Edgar Allan, 15, 70
Potter, Beatrix, 58
Practical goals, 129
Practical values, 46
Practicality, lack of, 46
Precise handwriting, 83

Pressure of handwriting, 62–66. See
    also Strokes, pressure of
consistent, 113
determining, 65
fading, 113, 119
firm, 164
heavy, 62, 64–65, 164, 187–89
light, 63
spotty, 113
Pretense, 69, 116, 177
Preyer, William, 16
Pride, 124
Printing, 98
Procrastination, 131
Proportion, sense of, 190–91
Pulver, Max, 16
Purpose, sense of, 40. See also Willpower

R's, flat-topped, 191
Rasputin, Gregori, 36
Rathbone, Basil, 87
Ravel, Maurice, 31
Reagan, Nancy, 52
Reagan, Ronald, 52
Recognition, desire for, 121, 151
Reality, 43
Regularity of handwriting, 19–22
    excessive, 21, 177
Remington, Frederic, 187, 189
Repartee, 113
Repression, 92, 136, 139–41. See also
    Retraced strokes
Research, ability for, 73
Resentment, 118, 153–54
Reserve, 7
Resourcefulness, 184
Responsibility, desire for, 138
Restlessness, 52
Retraced strokes, 51, 126–27, 136,
    139–41, 168–69
Rhythm, 16, 67, 183–84. See also
    Regularity of handwriting

Rightward slant, 58–60
Rightward-directed strokes, 54
Rigidity, 34, 75
Rockefeller, John D., 34
Roman, Klara, 18

Sarcasm, 113, 131, 156
Saudek, Robert, 17
Schoolroom model, 5
Scientific aptitudes, 195–96
Secretiveness, 72, 88, 159–60
Security, concern with, 54–60
Selectivity, 149
Self-assuredness, 114
Self-castigation, 132
Self-confidence. *See* Confidence
Self-consciousness, 31, 135–37
Self-control, 131
Self-criticism, 31
Self-deceit, 160
Self-discipline, 8
Self-esteem, distorted, 143
Self-protection, 72, 92
Self-reliance, 91–92
Self-underestimation, 129, 141–42
Selfishness, 140
Sensitivity, 112
Sensitivity to criticism, 125–26, 142–43
Sensuality, 65, 164
Sensuousness, 164
Sex, 50, 122, 163–73
Sexual distortions, 167–71
Sexual immaturity, 50, 55
Shakespeare, William, 184
"Shark's teeth," 178
Shaw, George Bernard, 58, 130
Shelley, Percy B., 59, 60, 128
Showmanship, 86, 87
Signatures, 85–96
    clarity of, 86
    crossed out, 94
    different from text, 88–90

embellished, 87
encircled, 92–93
illegible, 87–88
patched, 94
placement of, 90
underlined, 91–92
Simplification, 82, 128, 187, 190
Size of handwriting, 22–24
    variable, 24
Slant of handwriting, 54, 56–62, 145–46.
    See also Emotional responsiveness
    consistency of, 61
    left-handedness and, 61
    leftward, 60–61
    measurement of, 57
    rightward, 58–60
    variable, 62
    vertical, 58
Slow handwriting, 68–70, 71
Small handwriting, 23, 83–84, 135, 148
Social traits, 28–31, 120–21, 144–62
Solitude, desire for, 31, 149
Sonnemann, Ulrich, 18
Spacing of handwriting, 24–33, 146–47
Speech disturbances, indications of, 18
Speed of handwriting, 67–71
    how to determine, 70–71
Spelling errors, 69
Spontaneity, 8, 41
Spotty strokes, 113, 179
Stability, 20, 28, 34, 38, 61, 183
Star-shaped strokes, 132
Stinginess, 140
Streep, Meryl, 161–62
Strokes, 110–13
    curved, 111
    feathered, 193
    final, 114, 119–22, 193–94
    fragmented, 178
    glassy, 75, 170
    initial, 114–19
    pressure of, 111–13

sharp, 152
spotty, 178
straight, 111
unique, 184–85
weaponlike, 152, 173
Stubbornness, 73, 119, 127–28
Style of handwriting, two or more, 98
Stylized handwriting, 99
Superficiality, 131
Suppression, 139–40
Surname emphasized, 91
Suspicion, 153
Swit, Loretta, 50

T (letter), 123–33
T bars, 128–33
Talents, 182–96
Talkativeness, 159
Tangled lines, 25–26
Tapered letters, 77, 120, 194
Taste, indications of, 115, 186
Technical work, ability for, 83
Temper, 131, 151–52. *See also* Anger
Temple, Shirley, 86
Tenacity, 121, 131
Tension, 73
Thackeray, William M., 38
Thinking styles, 8, 67–80
Thread formations, 41, 76–78, 120
Thriftiness, 7
Tics, 118, 155. *See also* Barbs
Tied strokes, 132
Tight handwriting, 31, 135
Timidity, 136
Tolerance, 46. *See also* Open-
mindedness
Toulouse-Lautrec, Henri de, 188
Trickiness, 88, 178
Trump, Donald, 75
"Trunk Murderess." *See* Judd, Winnie
Ruth
Twain, Mark, 28

Unique formations, 184–5
Unlined paper, 34
Unreliability, 34
Upper zone, 43, 46–49
exaggerated, 49
neglected, 46
retraced, 47

Valentina, 45
Vanity, 124–25, 143
Variety, desire for, 26, 52, 148
Vernon, Philip, 17
Versatility, 28. *See also* Flexibility
Vertical handwriting, 58
Vidal, Gore, 78–79
Visionary, 129, 132

Weapon-like strokes, 170, 173
Westmoreland, General, 80
Whistler, James McNeill, 78
Wilde, Oscar, 81, 128
Willfulness, 130, 133
Willpower
strong, 129–30
weak, 130
Withdrawal, 61, 126, 135
Witticism, 113
Wolff, Werner, 17
Woodward, Joanne, 33
Word spacing, 28–31
even, 28
exaggerated, 30–31
narrow, 29, 147
variable, 28
wide, 29–30
Wright, Frank Lloyd, 191

Zones of handwriting, 16, 42–53, 54–55.
See also Lower zone, Middle zone,
Upper zone